Instructional Communication in Professional Contexts

Editor

Michael G. Strawser
University of Central Florida

cognella
SAN DIEGO

Bassim Hamadeh, CEO and Publisher

Todd R. Armstrong, Publisher

Anne Jones, Project Editor

Alia Bales, Associate Production Manager

Jessica Delia, Graphic Design Associate

Alexa Lucido, Licensing Manager

Natalie Piccotti, Director of Marketing

Kassie Graves, Senior Vice President, Editorial

Jamie Giganti, Director of Academic Publishing

Cover image copyright © 2013 Depositphotos/Nik_Merkulov.

Printed in the United States of America.

3970 Sorrento Valley Blvd., Ste. 500, San Diego, CA 92121

Contents

PART III.   Health   103

PART IV.   Technology   145

Chapter 8   **Current Trends and Future Directions   167**
David Westerman, Stephanie Kelly, Kyle R. Vareberg,
Kenneth T. Rocker, and Nicholas David Bowman

PART V.   Risk and Crisis   187

Chapter 9   **Background   189**
Jeffrey Brand

Introduction

Michael G. Strawser & Derek Lane

C ommunication remains a relatively young academic discipline according to contemporary standards. However,
despite our discipline's infancy in traditional higher education contexts, "communicators" have been practical problem
solvers for centuries, dating back to the beginning of recorded
history (Friedrich, 1987). As our academic discipline evolved,
numerous concentration areas arose that reinforced communication across the spectrum of human experience. Instructional
communication—the academic study of communication in
and through all educational contexts regardless of grade-
level setting or subject matter, with a unique emphasis on
the blended triumvirate of educational psychology, pedagogy,
and communication (Mottet & Beebe, 2006)—is one of these
foundational topic areas. What makes instructional communication research (ICR) unique is this melded research approach
with tentacles that reach into all other academic disciplines
and professional contexts, with an emphasis on education or
instruction writ large.

Unfortunately, instructional communication researchers continue to limit our potential impact, especially outside the academy, for a host of reasons (Strawser & Sellnow, 2019). The conversation surrounding the role of instructional communication is not new and has, in fact, become somewhat routine and predictable. Despite this repeated conversation, we find ourselves (yet again) at a crossroads because of the changing nature of education and the workplace.

A review of recent meta-analyses specific to communication education reveals interesting distinctions of our focus as those who study communication education and, more broadly, instructional communication. Starting in 2001, Waldeck, Kearney, and Plax revealed ICR research categorizations that center on student communication, teacher communication, mass media effects on children, pedagogical methods/technology use, classroom management, and teacher–student interaction. Nussbaum and Friedrich (2005), similarly, found student communication, teacher communication, mass media effects on children, pedagogical methods/tech use, classroom management, and teacher–student interaction as central foci of recent instructional communication research. Not surprisingly, Myers et al. (2016) found similarities as they explored the types of articles found in *Communication Education* from 1976–2014. Specifically, their results reveal an overwhelming focus on articles that focus primarily on undergraduate student participants and college instructors and discuss topics that include instructor characteristics, instructor classroom behaviors, student characteristics, student classroom behaviors, student learning outcomes, learning environment, mediated communication, program evaluation, and instructional content (Myers et al., 2016). Finally, in their 2017 content analysis of *Communication Education*, Conley and Ah Yun (2017) found that research published in this flagship journal tends to "derive most of its data from surveys, administered to college students, and predominantly focuses on refining and further exploring previous research topics in new contexts" (p. 451). While their participants did look extremely similar, with the majority of studies focusing on college students and instructors, their topic areas were represented uniquely. Specifically, Conley and Ah Yun (2017) found affective learning, public speaking, teacher immediacy, cognitive learning, pedagogy, communication apprehension, communication competence, communication across the curriculum, teacher clarity, teacher credibility, and motivation as the preeminent topics/keywords represented in *Communication Education*. Collectively, these analyses reveal a focus on a (a) particular participant population and (b) consistent instructional variables.

Purpose of This Volume: Expanding the Research Agenda

As you can imagine, for the purposes of this volume, these revelations are purposefully selected. Ironically, two major themes seem to arise when we consider the breadth and depth of analyses of instructional research. For one, we tend to focus our considerations on the flagship journal, *Communication Education*. And, embedded within this journal we tend to focus on Sprague's (2002) "E5" category (college students, predominantly in communication courses, and college instructors). We believe this type of research has been, is, and will continue to be valuable for instructional communication. However, we do believe that instructional research goes beyond these traditional contexts and that it is important to find synergy and commonality with those in other communication topic areas who are doing important instructional research. Additionally, we recognize that instructional researchers publish their work in journals other than *Communication Education*, in journals that may not even be communication centric because of the interdisciplinary approach to ICR. As a result, this volume was initiated to further discuss instructional research that transcends the typical college classroom and those distinctives predominantly explored by *Communication Education*.

This volume approaches instructional research from a broader perspective, moving toward what Sprague (2002) references as "bigger questions" that transcend our traditional university environment. Five professional contexts were selected to represent areas where instructional research has been prominent beyond the academy. Specifically, chapters in this volume address instructional research in the following contexts: (a) learning and development, (b) organizational, (c) health, (d) technology, and (e) risk and crisis. These contexts are not exhaustive, as other professional environments can be obvious environments for instructional research, but they do represent several distinct contexts where instructional research has been influential.

Our reality is indicative of a larger movement. We must evolve to address necessary changes needed to continue to expand the instructional communication research agenda. Most "instructional research to date examines communication among teachers and students in conventional classroom contexts. Although past and present research is prolific and informative, it is also somewhat limiting" (Sellnow & Limperos et al., 2015, p. 417). And while our more traditional, university-centered research still has substantial value, we believe instructional researchers must continue to expand and address those crucial questions highlighted by Sprague (2002) and other pillars of our discipline. As such, this volume is designed to address the current status of instructional communication as a necessity for professional contexts, not just college communication classrooms. This book highlights several areas where instructional communication researchers can, and should, expand a research agenda that transcends our typical context, thus increasing our relevance beyond the academy. The topics addressed in this text, health communication, risk and crisis, organizational, learning and development, and technology, present professional contexts where instructional scholars can explore communication in and through all educational contexts. Within each topical part there are two chapters—where have we come and where are we going. The following section provides an overview of each topic area addressed in this book.

Learning and Development

For obvious reasons, the connection between instructional communication and the education sector at large remains a primary area of study for instructional communication scholars. In their part, focused on learning and development, Angela Hosek, Scott Titsworth, Carly Densmore, and Grace Sikapokoo reinforce intersections between ICR and applied settings outside of the actual classroom. Focusing on learning broadly, the authors explore the connection between instructors and learning. Their approach focuses on the exploration of learning through the primary domains (cognitive, affective, and behavioral), and they position instructional communication as a means of continuing to prepare students for our modern professional landscape, where employers routinely desire communication competence from their employees. They believe that in the future, instructional researchers will continue to explore content related to employer-desired skills (e.g., listening, reading, writing, speaking, etc.) while extending our understanding of learning and training.

Organizational

Stephen Spates and Shawn Wahl discuss instructional communication through varied organizational contexts. Recognizing that instructional communication is multifaceted and widely applicable, Spates and Wahl argue that the connecting factor is effective learning. They answer questions surrounding the influence of schools, the role of the instructor, the functional role of language in education, as well as other pressing questions. They transition, then, to the exploration of trending organizational contexts, including health, technology, as well as corporate and finally technical professions. They express, rightly, the position that "no matter the discipline, organization, or profession, instructional communication practices are made for successful learning. Instructors who engage in approaches that promote authentic and sustainable learning will find success for their learning experience." The designation of future areas of importance for instructional researchers include technology and artificial intelligence, risk/crisis, sports, as well as the legal system.

Health

As Teresa Thompson, Nichole Egbert, Heather Carmack, Yan Tian, Angela Cooke-Jackson, and Michael Mackert illustrate in their chapters, health communication has evolved from an emergent subdiscipline to a thriving focus of communication. As an area of focus for instructional communication scholars, health communication is a robust area of study in part because of its sheer influence not just on college curricula but on interprofessional health practitioner training and patient communication. Their chapters discuss the ever-present reality that "health educators have a responsibility to their communities and publics to ethically confront and engage current and future health issues and crises, providing learning spaces for everyone to become more informed consumers and decision-makers." Instructional researchers, especially those who focus on health communication, can be genuine difference makers. As an area of instructional research, health communication must remain a staple of engagement inside and outside the academy.

Technology

In their forward-thinking part on technology, Nick Bowman, Kyle R. Vareberg, Kenneth T. Rocker, Stephanie Kelly, and David Westerman try to reign in the often-considered "*Wild Wild West*" of new educational technologies. Their chapters review the historical development and implementation of technology in education, through the instructional communication scholarship lens. They conclude, rightly, that "technology has always been 'normal' in the classroom, that it can be used well or not, and that we (instructional researchers and others) have always debated this use." Practically, they show that technology is and will remain a powerful force for education and that it is not a magic wand or panacea yet should be a continued focus for instructional scholars. In a plea to educators, they argue that "to effectively use technology to deliver education, technology must be chosen carefully to meet the learning objectives and accompanied by strategic instructional communication tailored to the specific CMC (computer-mediated communication) channel and technologies being used."

Risk and Crisis

In the last part of this volume, Jeffrey Brand approaches instructional communication in the professional sphere by first mentioning four distinct long-term realities that communication, as a discipline, must continue to seek. It is important holistically to consider how these challenges provide context for how instructional communication scholars should approach their research. The four challenges mentioned in Brand's chapters include establishing respect for the field (i.e., communication) in academic and public arenas; the need to create a research-grounded body of knowledge; a desire to generate knowledge that contributes to solving social problems; and finally, promoting communication-based theory and practice for use and awareness by nonacademic publics. We cannot ignore the fact that we must be conducting applied research that can be shared beyond our immediate spheres of influences. These realities provide a foundation for the remainder of Brand's argument. He thus addresses the role of instructional communication research in the risk and crisis context and provides insight into how ICR is used to study and solve risk and crisis problems. His first chapter explores basic risk and crisis concepts and demonstrates how instructional communication research meets risk and crisis needs. Brand's second chapter identifies new directions and potential avenues to expand risk and crisis situations.

The chapters in this volume strategically explore the historical development of instructional communication in unique contexts. However, it is also necessary to understand, holistically, how instructional communication research has developed and the roots of this subdiscipline in order to proactively engage in a conversation about our future. Therefore, the next section provides a brief history of instructional communication research as well as a picture of the present and a call to address our future.

Historical Development

Communication historians have suggested that contemporary speech courses for teachers were offered at Indiana University as early as 1892 but that such courses were common by 1920 (Cohen, 1994; Delia, 1987; Schramm, 1997; Smith, 1954; Wallace, 1954). It is remarkable, however, that communication education graduate programs designed to produce communication researchers that could develop instructional communication theory based on empirical research conducted in instructional contexts did not appear until the late 1960s. Over the next 35 years, several strong instructional communication graduate programs emerged that produced quality programmatic research used to improve instructional practices across multiple grade levels and disciplines. Unfortunately, communication education was dropped as a disciplinary emphasis from the 2004 reputation study because too few doctoral programs were offering a specialization in instructional communication.

The critical turning point for instructional communication as a doctoral specialty in U.S. universities seems to have occurred sometime between 1972 (when the International Communication Associated created the Instructional and Development Division) and 1976 (when we changed the name of our discipline's second oldest journal, *Speech Teacher,* originally published in 1952, to *Communication Education*; Friedrich, 1987).

Barker (1989) describes the key players, influences, and origins of two doctoral programs in communication education that focused explicitly on the interface between communication and instruction—one at Purdue University (1967) and the other at Florida State University (1970). According to Barker's personal account, the events that shaped the course of communication at two American universities—with a behavioral science influence—occurred because of the mix of personnel interested in communication education, grant funding from the U.S. Department of Education, outstanding resources, and enthusiastically committed graduate students.

The key players included Robert J. (Bob) Kibler, Larry L. Barker, Theodore (Ted) Clevenger, Jr., William D. (Bill) Brooks, and Gustav (Gus) Friedrich—all of whom were hired to teach at Purdue University in 1967. The early graduates from the Purdue program were William (Bill) Seiler (who was responsible for creating the instructional communication program at the University of Nebraska), Jo Sprague (whose critical teaching and learning scholarship set the agenda for instructional communication research for nearly 2 decades) and Don Cegala (who is best known for his research on patient education in health contexts). In 1970, Kibler and Barker left Purdue to join Clevenger at Florida State University in Tallahassee in order to create a new communication education graduate program. While serendipity and good timing were responsible for the two earliest communication education doctoral programs, the primary characteristic of those instructional communication programs that followed was the individual commu-nication scholar—and their students.

The next key event occurred 2 years later, in 1972, when the tradi-tional speech program at West Virginia University was transformed into an empirically oriented communication program designed to study the role of communication in classroom environments. Richmond (1989) explains that the antecedents of the WVU instructional communi-cation graduate program were Penn State's Speech Communication Teacher Workshop program and—not surprising—the Florida State doctoral program with an emphasis on communication in instruction. McCroskey and Richmond (1992) provide a concise rationale, complete with course descriptions, objectives, instructional strategies, and assess-ment protocols for the WVU instructional communication program for in-service teachers. It is worth noting that no instructional com-munication program, so far, has exceeded the standards established by those built at WVU from 1972 and culminating with the creation of a doctoral program in 2005. In fact, as can readily be obtained from data contained in research productivity reports published over the past several decades, no single communication researcher to date has been as prolific as James C. McCroskey (Edwards et al., 1988; Hickson et al., 2003). Furthermore, the contributions of McCroskey, Richmond, and their colleagues and students at WVU cannot be overemphasized. In a communication research productivity analysis spanning 1915–2001, WVU was ranked number one with 328 cites, followed by Michigan State University with 239 cites (Hickson et al., 2004). In a shorter analysis of research productivity (1996–2001), Hickson et al. (2003) suggest that the most common profile regarding institution is that one would be teaching at West Virginia University, holding a terminal degree from Michigan State University, graduating in 1988.

Major advances in the status of communication education research were made possible by two pivotal conferences held in the 1980s. The first, according to Friedrich (1987), was the Speech

Communication Association Regional Research Seminar that was held in Michigan in the fall of 1983 and the spring of 1984. Key participants included Gus Friedrich (University of Nebraska), Cassandra Book (Northwestern University), and Jerry Feezel and Rebecca Rubin (both of Kent State). The results of the seminar were published as a symposium entitled "The Scholars Anthology: The Research Agenda for Communication Education in a special issue of the Central States Speech Journal in 1985. The second critical conference was organized by Jody Nyquist and held on the University of Washington campus in July of 1985. The Summer Conference on Instructional Communication, as it was named, included participation from Friedrich, Book, Donald Wulff, Janis Anderson, and Ann Staton-Spicer. In his summary of instructional communication research, Friedrich (1987) enthusiastically described instructional communication as "an exciting and active area of research within the communication discipline, which has attracted a core group of scholars who are producing quality, programmatic work" (p. 9). These historical roots have led to the development of additional flagship journals, doctoral programs that emphasize instructional communication research, and other consideration. The next section identifies and assesses the current status of instructional communication.

Current Status Assessment

In their review of instructional and developmental communication theory and research in the 1990s, Waldeck et al. (2001) identify the scope, major theories, and major lines of research and outlets for publication, as well as the future of instructional and developmental communication. Over the span of nine years (1990–1999), 42% of the research published was related to student communication; followed by 31% related to teacher communication, and 10% related to both mass media effects on children and pedagogical methods/technology use. Less than

4% was related to classroom management and teacher–student inter-action. Sixty-six percent of all instructional communication studies were published in one of three journals: *Communication Education* (47%), *Communication Research Reports* (7%), and *Communication Quarterly* (12%). Waldeck and her colleagues criticized instructional communica-tion as not being programmatic, containing too much conceptual and operational overlap, and being largely atheoretical. These criticisms are consistent with those raised by Friedrich (1987) a decade before when he argued that instructional communication research suffered from many of the problems identified by Scott and Wheeless in the 1970s (variable analytic; atheoretical; nonprogrammatic; no focus on actual classroom behavior or student–teacher interaction). In a fol-low-up review of instructional/development communication published in 2005, Nussbaum and Friedrich echoed the sentiments of Waldeck and her colleagues and also argued that instructional research should become more balanced along the developmental continuum by moving outside college classrooms to include younger and older learners. They also criticized instructional research for being overly reliant on log-ical empiricism and called for the inclusion of more interpretive and critical traditions to inform instructional communication knowledge claims. Almost 20 years later, we still struggle with similar challenges.

Given the current status of instructional communication research-ers (many of whom are teaching at standalone MA programs) and the dearth of instructional communication doctoral programs, the future of instructional communication is nebulous at best. But it does not have to be.

A Nebulous Future?

This chapter thus far has traced the historical development of instruc-tional communication in order to assess their current status and anticipate the future of communication education research in U.S.

universities. While there has been substantial progress made with respect to knowledge claims that can be used to improve instructional practices (e.g., *Handbook of Instructional Communication*), there is some concern about the future. It is necessary for more doctoral programs to be created that focus on instructional issues—preferably issues that are fundable (e.g., NIH, NINR, NIDA). We suggest programs might integrate the trend to include more of an emphasis on ICR beyond the university classroom and through other professional contexts. New theories must be developed and tested that move beyond the application of interpersonal or mass communication theories in the university classroom. In the current political climate of Common Core State Standards (CCSS; which at the time of this writing are dying a slow death) and accountability, we must make *learning* the bottom line and determine the most successful strategies for improving learning outcomes no matter the educational context. For instance, there is currently a demand in medical and engineering education for assistance in improving curriculum, instructional strategies, and behavioral competencies. Instructional communication research has much to offer. We are, as Gladwell aptly describes it, at a tipping point. What can we do? What must we do?

Conclusion

Hopefully the tone of this chapter is not received as unintentionally dire. Quite the opposite is true. Instructional communication research can continue to be an influential area of study moving forward. Realistically, we must adapt to our changing context and climate and pursue questions that transcend the university environment without forsaking the good work accomplished within our college communication departments. This volume hopefully continues a conversation that has been ongoing for decades. How do instructional communication researchers lend our expertise to help solve problems inside and outside of the academy?

PART I

Learning and Development

CHAPTER 1

Background

Angela M. Hosek, Scott Titsworth,
Carly Densmore, and Grace O. Sikapokoo

Various publications have documented the rise of instructional communication research, which was born out of the social-scientific shift by several scholars in the communication field. The history of instructional research has then mirrored broader trends in the field, starting with a decided variable analytic approach, which has then progressed through rigorous debate on the role of various methodologies. Furthermore, it has continued into a gradual development of (sub)discipline-specific theorizing. Our purpose in this chapter is not to revisit that history in detail, for other sources such as Houser and Hosek's (2018) *Handbook of Instructional Communication*, Fassett and Warren's (2010) *Handbook of Communication and Instruction*, and articles by Preiss and Wheeless (2014), Sprague (2002), and Morreale et al. (2014), as well as the first chapter of this publication, all provide an excellent analysis on the field's rich history. Rather, our purpose in this chapter is to highlight the intersections between instructional communication theory/research, K–12 communication education and the workplace, and various applied settings outside of the classroom that lend research in the area of instructional communication scholarship. Our central objective of this chapter is to argue that those intersections, whether they be in the form of theories or specific research agendas, are productive areas for continued research and seek attention by instructional scholars.

Variations in Approach

On face value, instructional communication and talent development are closely connected to one another. In both the classroom and applied settings, instructors (or trainers) develop and deploy lesson plans with the intended outcomes of helping students (defined broadly) learn new ideas, skills, and behaviors. Much of the skills and behaviors that are emphasized in the field of communication, specifically in communication education within the K–12 setting, include the skills of listening and speaking when it comes to public speaking and communication competence (Strawser et al., 2022). With these different objectives and settings in mind, both traditional teachers and talent development trainers seek to find new ways and various methods, backed with evidence, to improve the student (trainee) learning outcomes. Though many similarities appear obvious among these settings, there are various key differences that are also apparent when comparing traditional classroom instruction with nonacademic instruction (see Curtis et al., 1986).

For instance, different traditions focus on different aspects within the education setting. When looking at the tradition of educational psychology, the focus is on the learner, specifically how the learning occurs (LeBlanc Farris et al., 2018). In other words, a focus on educational psychology in teaching and training contexts explores how student (trainee) traits influence learning outcomes related to what students learn. Moreover, the focus seeks to understand how the students (trainees) feel about what they are learning and the ways they can demonstrate what they have learned (Mottet & Beebe, 2006). In many trainings and workplace contexts, this approach can be seen when work teams are asked to take personality-based assessments (e.g., Myers-Briggs Type Indicator; Strengths Finder; Dominance, Influence, Steadiness and Compliance [DISC]) as part of organizational training. These assessments are often administered to highlight and gain insight into how each employee is different or similar when it comes to their work style, motivation in the workplace, and approach to team-based interactions (Indeed Editorial Team, 2021). Although, through taking these assessments and, in turn, seeking to understand the individual differences, they do provide some insight to the learning context, instructional communication trainers and practitioners are more interested in how the interactions between trainees and trainers influence learning outcomes (LeBlanc Farris et al., 2018).

An additional way to explore the learning context is through an emphasis on pedagogy: The focus is on teacher (trainer) behavior, the methods, and how those lead to learning goals. In this sense, the focus is typically on classroom behaviors, specifically looking at how teacher behaviors motivate learning, classroom management (e.g., managing student misbehaviors), and teaching methods (e.g., lectures, discussions, experiential activities). In both the classroom and professional contexts, this often looks like teachers and trainers building relationships with the students (trainees), managing time, getting to know trainee needs, and using various methods to engage learning (e.g., projects, activities). However, there are differences of temporality that are at work in both contexts. Traditional classroom instruction typically occurs over an extended period of time, which offers teachers the opportunity to get to know their students interpersonally, as well as gives them the ability to identify their students' various motivations and the tools to then build a classroom culture based on their students. This may occur differently in nonacademic settings. This difference may be due to how trainings often occur internally through divisions of human resources or through trainings that are purchased and delivered by external consultants. In the case of nonacademic instruction, the ability to develop relationships is reduced, and the overall teaching methods may be less tailored to individual group needs without the insight into each individual in the training.

Another way to view pedagogy is through the substantial body of research within instructional communication devoted to the messages that teachers use to enhance learning outcomes in the classroom with their students. In line with our goal for this chapter, we highlight content relevance and clarity as teacher (trainer) behaviors that intersect both the classroom and professional contexts (see Mazer, 2018, for a comprehensive list). Teachers and trainers engage in content-relevant behaviors to show students and trainees that the content is related to their personal needs, the goals they have set for themselves, and their career goals (Keller, 1983). Particularly in classroom settings, this is often executed when teachers take inventory and seek to identify what students' goals are for taking certain courses, using popular media to explain course content (e.g., video clips, news articles) and highlighting how information can help students when they set out to find a job and begin their careers. This is similar regarding the area of professional contexts, in that these behaviors tend to inform trainees how recommended behaviors can apply to career enhancement and improve workplace relationships. Regarding the area of student motivation, Millette and Gorham (2002) found in their research that interest and relevance are essential motivators to student learning in the classroom. In short, relevant behaviors that teacher and trainers can engage in can make content meaningful and useful across multiple learning contexts.

Teacher (trainer) clarity is another teacher behavior that transcends learning environments. Clarity occurs through a cluster of instructional behaviors that support the reliability of instructional messages (Mazer, 2018). Researchers and communication scholars have argued that clarity is perhaps the most important teacher behavior (Rosenshine & Furst, 1971) and generally promotes student learning (Mazer, 2018). Teachers (trainers) that use clear messages allow for students to learn more, fear misinterpretation less, and find value in the material and the teacher (Chesbero, 2003). When teachers and trainers present information in ways that are structurally clear when using written cues (e.g., outline on the slide) and oral cues (e.g., "This next point is important to know"), retention and positive evaluation for the content and the teacher occur (Titsworth et al., 2010). Ultimately, attending to pedagogical goals related to teacher behavior in the classroom and professional contexts is important for learning to occur. Looking at the learning process from a communication perspective, much of the learning regarding communication education has begun in K–12 education context. Understanding this context and the education that takes place in K–12 education, teachers (trainers) can understand what individuals have been taught since the beginning of the educational journey.

In reflecting on the goal set for this chapter, we highlight content relevance and how teachers set their students up for success in the workplace through understanding how communication education is giving students the ability to be successful in professional contexts. K–12 education has integrated communication education in the classroom. Instructional communication research has been studied and applied in the context of K–12 education. Teachers and departments of education have pushed for communication competencies to be implemented and met in K–12 classrooms across the United States. Much of this push for communication competencies to be met comes from the Common Core standards. The standards that were put in place emphasized the initiative to promote communication learning and communication education regarding speaking and listening (Common Core State Standards Initiative, n.d.). The initiative and standards that were put in place mirror what Hess et al. (2015) investigate: what is being taught through the integration of communication education in K–12. Through the Common Core standards of teaching communication education in K–12 spaces, students are learning and developing their skills in the areas of speaking and listening to aid them in their skills as communicators in the classroom and beyond into the workplace. Additionally, Hess et al. (2015) underline what teaching communication in K–12 can do for the future of the student when it comes to the skills they can attain and apply in the classroom and beyond. This notion supports what Morreale et al. (2000) argue, as highlighted by Strawser et al. (2022), in that "the development of communication curricula in K–12 education by highlighting the role oral communication education plays in developing students' translatable skills" (p. 247). These transferable skills that can be learned in the K–12 education context can help them as they grow and advance their education.

To emphasize the impact the communication education has had on K–12 education, Morreale et al. (2014) explore how communication education has evolved and made an impact: "These speaking and listening standards have the potential to impact the teaching of communication significantly and positively in many K–12 schools in the U.S." (p. 351). Through integrating the standards, students are able to communicate effectively, listen to others, and overall engage with others in the classroom. By teaching these skills in the context of K–12, are able to carry over these skills to their future journey in higher education or in their careers after graduating from high school. A study conducted in 2008 by Morreale and Pearson uncover the importance of communication education. Morreale and Pearson's (2008) findings uncover six main themes that argue for why communication education is important in K–12 and the higher education context: (1) It is vital to the development of the whole person; (2) helps to improve the educational enterprise; (3) encourages being a responsible citizen of the world, socially and culturally; (4) helps individuals succeed in their careers and in business; (5) enhances organizational processes and organizational life; and (6) addresses emerging concerns for the 21st century. Overall, these themes illuminate that communication education is imperative to the education of students in K–12 and beyond, in that what they learn transfers into their future endeavors. These themes give insight into what students are learning and how they can transfer their skills in the workplace. Ultimately, through communication education, the hope is that once the education has been advanced, the student can then take their skills into their career and lives beyond the classroom. However, to in order to have communication education be of significance in a student's life, transferability of the skills is key to their success in their field and personal life.

When exploring the transferability of the communication education implored in the K–12 education context, Hess et al. (2015) outline that it can aid in the development and success of students when they navigate the next phase of their educational journey in higher education and the workplace. For example, when a teacher in the K–12 education context gives their students a lesson on how to write, cite sources, and give the speech to a live audience, they are then able to practice what they learned in that lesson and are able to receive an evaluation of the overall practice of writing and giving the speech. Ultimately, when a student learns how to produce, and give a speech using what they learned, they can take those public speaking skills into their classrooms in a higher education setting, where they can develop their skills further and take them to the workplace. Then, in the workplace when they have to give a presentation, they can use the skills they have been taught throughout their entire educational journey, leading them to be successful in writing and presenting the presentation. This overall gives students the ability to be successful and showcases the learning process. However, for the success of communication education in K–12 to be reflected in students' abilities when it comes to the workplace, Strawser et al. (2022) state that communication scholars need to advocate and promote the education of speaking and listening in the context of K–12 education. To advocate for the teaching and learning of speaking and listening, Strawser et al. (2022) emphasize that teachers in K–12 should be trained and provided resources to aid in their teaching of communication. Additionally, partnerships and research can aid in the push and support for communication education in K–12 education (Strawser et al., 2022). By providing resources and teacher training (preparation for trainers), partnerships, and research regarding the communication education, development of student skills and their success in being a communicator can be greater—meaning that when a student starts off with communication education courses in K–12 education, they develop their skills throughout their entire educational career, which can then aid them in their skills in the workplace and beyond.

However, much of the communication curriculum (and that of most academic departments) is aimed at traditional-aged college students, However, this claim is contrasted with other training situations where the learners are, by and large, adults. In the research conducted by Curtis et al. (1986), they explain, "While teaching and training are similar, ample evidence suggests that each activity requires distinct methods that limit crossover. ... Androgyny, the art and science of helping adults to learn, is a difficult orientation to master" (p. 57). In addition to differences between learners, traditional classroom instruction and training situations offer differences that are based on the intended outcomes of the teacher or trainer. Whereas classroom instruction generally works from conceptual to practical, many training situations are designed to focus exclusively on immediate, practical application, and problem-solving outcomes from the individuals being trained. Additionally, the teaching methods employed by teachers and trainers vary depending on the needs of the students and trainees in both classroom and professional settings. In recent years, applied forms of teaching methods such as problem-based learning (PBL) and place-based education (PBE) feature real-world and service-learning projects tied to local school and/or community issues that give students exposure to clients and consequential outcomes. Through these two methods students can see firsthand how the content of what they are learning impacts them personally and translates to the world around them. Both of these teaching methods can be seen to transcend both the classroom and professional contexts.

On top of that, there are evident differences between academic and nonacademic teaching contexts that imply that any application of instructional communication theory and research to nonacademic settings should be critically evaluated. Although the underlying objective of teaching others may extend into both types of learning situations, theories (and underlying research) of instructional communication have generally been developed with traditional college-aged students as the prime audience and as the research population, with little K–12-aged students being researched in this area, much like nonacademic settings. Thus, application of instructional communication theory and research to nonacademic settings and the setting of K–12 education should be taken with care to determine appropriateness and validity of such application.

With our objective of highlighting intersections between instructional communication and applied training settings, an obvious approach would be to analyze existing instructional communication theories for potential applicability to nonacademic settings. With over 50 years of research and scholarship, such an analysis would be substantial. However, we feel that the approach, given the previously mentioned cautions about such application, would result in a consistent conclusion: that existing instructional communication research and theory may have applicability to nonacademic settings but should be undertaken with caution because of key differences between academic and nonacademic settings. Thus, we opt to take a different tactic and analyze what we view as boundary spanning theoretical perspectives—theories and perspectives that draw from instructional communication concepts to implement training in settings outside of traditional classroom environments, which include the workplace. In essence, in this chapter we hope to highlight research and theory that act as a bridge for instructional scholars and practitioners to see connections between instructional communication and diverse training contexts. For clarity, we organize this discussion around the three domains of learning in Bloom et al.'s (1956) taxonomy: cognitive, affective, and behavioral. For each domain we discuss a theoretical perspective that spans both instructional communication and nonacademic perspectives.

The Cognitive Domain

Bloom's cognitive domain is a taxonomy of processes and outcomes through which students attain knowledge of different types of information and also an understanding of how that knowledge acquisition occurred (see Krathwohl, 2002). When teachers and trainers are focused on this domain the goal is that students understand what is being taught to them and are able to comprehend the new information. For instance, in a communication classroom, when students are learning about communication theory, many students progress through predictable stages where they recall, understand, apply, evaluate, and eventually create knowledge about the particular theories. Furthermore, such knowledge of these theories can range from factual knowledge to conceptual, procedural, and even metacognitive knowledge. An additional example in the context of a communication classroom can be understood when students are tasked with learning about nonverbal communication. In this example students may first learn factual information about different types of nonverbal behaviors, which could include haptics (e.g., touch), kinesics (e.g., movement), or proxemics (e.g., how space and distance influence communication). With that in mind, students must learn about these facets of nonverbal communication before they are able to ultimately begin applying their new learned knowledge to interpret the meaning of others' nonverbal displays. In short, the cognitive learning domain addresses how students acquire and develop knowledge. With that being said, in communication classroom situations, such knowledge is typically identified in learning outcomes and assessed through quizzes, exams, and projects. For example, in group communication courses, students could be tasked with conducting a group project that applies what they have learned throughout the semester into the final project. In this practice, the teacher is giving the students the opportunity to be assessed through actual application and practice of how to utilize what has been taught to them. However, the cognitive domain does not stop here. It goes further in looking at various communication contexts beyond the classroom setting.

One example of cognitive learning objectives that reach to applied settings lies in various research areas of health communication. Specifically, there has been research conducted where practitioners and trainers attempt to improve provider and/or patient knowledge that is essential for improved care. Theresa (Terri) Thompson, editor of *Health Communication*, wrote in a 2018 *Communication Education* reflection piece, "Obviously, the goal of all health communication research is educational, in that scholarly investigation is focused on changing health related behaviors and communication within health care contexts" (p. 490). As noted by Thompson, medical residents are trained through on-the-job residency programs to reach competence in both clinical and relational outcomes. Consequently, such training programs focus heavily on the advanced stages of the cognitive learning domain. As such, this gives the medical residents the opportunity to learn and progress well into the domain of cognitive learning in order to apply, analyze, and create approaches to care that benefit patients. This training also includes approaches to communicating health information to patients that aid in their care.

One such example of scholarship emphasizing advanced cognitive learning for medical residents is Villagran et al.'s (2010) COMFORT model for communicating bad news to patients and their family members. COMFORT is an acronym representing communication focal points for health professionals during interactions with patients:

> **Communication**: The need for basic competency in dyadic communication, including verbal and nonverbal effectiveness and the ability to adapt messages to other participants in the interaction
>
> **Orientation**: The ability to orient patients to the specific condition(s) presenting in their case, its prognosis based on available data, and opportunities for potentially improving that prognosis
>
> **Mindfulness**: The ability of medical professionals to be mentally and emotionally present in the moment and not rely on stereotypes, scripts (real or implied), or preconceived impressions about the patient

Family: Recognizing that family and other personal caregivers are essential members of the care team and also that such care presents second-order challenges to well-being

Ongoing: Providing confidence that care of the medical professional will be consistent and ongoing through the course of the medical episode

Reiterative messages: Reinforcing key messages about any progress or milestones in care and repetition of the most important messages related to tasks, recommendations, and requirements for standard-of-care treatment

Team: Promoting broad awareness that health interventions involve multiple team members (including family) and ensuring understanding of various roles of those members

Villagran et al. developed the COMFORT model as an interactive and dynamic guide for medical professionals who deliver bad medical news to those in their care (e.g., terminal illness). Their model was developed as an alternative to another model, called SPIKES, which they describe as problematic "because of its lack of emphasis on important learning goals for health communication instruction such as critical thinking, ethical recognition, and advocacy" (p. 223). In turn, each of these elements are related to the cognitive learning outcomes. Through observation and analysis of effective and ineffective interactions between residents and standardized patients, Villagran et al. formed the COMFORT model to serve as a set of competencies for health care providers that are effectively used and dynamically integrated into various health interactions.

The COMFORT framework is a productive example of a grounded theory at the intersection of health communication training and instructional communication. For instance, Villagran et al. explicitly identify verbal and nonverbal communication behaviors associated with perceptions of immediacy as critical communication skills needed in provider–patient interactions where bad news is delivered. Of course, instructional communication scholars have generated a substantial body of literature on this issue. Furthermore, any framework attempting to help providers establish immediacy could draw on the valuable information from that literature. Likewise, when discussing mindfulness, Villagran et al. discuss the essential need for empathy and emotional support, all while recognizing the potential emotional toll such behaviors may place on the practitioner(s). When training residents and other providers to enact mindfulness in their role, the use of emotional response theory (ERT; see Mottet et al., 2006) can be evident in this interaction. For instance, Mazer et al. (2014) found that poor communication is associated with perceptions of less social support, more emotion work, and higher levels of negative emotions such as anger and hopelessness. Another study by the same author team also found that positive communication behaviors are related to increased perceptions of social support, less emotional labor, and several positive discrete emotions, for example hope (Titsworth et al., 2013). The ERT framework could provide conceptual models to help medical practitioners learn how their communication can potentially contribute to a climate of mindfulness important for their patient's well-being as well as their own.

Through this analysis, we feel that the COMFORT framework illustrates how a boundary-spanning model can usefully draw on instructional communication literature to help medical practitioners effectively develop knowledge from which they can achieve higher order learning outcomes. To crystalize this point, consider how some knowledge of immediacy and ERT could make two elements of the COMFORT model have concrete, data-based reference points for those being trained on the model. The interplay of instructional communication theory and research with the COMFORT model enriches how it could be taught to practitioners to enhance their opportunity for higher order cognitive learning.

The Affective Domain

Krathwohl (2002) characterizes affective learning as attitudinal change toward subject matter surrounding perceptions such as heightened attention, actively responding, and valuing. When students gain knowledge and engage in affective learning, their emotions and intensity of acceptance (or rejection) may increase in ways that influence their interests, attitudes, and discrete emotional reactions toward a subject matter and/or learning situation. A recurring theme of instructional communication research is that affective learning is a "central causal mediator" between instructor behaviors and cognitive learning. When instructors engage in behaviors that raise students' affect, they are far more likely to improve in cognitive learning outcome objectives. This lends insight into what scholars have explored and coined, which is understood as entertainment education.

Research regarding entertainment education is a theoretically driven application of entertainment-based messages to promote social good (see Singhal et al., 2003). According to Singhal and Rogers (2002), entertainment education involves the intentional placement of health messages within entertainment-based media, such as radio dramas, television shows, comics, and other sources. Although the intended outcome of entertainment education is positive social change (e.g., the appropriate use of contraceptives, or engaging in behaviors to reduce the spread of disease), the use of entertainment media is initially focused on achieving attention and driving attitude change toward such health interventions. In essence, entertainment education hopes to achieve behavioral outcomes by first influencing affective outcomes. Looking back at the beginning of entertainment education, entertainment education was born out of Rogers's broader theory labeled as diffusion of innovation. What Rogers describes is a process through which innovations, such as health-promotion interventions, are propagated throughout a society, culture, or group of people.

Looking back at Singhal's early work in entertainment education, it emerged and progressed from a focus on entertainment education broadly to more specifically examine how a specific type of narrative, called positive deviance, can be used to promote social good. Positive deviance is a perspective championing the notion that certain members of local communities are able to problem-solve and find solutions to larger problems (see Kwitonda & Singhal, 2018). When scholars and practitioners are able to identify positive deviants, such locally based knowledge can be integrated into social change messaging (e.g., entertainment education) to help diffuse innovative, locally produced solutions.

The interplay between positive deviance, entertainment education, and the diffusion of innovation is a powerful example of how affective learning plays a role in applied communication settings. By focusing messages on local positive deviants, messages promoting social change are able to have greater potential for impact because they are far more likely to result in positive affect toward new innovations. As explained by Kwitonda and Singhal (2018), messages about positive deviants are neither top down nor completely grassroots. However, these messages ultimately lie somewhere in between because they emanate from highly innovative individuals who employ strong critical thinking and problem-solving skills to tackle endemic social problems.

Of course, a significant body of instructional communication research has focused on affective learning, though in a way distinct from Singhal and colleagues. Many affective learning articles focus on teacher characteristics (e.g., nonverbal immediacy) that are related to students' reports of affective learning. Be that as it may, Singhal's focus on positive deviant messages is different in the sense that peer messages, not top down, are highly effective at promoting change. Although many instructional scholars have called for greater attention to peers, few studies have specifically examined how peers, rather than teachers, are connected to affective outcomes. One counterexample to that statement is a study by Russo and Benton (2003), who found that the perceived presence of peers in an online class was related to greater affect for students. Notably, peer feedback provides students an opportunity to improve their understanding of course concepts, which is additive as it reinforces the cognitive domain of learning (Hosek et al., 2017).

Ultimately, our analysis suggests that instructional communication researchers have generally approached affective learning from what Singhal and colleagues would call a top-down approach. What this means is that certain behaviors by teachers or trainers may influence the students' overall affective learning. Equally viable is the notion that peers influence affect, as is the case with numerous positive deviance examples described by Kwitonda and Singhal (2018). Nevertheless, the concept of affect is meaningful in helping to explain a type of learning that is related to positive deviance, entertainment education, and the diffusion of innovation. Moreover, the ways in which affect is integrated into academic settings, as exemplified in much instructional communication research on the topic, and nonacademic settings, such as with Singhal's work, could be mutually informative. In short, as teachers and scholars we should be looking for positive deviant behaviors more frequently in our instructional research programs, as this may inform what these behaviors look like in context in various industries.

The Behavioral Domain

The behavioral domain, also referred to as psychomotor learning, exists when students engage in physical activities. These activities are understood as involving discrete movements with skill, coordination, accuracy, and timeliness (Simpson, 1966). For example, think of a basketball player. As a student-athlete is instructed by a coach, their ability to perform basic skills like dribbling the ball, shooting, and defending the ball from other players increases in precision and effectiveness. Learning and improving on these basic skills can then lead them to the point where they are able to create impactful game play on the court during live game situations.

In comparison to affective and cognitive learning, instructional communication scholarship has devoted less attention to the question of how effective classroom instruction and student performance can boost behavioral learning outcomes. Moreover, a typical example where behavioral learning has been explored is in Sanders and Weisman's (1990) article where they sought to explore the connections between teacher immediacy and students' intent to continue studying a particular subject. Using a self-report measure of intent, Sanders and Weisman (1990) found that when teachers engaged in behaviors perceived as immediate, students were more likely to indicate a preference for continuing to study that subject matter. Although similar findings have been observed in other studies, the self-report measure of intended behavioral change does not necessarily demonstrate actual change. Nevertheless, the self-report measure approach is typical in much of the literature.

Instructional scholars have recently begun to explore more direct behavioral implications for instructional communication taking place outside of the classroom. In explaining the role of instructional communication for crisis and risk messages, Sellnow et al. (2015) noted that "[crisis] messages include the essential components for garnering the attention of receivers (or learners) in ways that motivate them to attend (affect), to comprehend (cognitive), and to take appropriate actions (behavioral) during high-risk situations" (p. 421). Sellnow et al.'s (2015) program of research has explored crisis communication in a variety of settings. In addition, a recent publication by Edwards et al. (2021) is a productive example of how their applied research focus meaningfully blends instructional communication with crisis and risk communication.

In Edwards et al.'s (2021) piece, they explore how a community of practice in agricultural communication uses principles of instructional communication to raise awareness of and action to mitigate risk of a highly transmissible disease in the swine/pork industry, specifically the African swine fever virus. Edwards et al.'s (2021) study uses organizational learning theory to better understand how the community of practice in this sector of agricultural communication improves messages to affect risk-prevention behaviors in that community. Based on interviews with members of the swine industry, they observe that the community of practice engages in organizational learning (OL) through mutual engagement, negotiation of joint enterprise, and shared repertoire. Mutual engagement refers to how members of the community organize connectedness. For example, the community must learn how to best connect members who represent diverse producers, medical practitioners, transporters, and processors, each who have a role to play in mitigating virus transmission. Negotiation of a joint enterprise is the extent to which members of the community have agreed-on objectives and courses of action to abate risk. Finally, shared repertoire is the extent to which the community has and shares knowledge, and also has processes through which to continually adapt and gain additional knowledge to mitigate the crisis.

In addition, Edwards et al. (2021) contend, "Instructional communication research clarifies how [organizational learning] operates in crisis planning and response by focusing more specifically on how instructional communication learning outcomes are addressed and achieved via [communities of practice] as learning communities" (p. 52). In essence, they suggest that communities of practice, particularly those responding to crisis events, use instructional communication principles to dynamically adapt to the learning and communication needs of the community while simultaneously promoting behaviors to mitigate risk. Effective organizations can open communication surrounding community knowledge that becomes (and is adapted to) all members of the organization, and in doing so may respond more effectively to crises.

The work on crisis communication in the works by Sellnow et al. (2015) and Edwards et al. (2021) are clear examples of how instructional communication perspectives are meaningful lenses through which to understand processes outside of the classroom. Whereas instructional scholars typically examine communication between and among students and teachers that occur in the classroom and attempt to draw connections between communication and learning, Edwards et al. (2021) meaningfully extend that analysis to an entire community of practice. As noted by Sellnow et al. (2015), such an extension in perspective raises numerous examples of how instructional communication can be extended to multiple types of applied and organizational settings. Such extension addresses some of the same basic questions of learning as instructional communication. This is due, in part, because of the change in setting, which tends to examine those questions on broader organizational and systemic scales. Such a shift in perspective has potential for a productive expansion of where instructional communication research may have impact.

This chapter has examined the connection between educational psychology, pedagogy, K–12 education in regard to how it is examining communication education, as well as the professional contexts. We also explored three areas of research that highlight learning outcomes similar to instructional communication, but in contexts and applications outside traditional academic environments. In each instance, such research recommends approaches for practitioners intended to raise cognitive, affective, and/or behavioral learning in the classroom and beyond. To close, we offer three final observations. First, each of the applications we reviewed appeared to integrate Bloom's three domains of learning rather than focus on a particular domain. In regard to what scholars have examined in the area of entertainment education and positive deviance, raising attention and promoting social change also requires some transmission of knowledge (e.g., how to properly use contraceptives). In addition to entertainment education, there has been research focused on how to prevent swine infections. In these instances, we see that both knowledge and affect/motivation is necessary in this process. A second observation we examined is that these applied contexts are more dynamic than typical classroom instruction. What is observed is that in each of the example applications, learners are more dispersed, and the approaches to effective instruction are more strategic than typical classroom lesson plans. The last observation we were struck with was that applications of instructional communication to these other contexts promoted reflection on how understandings of effective classroom communication might shift if we were to bring the types of questions asked in these nonacademic contexts back to more traditional settings. For instance, we ask the following question: How do students and teachers meaningfully interact with broader communities of practice? This question and idea are explored further in the next chapter. Another question we have pondered is how teachers and students shift between classroom skill sets in the same ways as proposed in the COMFORT model. We conclude that an expanded application of instructional communication to nonacademic contexts could be fruitful in nonacademic settings, while at the same time expand the types of questions we explore in traditional classroom and school environments.

CHAPTER 2

Current Trends and Future Directions

Angela M. Hosek, Carly Densmore,
Grace O. Sikapokoo, and Scott Titsworth

R esearch and industry reports regularly acknowledge that employers desire communication, teamwork, and relational and problem-solving skills from their employees. In fact, an academic foundation in communication often provides employees with competence in a multitude of areas such as interpersonal, intercultural, and organizational communication and the ability to create clear and concise messaging (Randall, 2018). As teachers we hope that we are guiding students to pursue passions, contribute to democratic society, and promote inclusion in personal and professional spaces, among a host of other goals. We hope that we are preparing them for successful professional careers. Yet, as teachers we may not regularly hear from our industry partners to know if, and how, these desires are being realized in professional settings. To be sure, universities and colleges maintain alumni relationships, collect alumni and industry survey data, and collaborate with industry networks on a global scale. Yet, the complex and rapidly changing needs of industry are often a bit slower to translate back to academic contexts in ways that allow for agile curricular change to meet industry needs and demands.

The COVID-19 pandemic has shown both educator and professional alike how quickly we can and often must adapt. As Corpuz (2021) notes, "To live in the world is to adapt constantly" (p. 344). Accordingly, researchers note that people and organizations cope with rapid changes by adapting and responding quickly (Burke et al., 2006). Hence, it makes sense that employers desire employees that are astute at using social media, can create and deliver digital and virtual presentations, and know how to troubleshoot technological issues (NACE, 2020). Essentially, Edwards (2021) argued that "technological skills are more important in a pandemic where physical social distance is best practice" (p. 3). In this chapter, we continue the work from our previous chapter, yet turn an inward eye toward the ways industry experts and professionals see instructional communication skills and research translating (or not) to practice in the workplace. To do so, we interviewed nine working professionals ranging from experts who recently moved from academia to the public sector, CEOs of international companies, and consultants with a collective 30 years' experience to gain their perspective on trends, needs, challenges, and innovations related to instructional communication knowledge and skills in the workplace.

As authors of this chapter, we too have personal and scholarly connections to the ways in which instructional communication is and could be engaged in professional contexts outside of academia. Collectively, we have decades of professional and research experience spanning corporate industry, academic administration, and teaching in the United States and globally. In addition to her academic credentials, Angela spent the early part of her career as a corporate training and curriculum designer in the aerospace industry that served clients in the civilian U.S. military and in the United Statets and Canada. She serves as director of the presentation skill program at Ohio University and is responsible for graduate teacher training. A portion of her research and training focus on instructional communication. Grace has served as the associate director for the presentation skills program at Ohio University, has facilitated graduate teacher training, and has also taught various communication courses. Prior to joining academia, Grace was a customer experience professional who developed customer service training manuals and conducted training sessions with sales and customer support employees in the South African insurance sector. Carly has taught a variety of communication courses, and her research interests relate to instructional communication, with a particular interest in communication apprehension and social support. Additionally, she is passionate about continual improvement as a teacher and helping students improve their communication skills inside and beyond the classroom. As someone whose experience has largely been in academia, Carly believes that this chapter is vital for educators with less industry experience as it provides insight into what professionals in industry are looking for from their employees. As an educator for nearly 30 years, Scott has conducted training in both academic and nonacademic settings. Like Angela, Scott has served as director of the presentation skills program at two universities and has also led training for other academic administrators on external and internal communication strategy. Scott has also worked with units inside the Scripps College of Communication at Ohio University to design training strategies that utilize virtual reality to improve relational skills in fields such as medicine and law enforcement.

Focusing on the ways in which instructional communication and education occur in professional contexts from the viewpoint of our industry partners and where we, as authors, see this area headed is vital for several reasons. Notably, employers desire communication skills competence from their employees. Also, it is necessary to know if the skills that students are receiving translate to the desired skills that employers are seeing and where, if any, revisions to concepts, contexts, and approaches need to occur. In this chapter, we explore skills and trends essential to instructional communication, with a particular focus on virtual learning and its impact on how students should be prepared to apply communication skills in the workplace. Then, we highlight the findings from our interviews with industry experts and share implications for the future of instructional communication in professional contexts.

Instructional Communication and Technological Competency

Employers continue to desire skills that are increasingly lacking in employees, such as listening, reading, comprehension, clarity, critical thinking, writing, information technology (software and hardware), mathematics, coordination, monitoring, judgment, decision-making, and active listening (Marand & Noe, 2018). We expect that instructional scholars will continue to explore content in these areas to extend our understanding of learning and training outcomes in these areas. Yet, we predict a significant focus will be on communication technology competency, and thus we focus specifically on this area before exploring the findings from the interviews with industry experts.

In many higher educational settings, universities, instructors, and students have embedded the use of technology in the learning environment. In doing so, students engage in what is termed *virtual learning*, which occurs when learning takes place through a means of technology (Lacka & Wong, 2021). Many courses in university settings have switched from face-to-face to an online environment due to the increase in the efficiency and popularity of online learning (Kaufmann & Vallade, 2020). As of the early to mid-1990s, distance learning and online education was implemented in higher education settings due to the developments and advancements in technology (Kentnor, 2015). The popularity of virtual learning increased due to technological advances and as researchers began to understand how virtual learning impacts student learning and overall experiences in the classroom (Edwards & Edwards et al., 2016; Kuznekoff & Titsworth, 2013). The impact of student virtual learning includes which types of technologies can lead to student success and substantial learning in the classroom. Additionally, many of the students currently taking classes are known as "digital natives," meaning they have grown up in a time of technology being at the forefront of their environment (Gallagher et al., 2020), and learning (e.g., reading, gaming, interacting) in a virtual space has typically always been an option. Yet, researchers indicate that many employees struggle to adapt and use new technologies. As we envision new ways of being as a result of the pandemic, these technologies are now more commonplace in our work and personal lives.

Virtual learning affords students the ability to use the means they are comfortable with while also promoting the learning of new skills. Virtual learning can promote new knowledge and skills embodied by students. By using, integrating, and promoting virtual learning in college-level courses, instructors can educate and challenge students to learn using technology and different modalities (e.g., VoiceThread, video chat [i.e., Zoom, Microsoft Teams, Slack]). This is essential, given that four in 10 employees lack digital workplace skills such as basic computer skills, collaboration software, and data analysis (Ismail, 2022). These modalities give students the opportunity to learn and communicate on different platforms with their instructor and peers. Through virtual learning, individuals can engage and communicate using technology in a time coined as the *information age* (Graham, 2019). Additionally, using technology and virtual spaces, individuals can communicate and obtain information faster. Working in a group or independently in a virtual environment has numerous benefits. Researchers indicate that working online can bolster collaborative learning by decreasing student apprehensions, increasing social skills, and promoting collaboration with peers (Brandon & Hollingshead, 1999). Furthermore, scholars have unpacked how virtual learning variations, motivations, and perceived immediacy in virtual learning environments (Carrell & Menzel, 2001) and classroom climate in a virtual learning environment (Kaufmann et al., 2016).

The ability to learn in a virtual setting and communicate on different platforms allows students to prepare for using these skills in their careers. Previous researchers have examined how online learning is used in the context of an industry-specific online learning center. Waldeck (2008) discovered that with virtual learning engagement there is increased satisfaction when individuals have been trained well and can utilize online platforms in their jobs. Waldeck's (2008) study highlights how communication skills, visual communication, and relationships are important for success in online environments. By providing students with the ability to take online courses and engage in virtual learning as part of their coursework, they may be better prepared when starting industry careers than their counterparts who have less experience, learning, presenting, and building relationships through these platforms Thus, virtual learning can be an integral part to industry work and performance. When working in a virtual environment, nonverbal communication is an important component because of the perceptions, immediacy, and relationships formed in the virtual environment (McArthur, 2021). Therefore, when implementing technology in the classroom, it is something that students may be used to and is a natural practice. Thus, virtual learning may be a way to promote learning in the classroom and show how learning takes place beyond, into their careers.

Instructional communication research highlights various skills that can translate into professional spaces, and virtual learning is a growing focus for scholars and practitioners. However, hearing from our industry colleagues provides additional complexity and support toward our goals in moving instructional communication forward as they see how these research translates in to practice (or not) on a daily basis. Next, we explore the findings of our interviewers with nine industry experts.

In Conversation With Industry Experts

To inquire about the ways in which instructional communication skills and behaviors are at work in the professional contexts, we interviewed working professionals in our networks. We asked each person a series of questions that focused on trends in teaching and learning in workplace spaces, innovative communication skills employers want from college graduates, topics they wish scholars were studying in their research, and what communication-related skills they wished the college experience focused more on to prepare students for their careers.

To analyze our interview data, we individually read the notes and transcripts from each interview and identified relevant themes. Then we met to discuss our initial reactions and finalized themes that grouped responses together in a coherent way. Next, we moved to interpretating how the industry professionals' responses reflected instructional communication skills and behaviors in the workplace. In order to capture the range of our interviewees, we asked each professional to describe their current position, any relevant previous positions, and number of years in industry, and as we share their ideas, we include this information with their exemplars.

Findings and Implications for Instructional Communication Research and Teaching

As we reflected on the interviews and what our industry colleagues had to share with us, we realized that instructional communication and communication teachers, in general, are providing future professionals with necessary and important skills. However, we may need to revise our framing, focus, and the types of application opportunities we provide for students to ready them for their careers. Our industry colleagues highlight the ways in which we need to prepare students in ways that are increasingly attuned toward technology to achieve presentation skills competence, rhetorical goals, and relational goals that prioritize inclusion and access.

Presentation Competence: Building Behaviors and Choosing Modalities

A first recurrent theme from our industry experts focused on the need to enhance presentation skills competence. In particular, our interviewees stressed the importance of students knowing how to use multiple modalities to deliver information. For example, Bill Zingraf (CEO, Strategy Breakthrough Transformation Innovation [SBTI], 13 years' experience) captured this need when he said, "People don't remember what you say but how you make them feel, and not doing presentations well makes or breaks careers" (B. Zingraf, personal communication, September 23, 2021). Bill and others suggested that more focus on nonverbal communication is needed in ways that communicate confidence and approachability. In many ways, this is tied to notions of immediacy, approachability, and rapport that are foundational aspects of instructional communication. To this end, they noted that it is not enough to be able to share content during a presentation; employees need to create an environment where people want to ask questions and want to get involved in the content. To achieve this goal, they suggested more emphasis and training in nonverbal presentational skills.

Although, our industry experts agreed that digital and virtual communication is fully integrated into the workplace, several suggested that we have yet to figured out how to harness certain elements for workplace communication. For instance, Bill suggested that more training needs to occur around the visual aspects of virtual communication and presentations, which is essentially tied to nonverbal communication. He indicated that more training needs to occur surrounding virtual presentation backgrounds, lighting, managing distractions (e.g., construction outside a house), and how to look at the camera instead of at one's own image. In other words, the production of visual communication and their processes are now equally as important as the content of the message, the credibility of the speaker, and the engagement of the audience.

In addition, the industry experts we interviewed discussed the benefits and struggles they encountered as they relate to the influence of technology on workplace engagement. Bill discussed the ways technology, in particular phones, have challenged how we view engagement and our relationships with others in the workplace. Bill used the analogy of the camera:

> Our technology reflects how the culture has changed. For so long we wanted great zoom lenses for our cameras to capture the distance through photography and see the expanse views, but now our focus is on selfies and filming ourselves doing daily activities and, in my opinion, it has made our focus narrower. I believe we have shifted our focus from wanting to see and know our outward surroundings to a more internal focus on headphones and staring at social media. In doing so, we have changed how we interact with the world and this change has made communicating more challenging, especially during presentations and meetings in professional settings.

In his argument, Bill shared that during meetings or presentations he observes presenters with little knowledge of what is happening in the audience when they use their phones to hold presentation notes or take notes during meetings. Bill argued that when the focus is on the self and on one's own experiences (on their phones) it makes it difficult to help others understand how skills like audience analysis remain valuable and necessary for rhetorical and relational purposes in the workplace.

When we think about engagement and participation, variables that are hallmarks of instructional communication research and teaching, the experiences of our industry experts show us a way to rethink the methods we use to teach these concepts. Although it would be easier to think that we should continue to teach students to focus on the needs of the audience and adapt their messages accordingly, we may be missing an opportunity to connect the self(ie) focus of contemporary technology to achieve this goal. Given that the focus for many of us has turned inward to our self(ie), it makes sense that we (re)think how we train, for example, presentational speaking. Perhaps we ought to begin with acknowledging and being honest about the fact that we typically are focused on our own thoughts and ideas before that of our audience. This can be problematic because this focus can make it hard to identify the needs of the audience or fully recognize that the speaker needs to (and be motivated to) adapt their message to the needs of the audience. Traditionally we have taught students to make the audience the center of their preparation and that every decision they make should trace back to the needs of the audience (Titsworth et al., 2020). Although this remains true, it may be time to redesign the starting point of our curriculums and training workshops to start with the self-focus and the ways in which it benefits and hinders our ability to meet our pre-sentation goals. In doing so, this may alleviate the frustrations expressed by our industry experts (and teachers) when presenters appear to be out of touch with their audiences. When we acknowledge the reality that our focus has turned inward, and that we need to turn outward to understand our audience, it creates space to identify and develop skills with different modalities to achieve our instruction goals in the workplace. Next, we share how instructional communication can be leveraged to prepare pro-fessionals for using multiple modalities in the workplace.

Our industry experts' comments reflected a sense that incoming professionals need to understand and be able to use multiple *modalities* to communicate messages. Modalities refer to the ways in which communi-cation takes place (e.g., phone, computer, face-to-face, etc.) in a job setting. Many of our experts mentioned this aspect of workplace communica-tion and noted that society, in general, has become more technologically advanced, and companies are focusing on conducting more work using various modalities (e.g., Microsoft Teams, Zoom, Slack; S. Tikkanen [Facebook; 2 months, 8 years in academia], personal communication, September 23, 2021). Different modalities come into play in workplace activities such as new employee onboarding, virtual team management, team meetings, group work, remote work, interacting with outside stakeholders, and personal investment to the company.

Relatedly, when onboarding takes place, new hires often engage in virtual training and learning (S. Tikkanen, personal communication, September 23, 2021; K. Atwell [leadership development, organizational design, and professional coach, 40-plus years of experience], personal communication, September 24, 2021). Through the onboarding experience, new hires learn information about the company, their job, and company expectations, usually through an online platform. Our experts suggest that this approach leads to employee retention, knowledge, and application (S. Tikkanen, personal communication, September 23, 2021; K. Atwell, personal communication, September 24, 2021). When speaking with Stephanie Tikkanen, who holds a PhD in communication studies, she emphasized that by encouraging virtual learning in the classroom, students can learn how to be a learner in this setting before being placed in this context when they start their careers—where the stakes are higher for the company and the employee. Mary pointed to the notion that students often do not understand how to learn and *then* apply what they have learned from passive viewing in a mediated setting (M. Hettinger [senior consultant, 30-plus years of experience], personal communication, September 24, 2021). Hettinger noted that students often view and hear the concepts, but do not apply what they learn beyond the classroom (M. Hettinger, personal communication, September 24, 2021). This can be likened to watching videos on macrons on YouTube but not being able to translate what you learned in to practice. The lack of learning and application synergy leads to miscommunications, misunderstandings, and struggles in the workplace. Hettinger suggested that teachers need to emphasize the *learn and then apply* concept, through this idea of "think, feel, do." For example, have students think about and ways to avoid implicit racial bias during salary negotiations by reading articles and texts, then attempt to feel what this might be like through testimony and personal accounts from those that have experienced it, and finally engage in activities (virtually on in the classroom) that have them simulate this experience with peers and working professionals. Teaching this concept early can help when individuals are no longer memorizing concepts for the final exam but can move toward application in the workforce. Thus, when using varying modalities, students can learn the concepts in multiple ways and apply them when they are face-to-face, listening to onboarding training, and much more. In all, envisioning these possibilities will assist in productivity and efficiency. Next, our experts addressed the need for quality communication as an essential skill needed for incoming employees.

Industry experts explained that quality communication on multiple mediated platforms allows individuals to be effective and encourages productivity and efficiency at work (M. Price [senior training consultant, 15 years of experience], personal communication, September 24, 2021). Monica Price explained that she is seeing more deficiencies in quality communication. Specifically, she receives emails that are sent throughout the organization with no capitalization, punctuation, or clarity (M. Price, personal communication, September 24, 2021). Price notes that even though a communication exchange is happening, it is not one of quality. Karen Atwell offers another example. She shared a story about an employee named "Jessie" who emailed a company two times to order materials, and when "Jessie" did not receive a reply, she did not follow up and never ordered the needed materials. When Atwell and other employees told "Jessie" to make a phone call to the company (which she had not thought to do), she was able to learn why no one responded and the materials were ordered (K. Atwell, personal communication, September 24, 2021). This example illustrates how many Millennials and Gen Z employees prefer to use messaging (e.g., email, text messages) to communicate versus calling on the phone. Researchers have found that Millennials and Gen Zers may experience phone apprehension, which is a fear of having to speak to someone on the phone. This fear occurs because people are nervous about potential faux paus that could take place on the phone, thus leading them to choose different means of communication (Wayne, 2014). In this example, "Jessie" may not have realized the implications of only sending an email, and how using different modalities could lead to a different outcome (e.g., talking to an actual person to get a response). However, Atwell suggested that teachers can prepare students by engaging them with different modalities to communicate with others and to recognize that the way they prefer to communicate may not always be the most efficient or reliable.

As instructional communication researchers we understand that teachers have learning outcomes and objectives to teach their students, oftentimes mandated by other policy boards (e.g., state policy, university general education requirements, discipline associations). As instructors, we are tasked with how to teach our students what will be helpful to them when they leave our classrooms. Instructional research has uncovered how practical application can assist students in understanding the implications and effects of what they are learning (Alexander & Reynard, 2008; Miller & Wieland, 2018; Root, 2018). Knowing what practical applications would be beneficial can, in turn, assist in teaching skills and etiquette. Furthermore, this could help in eliminating the poor quality of communication and increase student proficiency in varying modalities.

By having students work through group tasks or assignments using various modalities, they can learn how to manage conflict, work together, and, overall, communicate effectively (K. Atwell, personal communication, September 24, 2021). Having students work in an in-person, face-to-face setting allows for group dynamics to form because body language plays a role (K. Atwell, personal communication, September 24, 2021). The "data" within our messages is different depending on if the communication is mediated (face-to-face) or in person (face-to-face). Ultimately, by under-standing the benefits and challenges that come with each modality, students can select the mode that meets the needs of the context and relationship. Importantly, being able to explain and demonstrate that students know how to use these modalities can make students more marketable when seeking jobs (C. Francis [talent development consultant, 15 years of experience], personal communication, September 24, 2021).

Rhetorical and Relational Goals

A second recurrent theme from our industry experts addressed the need for *goal-oriented communication* that ties well to how instructional schol-ars view rhetorical goals in the teaching and learning process. Our experts framed goal-oriented communication as messages that are clear, direct, and relevant to the people involved in the interaction. Content relevance is defined as content that is personalized to the needs and interests of the audience and satisfies their personal goals (Mazer, 2018). For example, Chuck Francis (personal communication, September 24, 2021) discussed the importance of data visualization and project management as com-municative skills required by business leaders to make meetings more efficient and effective: "In corporate meetings, you do not have a lot of time to present, so you need to learn to be efficient, simple, and visual." Hence, the content of the presentation and the effectiveness of the com-munication helps to achieve the intention for the meeting.

Some of our experts discussed that students should have the ability to produce content that is simple and well written for people in the work-place (B. Jones [executive coach and author with 40 years of experience], personal communication, September 27, 2021). Beverly Jones (personal communication, September 27, 2021) refers to these skills as basics for deep work that involves reading, writing, and communicating. She also stated that employers and leaders are monitoring these behaviors with a renewed interest because "people don't write as well, which leads to more wasted time spent on communicating than is necessary," and the aim of efficient communication is to increase the return on investment. Therefore, students need to be trained on how to use verbal and nonverbal communication to deliver information that connects and resonates with professionals or their target audience.

The relational goal of developing immediacy, which is a psychological closeness between teachers and students (Richmond et al., 1987) in the classroom emphasizes the importance of being able to connect to others. Jo Spurrier, one of our experts, explained how having the ability to speak and connect with people is more valuable now than it was in the past (founder and CEO of Berkana LLC, 34 years of experience; J. Spurrier, personal communication, September 27, 2021). An increase in teacher immediacy increases students' interest in learning and tends to increase a student's motivation to learn long after the student has completed their studies (Richmond et al., 2018). As an employee, the student will not only find it easier to relate to their colleagues, but this will also help them to achieve their set milestones and keep their colleagues motivated and connected. Developing a connection with your colleagues and superiors helps to cultivate a team that "can do more with less" (C. Francis, personal communication, September 24, 2021).

Relational goals can also relate to students forming relationships and actively participating with others as part of their learning. Student learning and development takes place through engagement and participation. Student participation includes preparation, contribution to discussion, group skills, communication skills, and attendance (Dancer & Kamvounias, 2005). Engagement occurs when students are intrinsically motivated and are committed to learning using various strategies and being self-regulated (Harris, 2011). Having the ability to engage and participate on various platforms and through a variety of opportunities, such as an internship, provides young graduates with the chance to learn about the importance and relevance of communication through experience (J. Spurrier, personal communication, September 27,2021; B. Jones, personal communication, September 27, 2021). Further, Jones advised that providing fellowships over the summer for students could help them remain engaged with the industry while keeping instructional communication researchers informed of trends as students come back to report to the home departments. For example, internship coordinators can facilitate a colloquia for recent interns to present and showcase what they have learned "on the job" to their peers in a setting that at once practices presentation skills, facilitates information sharing, and enhances interest in internships. Internships have been impacted by the pandemic, and providing a showcase experience can enhance motivation and interest in pursuing them as employers engage and invest in these opportunities in the future (Feldman, 2021).

Another relational trend that our industry experts identified was how communication in the workplace is being (re)defined through daily lived experiences. For example, Francis recalls how he struggled to show the value he hoped to bring to a company with his undergraduate communication degree; as a result, his recommendation is to incorporate courses such as project management that require communication skills to discuss business outcomes and delivery (C. Francis, personal communication, September 24, 2021). In this way, communication studies students understand ways to see their work in activities that match specific organizational needs and roles (e.g., project management). Cat Russell also challenged how she has understood professional communication to be taught at the college level, which is from a very White, and in her view, prejudiced perspective that has excluded people of color and other marginalized communities (human resources liaison for strategic human resources programs, 11 years of experience; C. Russell, personal communication, September 28, 2021). However, she acknowledged that this perception is changing as people from marginalized communities are speaking up, contributing to discussions, and bringing their own perspectives to the classroom. These types of conversations are increasing and will soon spillover into boardrooms, if they have not done so already. Therefore, recognizing these different relational perspectives in the classroom and empowering students to engage and participate will help students to do so when they enter the workplace.

Instructor narratives have helped students retain information from their classes, making them more informed students (Kromka & Goodboy, 2019). Hence, storytelling is a recognized learning opportunity (C. Russell, personal communication, September 28, 2021) that enables the building of rapport and relationships in the classroom. Rapport is a relational construct that produces a positive instructor–student relationship (Frisby & Martin, 2010). Webb and Barrett (2014) organized five themes that instructors use to build rapport: attentive behaviors, common grounding behaviors, courteous behaviors, connecting, and information-sharing behaviors. These themes are similar to the humanizing practice and connection that storytelling brings to the classroom (Astiz, 2020), teaching students to connect with people as people first. Spurrier discussed the importance of connecting with people at all levels, especially as the workplace has become increasingly virtual during the COVID-19 pandemic (J. Spurrier, personal communication, September 27, 2021). She also suggested that "high-touch" behaviors, such as being articulate and connecting with people, can promote, courteous, attentive, and expressive interactions that are currently in demand and can help new employees be successful in the workplace. Jo shared an example from Disney about how the company now hires people who naturally want to create happiness and are passionate about the Disney brand, as opposed to having to train them to feel that way about the brand. As a result, Disney's strategy has improved the delivery of their customer service (Graham, 2021). Therefore, training new employees the Disney way is not challenging because they hire people who are engaged, happy, and willing to serve, and communication students could learn from them.

Recognizing and acknowledging people from different ethnicities, backgrounds, abilities, and socioeconomic status is part of ongoing strategy to create inclusive and accurate learning experiences in the classroom (Manning et al., 2018). This is aligned to some of the comments on innovative communication skills made by our industry experts. Kirby (2016) states that a class that has continued discussions about race/ethnicity is a space where authentic communication occurs. Therefore, by acknowledging the differences in ethnicities and backgrounds, students will be able to advocate for all types of people and use their future positions as opportunities to make organizations more inclusive. Teaching students about their legal protections, reporting chains, connecting with people, monitoring trends on professional platforms (e.g., LinkedIn), understanding what microaggressions are, and introducing students to the business sector early are what instructors should be sharing with their students as preparation for the workplace (B. Jones, personal communication, September 27, 2021; C. Francis, personal communication, September 24, 2021; C. Russell, personal communication, September 24, 2021; J. Spurrier, personal communication, September 27, 2021).

Implications and Next Steps for Instructional Communication Scholars, Teachers, and Practitioners

The industry experts we interviewed were unwavering in their view that academic institutions and businesses should pursue and maintain collaborative partnerships. In doing so, these partnerships will inform changes to academic curriculum in ways that prepare students for the workplace. Partnerships provide students with tangible opportunities to acknowledge the relevance of a communication(s) degree and communication as a skill (J. Spurrier, personal communication, September 27, 2021). Further, the involvement in an organization allows students to understand how effective communication (or lack thereof) contributes to a company's return on investment (C. Francis, personal communication, September 24, 2021). Also, academic institutions thrive when they are viewed as thought leaders and forward-thinking institutions that produce highly competent, effective, and engaged communication graduates.

As instructors we are teaching our students the skills necessary to be successful in their future careers. Through partnerships, instructors can understand what they should be and need to be teaching their students. These partnerships can also give students the opportunity to be evaluated outside of classroom context. Being evaluated by an industry professional offers opportunities for students to emphasize what they are learning and why it is vital to their success in a specific career. Organizations can also benefit from these experiences by working on specific projects that require real solutions that can be tackled by student project teams. In programs that have established internship experiences, perhaps engaging in mock job interviews where both industry contacts and faculty provide feedback on the performance would prepare students to position the viability of their degrees. These relationships will benefit communication students and partner companies in a reciprocal relationship.

Another trend our experts discuss surrounds the need to keep up with future trends. For example, academic institutions need to remain competitive with organizations that have developed training academies that provide credentialing and continual education courses (e.g., Google). Communication competence is evolving, with growth in technology enabling this change. In her interview, Beverly Jones (personal communication, September 27, 2021) mentioned how a daily review of LinkedIn could help communication scholars monitor communication trends: "Engaging and exchanging information on this platform is an easy and affordable way to keep up with the trends in the communication field." Further, understanding these trends helps to identify future opportunities for student engagement, practice, and internships that will better prepare students for their careers.

Many of our industry experts indicated that being able to adapt to multiple audiences and modalities will benefit new employees as they begin their professional careers. As researchers and teachers passionate about student learning and career success, we are invigorated by the possibilities that these ideas hold for the future for students, teachers, practitioners, and instructional scholars. For example, instructors provide their students with readings, assignments, and evaluations to assess their knowledge and skill attainment. We know from previous research that public speaking and hybrid communication courses lead to "reduced public speaking anxiety and increased self-perceived communication competence and connected classroom environment" (Broeckelman-Post & Pyle, 2016, p. 210). Knowing this, implementing various modalities can support students in improving their communication skills. However, with the move to more online communication, it is crucial to prepare students for communicating and presenting using multiple and varying modalities. In this sense, creating courses that feature opportunities for both online and in-person presentations will help address several of the issues expressed by our experts. By integrating online learning in the classroom, students can learn how their perceptions impact their learning and others' perceptions of them and minimize their "zoom fatigue" (McArthur, 2021, p. 3; Nadler, 2020). Through virtual learning students can learn how to use their nonverbal communication in a way that engages their peers, showcases effective communication, and reduces the fatigue of being online, prior to entering a job where virtual learning and online engagement is an essential component (McArthur, 2021).

As we conclude, we hope you have new insight into the kinds of communication knowledge and skills industry experts desire in their employees and how instructional communication and education experts can meet these needs. We hope this information sparks new and needed conversations about curricular revision and industry collaborations. Finally, we hope each of us will take time to reflect on the instructional habits, biases, and practices that may be tried and true but that can also hold us and our students back from finding new approaches and possibilities inside and outside the classroom.

PART II

Organizational

CHAPTER 3

Background

Stephen A. Spates & Shawn T. Wahl

When you think of instructional communication, what comes to mind? Do you think of a classroom? Do you visualize a teacher speaking to a group of students while they sit at their desks taking notes? Most people envision a traditional classroom environment with this type of exchange. However, instructional communication can move beyond that classroom and into a varied number of professional contexts. Organizations are filled with practitioners, applied scholars, and trained professionals who must use instructional approaches to reach desired learning outcomes.

In this chapter, instructional communication will be looked at from a broad range of organizational contexts. The purpose of this chapter is to show the connection between instructional approaches and professional contexts that cover a wide range of organizational contexts. Although the professional fields vary, you will see a connection of instructional approaches that center in effective learning, no matter where the learning takes place.

First, a history and overview of the field will be provided. While the history is given, some core questions will be presented that are centered on a seminal article by Sprague (1992). Each of these questions will be highlighted and discussed to provide a foundation for understanding how instructional communication concepts can be trusted across many disciplines. After that, current trends within instructional communication will be highlighted. These trends will cover several professional fields, including health, technology, corporate, and technical professions. Finally, a conclusion will be offered for this chapter.

History and Overview

Instructional communication is a subfield of communication research that evolved out of its parent field, communication education. Specifically, instructional communication was developed to address communication messages that were rooted in instruction but applied to all levels and fields of learning. Sprague (1992) noted that instructional communication can be traced back to the 1970s where there was an evolution taking place in the field. A shift began to take place, in paradigms, leading college programs to change and make room for this new research area. As people began to ask more questions, and align with critical theorist approaches, the field of instructional communication took form.

At the inception of instructional communication, the purpose of its development was to provide a more practical way of approaching communication for educators at various levels and fields. The function of communication was to be consultative and strategic, allowing those from different schools of communication a way to reach their organizational goals. To fully understand the history and overview of the field, one must think about the questions that have previously been asked. Let's take a closer look at a pivotal piece by Sprague (1992), which asks a series of questions that were considered unasked at the time. Before engaging in instructional communication, one should reflect on these questions to prepare themselves.

WHY DO SCHOOLS EXIST?

Traditionally, schools have been organized structures where learners go to increase knowledge about a certain phenomenon, to better engage with various functions of society. The expectation is that those who complete their education are better equipped and ready to move up the social and economic ladders, contributing to their community at a higher level. While this can be true, Sprague makes that argument that most school environments only prepare learners to work within the current structure, as it is. In other words, it reinforces the current structure of society, benefiting those who create and develop the curriculum.

Instead, schools should be organized spaces where the learner engages in asking questions, even beyond the academy. For the educator preparing learners for different professions, this question should be central to instruction. Instructional communication, in professional contexts, allows for communication to be strategically used for learning and practical application. Learners, therefore, should be equipped with knowledge but also the motivation to continue asking the right questions. This is where instructional communication intersects with another subfield, organizational communication. By dedicating efforts toward asking the *right* questions, instructors can better serve their students and produce a higher quality learner. Deetz and Mumby (1990) noted that engaging in critique of questions can help reveal biases and imbalances within a structure. Thus, instructional communication should be designed to mold the learner and the learning experience.

WHAT DO TEACHERS DO?

The author discusses the historical understanding of teachers, describing the instructional role as a collection of technical skills. Often teachers learn along the lines of a social rapport development. As a result, teaching excellence is rooted in presentation-based behaviors. For example, research on immediacy in the classroom has received much attention. Studies show that instructors can produce higher instructor satisfaction when engaging in behaviors that promote interpersonal closeness (smiling, close proximity, use of touch, etc.). However, the connection to learning is filtered through behaviors that arouse the student first, then motivate, ultimately leading to achievement in learning. While these connections can be useful, the author discusses the challenge of reducing the instructional role to presentation and well-trained behaviors. By engaging in this perception, instructional communication is diluted in substance. Educators are not able to fully realize their instructional potential when fully focused on communication behaviors that connect with relational goals.

In response, the author discusses the importance of using communication principles to view the teaching role as a manager of learning and not just a presenter of information. This is hallmark to instructional excellence in professional contexts. Sprague's call for action includes perceiving the instructional role as one that is naturally intellectual. This is essential for educators as it does not reward the instructor role with an elitist power, but rather a necessary amount of understanding to manage effective learning environments. Instructors, therefore, become essential contributors to the curriculum and experience of the learning environment. This places effective learning back into the entire learning space and gives agency to each part of the structure (instructor, student, and environment).

Within professional contexts, instructional communication begins to shape the learning environment. This makes the communication style of the instructor just as important as the information they share. Using both aspects together can impact the learner in a way that has a deeper impact.

Depending on the discipline, processes and approaches can be learned in a way that fits learners' goals. Instructors who structure their learning spaces with this in mind have a better chance of instructional success.

WHAT IS THE NATURE OF DEVELOPMENT?

Early research in communication education, and even instructional communication, centered on development as something mainly based in cognitive function. Developmental modes were noted as the overwhelming reference to instructional development approaches. This bias in the research is noted by the author as concerning, noting that it does not take into consideration the differences in development. Cognitive-based development approaches, while useful, cannot be deemed universally effective or acceptable. By doing so, instructors engage in an ethnocentric bias that does not structure an inclusive learning environment.

Socially based approaches to learning, he argues, are more useful and position communication as more central to the learning process. In terms of professional contexts, communication can be increased in utility, as educators with knowledge and experience can incorporate experiences into the curriculum. With cognitive-based processes, learning is restricted to models and psychological behaviors. However, he then argues that socially based learning allows for development to incorporate the interactions as a part of instruction.

WHAT IS KNOWLEDGE AND HOW IS CURRICULUM ESTABLISHED?

Traditional thoughts on knowledge placed the learner as a collector of knowledge, provided by the teacher in their given curriculum. The epistemological position was rooted in the understanding that knowledge was wholly present and available for use. As knowledge is collected, it is the role of the teacher to provide that knowledge to the learner. With this thought in mind, Sprague argues that instruction becomes a mere transactional form of information. Pointing to Freire's (1972) work, he referred to the instructor–learner relationship as a bank. If knowledge is something given, then a teacher is like a banker who deposits knowledge into learners—a mechanicalized set of interactions where knowledge is passed down, without much room for question.

Instead, he called attention to the need for knowledge as social construction between instructor and learner. Within this position, knowledge is something created by both persons. By recognizing both people as cocreators, it shifts the position that learners only receive instruction and do not contribute to the learning experience. The instructor's role also shifts into one that interacts with the learner, creating a fresh learning experience each time. This position is of substantial benefit as it allows for a more organic creation of knowledge.

In professional contexts, learners can be recognized for their previous experiences and the understandings that they have when entering a learning program. Instructors can also build on that previous knowledge by applying it to current concepts and providing understanding for new concepts. This feeds into the discussion earlier of developing learners who still seek to ask questions and examine their structure, beyond their academic journey. This critical approach to learning improves instructional communication for professional contexts, allowing for organizations to use their educators, trainers, and consultants as instructional communicators—a benefit to the organizational structure.

HOW DOES LANGUAGE FUNCTION IN EDUCATION?

In early traditions of instructional communication, it was thought that language was simply an organized way for conveying a message. To some extent, many still subscribe to this position. In this view, language is a neutral part of the communication process, an inactive tool for distribution of information from one person to another. However, the author notes the problem with this position. Pointing to the work of Giroux (1988), language is noted as a technical way for individuals to reach understanding. This reduces the utility of language to a technical resource.

Instructional communication instead benefits from a position that views language as a way of creation. Language, therefore, functions as a product of interactions between participants. For instructors of professionals, language is essential as a function of education. Part of instructing for different professions is learning the language of the organization or role. Instructors enhance the learning experience by helping learners understand the language of their future profession. This is not for the purpose of clarity but to reach shared meaning. Instructors can use language as a marker of educational success. Learners can reach a higher point of knowledge by learning the language that helps describe and explain their role with the organization.

Further, Sprague highlights the importance of voice, as it connects with language. He noted that language can function as a marker of educational success when learners can take information and translate it into their own understanding. The voice of the learner serves as an output of language learned and understood. Instructors can also adjust their language for instructional clarity. Depending on the learning demographic, certain language use must be clarified, explained, or reduced to reach shared meaning. As a result, the voice of the instructor should be used in a way that promotes learning.

HOW DOES POWER FUNCTION IN THE CLASSROOM?

At the beginning of the discipline's research, instructional communication looked at power as a form of control. Traditionally power was in the hands of the instructor, and that power was used to control the management of the learning space. As a result, educational processes were perceived as spaces to be managed. Learners were viewed as individuals whose behaviors and responses should be trained into submission. Even positive behaviors such as feedback and evaluation are skewed by the traditional bounds of power. This carries an impact for learning environments, where instructors hold an imbalance of too much power and take on a manager role.

The author also points to Luke's (1974) work, which explains the challenge of a one-, two-, and three-dimensional view of power. In all views, the individual in power finds different ways to get the person not in power to comply. This kind of approach to power is noted as concerning because the learner is focused on compliance while the instructor creates an atmosphere of indoctrination. Literature on the hidden curriculum supports the notion that power dynamics allow the instructor to set up learning that promotes a reinforcement of biases and preferences.

To achieve authentic learning experiences for professions, teachers should strive for power dynamics that are attentive to social, economic, and political factors. This should center learning that encourages interaction and instructor–learner relationships that go beyond surface dynamics. Instructors should encourage the use of voice and autonomy with learners, providing opportunities to navigate the educational experience. This will provide a healthy educational structure for everyone that restores the power among both people.

For new educators and instructors, this historical article is one that should serve as the foundation of your instructional approach. By engaging with these questions, you can develop the groundwork toward an authentic instructional experience. It is essential to think about how your role and learning environment can impact the success of the learner. The impact of the learning experience can last outside of the classroom as learners understand how to use their voice, speak the language, and contribute to the dynamics of their organizations.

Current Trends

While the historical work in instructional communication provides a help-ful foundation, it is essential to look at where the field is currently. Next is a varied collection of the ways instructional communication is used in pro-fessional contexts throughout organizations. You will see a few examples of the trends within the discipline. At the end of this chapter we will dis-cuss how the discipline has evolved and what it means for future research.

HEALTH

Within health care, communication is a growing area of study. The unique environment of a people gathering for the purpose of one's well-being calls for attention to message and information sharing. Specifically, communi-cation scholars have called attention to how communication is useful for better training and improvement of patient–provider interactions (Wanzer et al., 2004). In fact, the authors noted that the importance of communica-tion in health care is substantially high. Think about the interactions that take place. A patient typically seeks information and clarity about a health topic, and a health professional shares that information with the patient for compliance and improved health outcomes. These do not always go as smoothly as they could.

Through instructional communication, Donovan et al. (2017) write that health care professionals can learn how to deliver information and better understand the patient. Additionally, the health care environ-ment benefits from better communication training as they can improve scores in satisfaction, compliance, and response. These are all challenges to health environments and cannot be solved through traditional man-agerial training. Instead, instructional communication approaches are necessary so that health professionals can increase their ability to build a rapport and develop a professional relationship with those they serve. The result of improved patient–provider relationships has already been linked to increased accuracy of diagnoses, reduced severity of conditions, and patient trust.

Growing trends in health communication research have merged with the instructional communication field to address the need for increased learning in this area. This work includes topics like collaboration work among health care teams, patient centeredness and empowerment, mobile health, and health campaigns. These areas help address some key challenges in health and instructional communication. Although health care providers understand the importance of communication, research is happening to address why communication is necessary to the health care professional's education. Best practices for delivering communication skills training and how communication skills impact overall health outcomes are current areas of research. Scholars are trying to solidify the legitimacy of overt communication behaviors in health care practices. Such research builds a stronger argument for adding direct communication courses into the educational curriculum of those pursuing health care professions.

A key article by Donovan et al. (2017) set the path for what research is taking place today. The authors called for scholars to draw their attention to arguments that help describe and explain the benefits of adding communication into the health care training plan. Health care professionals are not fully aware of how communication is necessary to the provision of health care. Specifically, because the attention is mainly on the improvement of health outcomes, instructional scholars' task is to show a connection between communication behaviors and health outcomes, or patient satisfaction.

Thompson's (2018) article also speaks to the need for more research in health communication to focus on instructional spaces. The author discusses the benefits of collaboration between health and instructional scholars finding ways to answer questions that can enhance the health care field's desired outcomes. Attention is also called to instructional messages that are delivered outside of the classroom. Given the practical nature of the health field, there are many opportunities for learning outside of the traditional learning classroom. This is essential to professional contexts, as classrooms may not always be the primary space for instruction. For health care professionals, training and learning experiences take place interactively. As an example, nursing students participate in a series of active learning sessions known as clinicals. In such a set-up, students learn as they interact with other individuals. Lessons are interactive and hands-on, not like the traditional classroom environment. As a result, instructional communication practices can be essential to the culture, success, and maintenance of desired educational outcomes.

Along the lines of instruction, the amount of education an individual has can impact their ability to trust or understand the medical information they're receiving. Chen et al.'s (2019) work on health literacy and trust sheds light on the need for quality information for certain populations. The authors conducted a study that looked at how health literacy was associated with trust in, and use of, health information from different channels. After conducting a large-scale survey data collection, they found several significant associations. While individuals with high health literacy were more likely to trust health information from health professionals, they were less likely to trust information from television, social media, and blog outlets. However, those with low health literacy were found to put more trust in television, social media, and blog outlets and less trust in health professionals.

The findings of this research bring the challenges of health literacy to light, as health literacy can impact an individual's ability to evaluate the quality of health information they receive. Specifically for those who are more trusting of media outlets, the risks can be high, since these channels have greater amounts of misinformation and disinformation. Such findings bring more attention to instructional communication's value in the health profession. Scholars extend the reach of communication research by connecting to fields where communication is not centered. By addressing such gaps in the field, health professionals learn the full value of communication-based concepts.

For example, to address the concerns of the article's findings, the authors note that health professionals can adjust their communication style and design of health messages. For those with lower health literacy, health professionals should learn how to adjust their communication to assume the presentation of media outlets but maintain the accuracy of the information provided. They also utilize those same outlets by carefully selecting a popular spokesperson to represent the topic of that message. By learning how to make these types of communication adjustments, health professionals can increase their message effectiveness and reach populations where they are failing.

These suggestions and works are rooted in the practices of instructional communication. Learning how to deliver communication and develop the skills to get a message across effectively are essential to success in the profession. Health organizations have not historically included communication behaviors as a direct part of their curriculum. However, these and other studies have contributed to the evolution of the health care field. Health educators are starting to see the value of communication concepts in their professional practices. As a result, they're in need of more research and evidence for communication's inclusion into the instructional training of health care professionals.

TECHNOLOGY

Research is developing in a fairly new, but unique, area of the communication discipline. Known as human-machine communication (HMC), this exciting field introduces the idea of communicative interactions between human and artificially intelligent machines. While this field is expanding in its research production, it does not come without challenges. Scholars note that this research breaks the normal expectations of communication behaviors that take place between humans (Edwards et al., 2017). They further explain that scholars must invest in learning these relationships now as more fields begin to explore and adopt machines into their normal operations.

Furthering their work, Edwards et al. (2018) discussed the need to look at HMC and its application in instructional contexts. As the classroom environment continues to evolve, educational programs are investing in machines and artificial intelligence (AI) for student learning. In these types of structures, the instructor takes on a role where they manage the machine as it primarily communicates with students. For this kind of classroom learning, the communication style of the machine must take on communication behaviors of humans. In order to do that, these machines must follow a communication script, which is a series of communication exchanges in the same format as takes place between humans. This is created through a spoken dialogue system (SDS), which is similar to the use of a chatbot. As a result, the machine is now a co-instructor and a contributor to the learning environment.

Likewise, the human instructor can engage in script design that allows for human-like exchanges. In other words, the script can be crafted in a way where natural conversational exchange takes place, rather than mechanical. This promotes greater certainty among human students as their levels of comfort will increase than with a more machine style of communication (Edwards et al., 2016; Spence et al., 2014). It also allows the instructor, while scripting, to examine the use of power dynamics as it relates to language. This includes any part of dialogues that could be considered as othering, which promotes an oppressive structure (Fasset et al., 2007). Instructional communication, therefore, takes on a role that builds a new type of classroom, one that is mediated by machine, moderated by humans, and guided by the interactions of both.

This is where the human–machine interaction stretches beyond the classroom, even though it is a tool for the classroom. Different professions have codes, jargon, and exchanges that are unique to their fields. When using machines, the scripts will not be the same across fields. Instructors are still necessary to develop and maintain scripts that allow for the machine to interact according to human expectations. Such training is rooted in a knowledge of communication. When machines are adapted for use, they must be programmed for interaction. Communication is necessary in order to properly program the machine for effective exchanges with students. Institutions invest in individuals who can provide the right instructions to the machines.

Organizations in health, engineering, computer science, and hospitality are already making investments in machines for human interaction. Although these new additions to the organization may cause disruption in the traditional employment structure, communication professionals have the opportunity to take advantage of new territory in training and consulting. Machines have to be tested and monitored for quality communication exchanges. This creates a need for communication scholarship and reinforces the importance of understanding instructional communication.

As machines are implemented into different professional contexts, the authors note parallels between human–machine communication and instructional communication: immediacy, credibility, teacher clarity, and humor. Immediacy speaks to the idea of psychological closeness. This can include verbal and nonverbal behaviors that impact the perception of closeness in a relationship. Instructional communication has already established a long line of research that connects immediacy to desired learning outcomes. The majority of previous research looked at immediacy from human instructors. Now, research looks at immediacy behaviors of machines in their various professional contexts. Machines are designed to provide a level of perceived closeness to gain the trust of human partners. With that understanding instructional communicators are essential. By knowing communication behaviors that promote immediacy, we can develop, observe, and maintain a level of immediacy for machines that can be well received by humans.

In the classroom, an instructor's level of credibility is a necessary aspect of their ability to be successful in that role. Instructional credibility, which can be divided into three parts—competence, trustworthiness, and goodwill—is tied to positive classroom behaviors (McCroskey & Teven, 1999). The development of credibility is noted by the amount a machine engages in behaviors like social presence, interaction, and accurate message exchange. By engaging in these behaviors, machines can build up a level of trust that would even allow them to maintain credibility when making a mistake (Salem et al., 2015). This is the same pattern that can be found in human–instructor classrooms. As a result, machines have a better chance of keeping a role in the learning process due to their ability to gain and keep credibility.

Teacher clarity can be described as the level of concern for fidelity in messages through instructional behaviors (Powell et al., 1990). The clarity of a message is essential to effective learning for instructional communication. For students to successfully learn, they must understand the information being shared. Along those lines, the clarity of messages is impacted by factors of vocalics (e.g., tone, pitch, accent), which can help or hinder a students' ability to learn (Niculescu et al., 2013). While these concerns carry certain levels of risk with human instructors, these factors can all be adjusted for machine instructors. In fact, Edwards et al. (2018) noted that this is an advantage of the machine instructor and questioned the impact on instructor identity and authenticity.

Humor, although sensitive to appropriateness, is also tied to learning. Students report higher levels of enjoyment and social attraction when proper humor is incorporated into instructional behaviors. The same findings are shown for machines (Mirnig et al., 2017). Such findings reveal a parallel to instructional effectiveness in communication. When used properly, humor can be a useful tool for learning. As a part of its script, machines can use humor to increase social interaction and even connect with immediacy. Such behaviors allow for better communication exchanges. Instructional communication becomes an essential tool again for professions, as instructors must be knowledgeable as to what is considered humorous, yet professional, for the machine instructor.

CORPORATE TRAINING

Research in organizations with professional trainers shows that influence, a communicative behavior, has a major impact in successful corporate training sessions. Mathis (2020) found that trainees were able to find a training session effective when the trainer incorporated communication behaviors (e.g., immediacy) and connected the training to real-life examples. In the article, it was noted that training sessions will continue to play an essential role in organizations, even into the future. In order for organizations to maintain an effective training program, the instructional communication of trainers must be given attention.

When thinking of the trainer as an instructional leader and organizational influencer, the idea of power and relational dynamics must be addressed (Mathis, 2020). Power is described by Vince (2014) as a concept shaped by context and relationships. In other words, no individual is more or less powerful by nature. Instead, power is socially crafted by the members in that space and time. Therefore, training opportunities present a certain power dynamic. The trainer holds a certain level of instructional "power" over those being trained. This is attributed to the knowledge they have and their identification with the organization. While those being trained are not completely powerless, they do hold less power, until their knowledge and understanding increase. The effectiveness of training gives trainees power as they must confirm the quality of training processes and programs. This creates a learning dynamic for both members to work together rather than a hierarchy of power that promotes oppression.

Instructional communication intersects with organizational communication work in this context, as trainers are organizational members.

As trainers, these organizational members can also be argued as organizational leaders due to the amount of influence they have in these interactions (Mathis, 2020). Literature is growing that draws attention to these individuals and their processes used. When conducting training, these individuals are invested in getting trainees to understand and identify with the goals as well as the organization. Much like the machine instructors noted earlier, instructional design and script is a strategic process for reaching optimum effectiveness.

While conducting research on organizational trainers, Mathis (2020) found that attendees had several reactions in connection to instructional communication. One finding was that they were able to see attending training as more than a compliance behavior, when they were able to identify with the training content. By only interacting out of compliance, instructor trainers can expect only low levels of relational power and influence. This is also in line with communication literature that speaks to the power and influence of relationships between working individuals (Mottet et al., 2006). Scholars are looking into the instructional environments of corporate trainers to investigate how trainer influence and relational connection enhance the training experience.

TECHNICAL PROFESSIONS

In technical and scientific professions (e.g., engineering), students are not only outside of the traditional learning classroom, the learning goals are different (Danells, 2000). Students in technical professions receive instruction that prepares them for the job but also prepares them for the careers in their specific profession. This can include the knowledge, skills, language, and cultural aspects that are a part of that career. As a result, research in instructional practices can differ, focusing on the specific skills and knowledge points that will directly lead learners down a path. Research that speaks to this unique type of learning is growing.

When students in technical professions engage in their learning programs, instructors must consider the goals of the course and the future career of the learner. In other words, they are concerned with the parts of knowledge that will help equip students with the skills to carry out their responsibilities. However, in addition to skills, instructors are also concerned with the learner's ability to explain and engage with others about their work (Danells, 2000). This creates tasks that fuse professional and technical aspects. For learners this is necessary to truly learn the material. Students who did not connect with the material in a way they could explain made a distinction between learning in the "classroom" and learning for "real-life application." As a result, the author noted that technical instructors should make it a point to see the connection between classroom materials and application in their actual careers. Without that, certain useful concepts may be lost.

Building on that work, current research looks at how technical communicators can engage in certain behaviors to enhance their identities and promote overall organizational values. Technical communicators (TCs) are communication practitioners who can work in various fields and professions. As practice-based professionals, they are often tasked with the problem-solving responsibilities of creating clear messages from the organization to the user in a clear and practical way (Barnum, 2011). In this aspect, the TC is an instructor but also a translator to the user, helping them learn and achieve their goals through clear direction. Wilson and Wilford (2017) describe the technical communicator as "almost always located at the nexus of data, language, and meaning, trafficking in expanding economies of information within organizations" (p. 5).

Martin et al. (2017) used an ethnographic approach to investigate how TC can help enhance an organization's overall goals by tailoring the communication to user advocacy design. The authors discussed eight practices that TCs can use to promote user advocacy: (1) Help stakeholders understand the benefits of good user research processes and experiences;

(2) connect user needs to organizational goals; (3) articulate how content and design decisions align with known user characteristics, needs, and wants; (4) help stakeholders identify the root cause of perceived problems before determining and implementing a communication solution; (5) demonstrate how user advocacy promotes a culture of continuous improvement; (6) create and consistently reference a representative user identity; (7) discuss multiple user pathways and work processes; and (8) frame content and design questions in a scenario- or task-based manner.

By engaging in these practices, the authors noted that TCs can better represent their identity. They found three benefits overall, including better understanding of technical communication work, clearer connections between values and TC work, and more positive identities. However, the key benefit is that they are able to show value for their role by being able to explain their role to non-TC individuals. The interaction between TCs and non-TCs shows another construction of organizational context. Although technical communicators can work in various organizations, it is their interaction with everyone that shapes their identity and the quality of learning (Martin et al., 2017).

Another study looked at the perceptions of TCs according to TCs and subject matter experts (SMEs) (Rice-Bailey, 2016). The author looked at how they both categorize and value the role of TCs. The findings revealed several characteristics of the TC. SMEs found typically described TC roles as an investigator or educator. Much of the data showed that SMEs characterized their TCs by the way they asked and gathered information. This spoke to the investigative characteristic. They were also noted as those who wanted to make sure their translation of information connected well to their audience. This aligns with the research noted earlier.

As educators, TCs were explained as knowledgeable and competent when they could clearly articulate their role, or responsibilities, to the SME or external audiences. In this case TCs are evaluated on their ability to communicate with multiple stakeholders in a way that is clear and promotes shared meaning. As a result, technical communicators play a multidimensional role in organizations. Their instructional communication approaches are even more complex as their organizational interaction is higher. Depending on the type of profession they work in, translation may take place at a higher rate on a normal basis.

Instructional communication among these practitioners brings an important collection of knowledge, skill, and practicality. Instructors for TC students are encouraged to continue teaching students how to excel in their careers by perfecting the way they communicate their role (Rice-Bailey, 2016). Students must learn how to articulate their role and quickly explain themselves to those outside of their profession. This goes beyond traditional classroom learning and helps prepare students for the applicable parts of their career that will help provide their value. Research continues to grow in areas that show how TCs are able to communicate their value with different roles in the organization, such as a project manager or external stakeholder (Mallette et al., 2019).

Conclusion

Hopefully when you think of instructional communication now, you picture something beyond the traditional classroom. Instead of picturing an instructor providing information to students at a desk, maybe you picture a set of communication behaviors and practices being used by instructors in a number of professional contexts. Instructional communication is not bound by the walls of the classroom. In fact, this chapter has shown that instruction is taking place well beyond the normal learning experience. Whether you are a student who's learning about the field, a new professional taking on an instructional role, or a practitioner preparing for an instructional project, this chapter applies to you.

The purpose of this chapter was to provide a history and overview of instructional communication for professional context and then discuss some current trends in the field across some organizational contexts. While many organizational contexts provide spaces for instruction, those in an instructor's role should be focused on creating a learning experience that promotes coconstructed learning. By decreasing a focus on technical teaching skills and increasing collaboration, instructors have a better chance of reaching learning that continues beyond the classroom environment. Likewise, technical communication must consider the multidimensional aspect of learning, making sure that learners are equipped with the skill and ability to clearly articulate their role. No matter the discipline, organization, or profession, instructional communication practices are made for successful learning. Instructors who engage in approaches that promote authentic and sustainable learning will find success for their learning experience.

CHAPTER 4

Current Trends and Future Directions

Stephen A. Spates & Shawn T. Wahl

Instructional communication has evolved in its use across professions. However, where is instructional communication going the future? How will it be necessary to certain fields as they evolve into nuances of society? Such questions warrant attention and conversation about the future of instructional communication within organizational contexts.

In the last chapter, we provided a history and overview of instructional communication in various professional contexts. We talked about current trends and what's currently taking place in the field. Specifically, we highlighted Sprague's (1992) work, which called for instructors to think about the learning experience they provide in a way that constructs an educational experience with the learner. In order to do this, he posits six critical questions: (1) Why do schools exist? (2) What do teachers do? (3)What is the nature of development? (4) What is knowledge, and how is curriculum established? (5) How does language function in education? and (6) How does power function in the classroom? Instructors should ask these six questions before engaging in instructional exchanges. The answers ultimately shape how instructors approach learning and their audience of learners.

Since that time, instructional communication has grown and evolved. As research is produced, scholars take the time to reflect and encourage others in the field to revisit these questions. Calls for a refreshing of the field have happened in the past, but most have pointed to these questions as a motivation to continue the work. However, some scholars are ready to move forward. Witt (2017) noted that instructional communication scholars need to start thinking and moving beyond these historical questions. He argues instead that it's time to move into new contexts, with deeper questions, that will further the field and broaden its reach. By using a variety of scholarly voices, and opening our minds to nontraditional approaches, there can be room for new inspirations for the field. It is in that spirit that we present this chapter.

In this chapter, we not only want to discuss the field, but discuss what's coming. This will pertain to what teacher-scholars can expect in the coming years from this field. For this chapter we will focus on three broad organizational contexts: technology and artificial intelligence (AI), higher education institutions, risk/crisis, sports, corporate training and the legal system. Each section will discuss how instructional communication is utilized and how that can impact the future of the field.

Technology and Artificial Intelligence

As technology continues to evolve, machine-based interactions will become more frequent among humans. Comfort with technologies such as smartphone applications (apps) and AI voice-command devices like "Siri" and "Alexa" have increased among human users. In fact, organizations like Uber have already developed and piloted programs like the driver-less car, allowing for riders to receive rides from artificially intelligent motor vehicles. Innovations like this call attention to the development and usage of robotics, machines, and AI. As these machines are created, they must take on human likeness to interact with their human partners. As a result, future research in instructional communication can address how these programs and devices can learn to interact with humans at a high level.

To address this instructional communication within human-machine communication (HMC) will be essential. In their 2017 work, Edwards et al. stated that machines will continue becoming a part of society. In fact, it is necessary that communication scholars are a part of that process, moving forward, so that these machines receive the characteristics that will make them human friendly. Specifically, the authors looked at how machines will be added into classroom environments. However, they pointed out that for machines to be effective in their interactions with students, instructional communication approaches must become a part of the machine's programming. For example, a machine's interaction with students should be modeled after a human teacher–human student exchange. For that to take place, a machine must learn the behaviors that would make that exchange similar. Whether it's the use of voice, dialogued responses, or providing answers to questions, machines will need to learn these characteristics from instructional communication scholars.

Likewise, the use of machines in various professional contexts will also benefit from the use of instructional communication. Let's go back to the example of the driver-less car. Think about driving concepts like navigation, rerouting, the occurrence of an accident. Human riders will need to interact with their AI-based vehicle in a way that reaches the same results with a human driver. As a result, instructional communication research should investigate how these programs and devices will be able to provide high-level learning or teaching to the user. More organizations are adapting these devices to their operations. Such research investigations will only help contribute to effective exchanges.

Within health communication and technology, instructional communication practices have been found useful. A recent study by Warren et al. (2021) noted that instructional communication brings useful approaches to mHealth and patient–provider communication exchanges. By applying the IDEA model (Sellnow & Sellnow, 2019), which stands for internalization (perceived value/relevance), distribution (delivery of the narrative through various channels), explanation (providing accurate information clearly to various audiences), and action (specific steps to mitigating risk and reducing harm), physicians could provide better quality care for patients. The study found that the model, originally theorized for instructional communication, applies to health communication contexts, including the use of mHealth. Physicians using mHealth technology will not only benefit from using advanced technology devices, but will diagnose patients with complex health conditions (e.g., POTS).

In this context, instructional communication can be a useful tool in helping increase interactions between providers and patients. Future research should investigate how the IDEA model works for effectiveness in mHealth communication for other patients. By employing the model, physicians will be able to approach health problems in a way that works with the patient and works toward better health outcomes. Scholars in the field will be a commodity among health professionals, as more health care environments adapt mHealth services. The success of the model, within health contexts, would be how the IDEA model promotes communication practices. Internalization refers to physicians' ability to show care and compassion to their patients (Warren et al., 2021).

As organizations evolve into tech-based, computer-mediated operations, instructional communication will become increasingly necessary. This can be an advantage for the practical scholar who studies instructional communication but desires to build a career outside the academy. As technologies become more advanced, machines will need to learn how to communicate. Once they learn, they will have to be managed in their operational exchanges with humans. Therefore, instructional scholars are a necessity to the success of these devices across professions.

Along these lines, changes in technology will also produce a change in workforce roles and positions. Technological liaisons, those who can develop and manage machines, will become a normal part of organizations.

While these positions exist in some areas already, more research will need to observe and explain instructional communication approaches for emerging fields where the user experience (UX) will be a new landscape.

Higher Education Institutions

Although instructional communication is rooted in the classroom, the field of education has seen a shift from the traditional classroom experience. Specifically, a significant increase in online learning and alternative classroom experiences have increased in the last 10 years (Allen & Seaman, 2015). Students are searching for alternative educational experiences that reach beyond the classroom. Likewise, there's been an increase in technical education programs that allow for students to learn a trade. As a result, instructional communication approaches no longer focus on the traditional in-person classroom. Instructional communication research in online learning and other alternative classrooms has reflected the changes of higher education. For instructors, this reveals a variety of professional paths and opportunities for new teaching careers.

In the online learning context, several research studies have addressed regarding creating effective learning environments (e.g., Kaufmann et al., 2016). However, Chatham-Carpenter (2017) brings attention to the need for more instructional communication research in this area. Since higher education institutions have broadened their offerings, students have taken courses that employ a number of alternative teaching strategies. In addition to online classroom learning, students have enrolled in courses that incorporated virtual and augmented realities (Kelly, 2016). This brings a variety of new elements into the learning environment, including advanced technology, machine-mediated learning, and innovative pedagogical strategies. As such, instructional communication scholars are called on to take the lead for research in this area (Chatham-Carpenter, 2017).

Although we discussed technology earlier, the impacts of teaching innovations are essential here. Essentially, new advancements and attention beyond the traditional classroom call for investigations into new territories. How can instructors build classroom community in these alternative classrooms? How can institutions provide quality learning experiences for various students from different backgrounds? While these advancements bring excitement and innovation, there are also new challenges. Privacy, security, and online bullying are noted as possible obstacles to online learning environments. Other concerns of accessibility are raised in thinking about how students will be provided the devices needed to learn in these new ways. Instructional communication scholars would be wise to start thinking about how these questions can be answered and how communication can address these concerns.

When we start to ask the questions that have not been asked, or have been overlooked, a new world of possibilities opens. Sprague's (1992) work is referenced as the motivation to pose new challenges to instructional scholars. Earlier we noted the impact of new technologies on educational institutions. However, another major shift in this profession is in the conversations on diversity, accountability, and social justice. Significant events around the globe have forced educational institutions to rethink the way their campuses operate. Through student protests/demonstrations, public scandal, and several terminations of educational leaders, individuals have been awakened to injustices within the structure.

In their work, Rudick and Golsan (2016) address the vacancies in instructional communication related to these concerns. The authors pose three challenges to instructional scholars to draw attention to these gaps. First, they challenge scholars to move conversations from a language of diversity to language of difference. By doing so, scholars will need to discuss how difference is constructed through the use of communication. As a result, conversations will need to address power dynamics, discrimination, and bias in this organizational structure. This is a complicated charge, as these conversations have been ignored for years and current structures do not provide motivation to address areas of difference. Success in such a conversation would take the leadership, knowledge, and perseverance of communication scholars. Instructional communication should inform us on best practices to carry out these conversations.

The second challenge to scholars is to be more accountable in research needs of populations that scholars are using or working with (Frey et al., 1996). In other words, future scholarship should make sure that research is conducted in a way that holds itself accountable to the populations it is supporting (Rudick & Golsan, 2016). Too often research takes place in a way that takes advantage of populations, specifically underrepresented populations, then keeps that knowledge out of reach. Instead, scholars should be thinking about the ways they can conduct their research to keep the process and the findings salient to the community. This means that approaches such as ethnography, participatory action, and inductive research should be employed as approaches to scholarship. This also means that these methods are important to teach in the classroom as legitimate forms of research.

The third challenge, and probably the most significant, is for instructional scholars to actively invest in research for social justice. As society continues to publicly address issues of oppression, scholars should actively be working as change agents in, and out, of the classroom. No longer can knowledge pertaining to challenges of structural and systematic oppression be left up to one class in diversity, or instructors from underrepresented communities. Scholarship must fully connect to social justice in ways that will benefit students. To do this, scholars must unite and join the shift in educational priorities. Instructional scholars should be the leaders of these conversations and the examples for other disciplines to follow. Therefore, the future of instructional communication should seek to investigate more research questions that challenge the status quo and lead to equity in educational structures.

Risk and Crisis

It would not be right to think about future advancements in instructional communication without mentioning risk and crisis. Every organization is vulnerable to crisis events and holds various amounts of risk or harm. How do these organizations teach their members in preparation for crisis? What kinds of messages are effective in risk and crisis training programs? How do organizational relationships impact the way crisis management plans are received or dispersed? These are just some of the questions that should guide instructional scholarship in this area. Let's look at this area and see the possibilities of the future.

Within professional contexts, organizations must be aware of their vulnerabilities. Once aware, communication can help develop plans that address the occurrence of a risk or crisis event. However, when an organization experiences an unplanned event that results in heightened perception of risk or threat, that organization is in crisis (Seeger et al., 1998). When crises occur in organizations, instructional communication approaches can be employed to help mitigate further risk or harm (Sellnow et al., 2012).

When organizations experience a crisis event, the messages sent are essential to reducing the amount of further risk or harm. Organizations are also concerned with the amount of uncertainty that may be associated with an event. Therefore, instructional communication practices have become a necessary approach to helping manage crisis events. Edwards et al. (2021) noted that instructional communication approaches helped manage crisis events in biosecurity's teachings for meat industries. When instructional communication competencies were employed (e.g., clarity, credibility, and consistency), learners were more likely to develop knowledge. The success of the response to crisis can be found in the quality of information messages shared during learning and training periods. This highlights the need for instructional communication theory and practice in professions far beyond education.

When thinking about preparedness plans, or campaigns designed to educate members on preparedness, instructional communication is useful. Johansson et al. (2021) found the IDEA (internalization/distribution/explanation/action) model useful in crisis communication. The authors conducted a study to test a campaign's effectiveness when the model is applied compared to a control message. Results showed that messages were more effective among members when instructional approaches were applied. In other words, instructional communication-based approaches to crisis management are more useful for receiving audiences.

When a crisis event occurs, individuals may need help and support to cope with recent traumas. However, this can be difficult for disciplines where communication principles lack. For example, STEM (science, technology, engineering, and math) fields trail in their resilience when dealing with crisis. Shay and Pohan (2021) found that communication behaviors, as applied by instructors, were the most useful for STEM instructors during the switch to online learning during the peak of the COVID-19 pandemic in 2020. Students struggling to cope with changes needed support and relational interaction to get through the trauma of the crisis event. This brings attention to the need for collaboration among instructors at institutions. Those in STEM fields can learn more about student-centered approaches by working with communication scholars and collaborating with campus teaching support centers. In this way, communication scholars are not only useful to students but to their coworkers and administrators. More attention is needed to research how institutions can collaborate with communication programs for instructional support across departments.

Sports

Like many fields, sports have seen an increase in the number of members (players) expressing their dissent of the current structure within their league or association. As a result, there's growing conversation on power dynamics of players, coaches, owners, and administrators. Topics like social justice, sexual assault, mental health, and drug policies, leadership must be addressed appropriately and professionally. In order to do this, instructional communication practices should be applied. While the sports communication field is growing, not much research intersects with instructional communication scholarship. Let's look at a few ways this can take place.

Over the past few years, more research is drawing attention to attitudes and responses of current and former athletes. These studies have highlighted a variety of challenges faced by professional and student-athletes. Some of those challenges include relationships with coaches and trainers, or disagreements with administrators. In their work, Rey and Johnson (2021) found that there were eight main triggers to college athlete's dissent, including dissatisfaction with health information provided by athletic trainers. The authors noted that instructional communication practices should be employed to help trainers provide better quality care to athletes. This creates an opportunity for instructional scholarship (and collaboration with health scholars) to investigate the communicative behaviors of athletic trainers when providing information to athletes. It was also noted that more education would benefit teams when it comes to having difficult conversations between players and coaches (e.g., playing time or inequity in treatment).

Along the lines of difficult conversations, sports communication scholarship has shown a significant number of injustices as it pertains to race relations and social justice. Specifically, the National Football League (NFL) has seen an outcry from fans questioning the leadership's practices in hiring. Over 50% of the NFL players are African Americans, yet there are currently only three Black head coaches in the NFL. The NBA has 12 Black coaches, with 74% of the NBA being Black players. Other than the MLB, the proportion of minority players far outpaces that of minority assistant coaches or head coaches (Cunningham, 2021). Some leagues are far worse than others; among women's college basketball programs, minorities are nearly four times more likely to be players than they are to be a head coach (Cunningham, 2021). African Americans are perceived more as players, assistant coaches, or recruiters (Anderson, 1993; Brown, 2002) than they are for head coaching roles (Cunningham, 2010). The lack of players seeing variety among coaches creates a power dynamic that impacts players, even on the field.

Because most athletes are minorities, African American coaches are given the responsibility of connecting with these athletes. "Wulf believed that it is generally acknowledged that one of the major tasks of the African American assistant coaches was to recruit African American players" (Brooks et al., 1996, p. 96, internal citations omitted). Although recruiting does not lead to head coaching jobs, connecting with players is an important task, one that can determine the greatness of a coach. Coaches are responsible for developing athletes' mental, physical, technical, and tactical abilities, and, of course, winning (Becker, 2009). The greatness of a coach comes along with being able to put all of this together. That includes helping athletes improve their performance, making them better people off the field, smarter on the field, and overall winners. The first thing athletes do when they join a team is familiarize themselves with their coach, the coach–athlete relationship, the environment, and the system (the four dimensions; Becker, 2009). A relationship is based on how a coach communicates with their players. A coach also initiates the nature of the relationship and communication because they have power, and they set the tone. The coach's power comes from having the ability to sit or start a player, punish players, and teach athletes things to excel. Coaches can teach athletes many life skills, and effective communication is one of the most valuable, especially in the sports world (Johnson et al., 2011). Since a natural part of coaching is training, development, and mentorship, instructional communication scholars should take interest in how these approaches are used within various sports.

In every sport there are time limits, so coaches and athletes have the task to communicate within an allotted time, and wasted time can have huge implications for them. Therefore, coaches have to be able to efficiently communicate with players to minimize losses and maximize success (Johnson et al., 2011). A great coach will find ways to break down complex ideas in a simple way so that younger athletes can not only understand but execute (Becker, 2009). Becker reported, in their study of athlete's relationships with coaches, that athletes repeatedly discussed how their coaches communicated basic performance information, player roles, expectations, team goals, individual goals, and a common team vision: "We knew exactly what coach wanted us to do in terms of getting better, improving, and helping the team" (Becker, 2009, p. 107). "No relationship, whether on the playing field or off, can blossom without communication and the relationship between players and coaches is no different" (Johnson et al., 2011, p. 2). Athletes also noted that great coaches knew how to communicate directly and indirectly. Direct communication is placed under the umbrella of interpersonal communication and includes one-on-one communication. Indirect communication happens nonverbally. The athletes in the study said that great coaches were able to use these forms of communication in a clear and concise way. The quality of these coaches' communication was also described as honest. Great coaches were able to tell a player or athlete what they needed to hear in a constructive way instead of telling them what they want to hear. Great coaches also communicate in an appropriate and positive way: "You have to have constructive criticism, but you don't want to have a coach who continually bangs on you until you wear down" (Becker, 2009, p. 109). Positive or negative, athletes said that they appreciate a response from their coaches: "If the coach just stands there and watches, you never know if you're doing something right. It's nice for coaches to show a bit of emotion and not be so stoic that they can't be human as well" (Becker, 2009, p. 110). The athletes felt that their coaches were human when they expressed emotions. This relates back to clarity and immediacy behaviors that help instructors reach success in the classroom. The same characteristics should be employed by coaches.

Sports at every level is a business, and coaches' lives can depend on their success; therefore, their athletes play a critical role in their lives. But a successful coach will not use their athletes as a tool. A successful coach will care about athletes as people and not just people who help them win games. Players are people first, and great coaches make time for the person as well as the player (Johnson et al., 2011). The motivational factor was also important for great coaches in Becker's study. Athletes said that a coach motivated them to learn the game, work hard, and reach their full potential: "When you have a coach that is super motivating, it makes you want to play for them" (Becker, 2009, p. 109). A coach has the task of finding the trigger in each athlete to bring forth their best work, because each athlete will respond to different triggers. "Some athletes need to be pushed, some need space," according to Tara VanDerveer, head coach of the women's basketball team at Stanford University. Being a good communicator is not only being an effective speaker but an effective listener also. These athletes experienced coaches who were not open to conversation: "You could go into the coach's office, and he would be all ears" (Becker, 2009, p. 93–119). This creates a comfortable atmosphere that enhances relationships (Johnson et al., 2011). But being available to athletes and other coaches is only as effective as the communication that takes place in any setting. The communication process is not a one-way street; it involves a sender of a message and a receiver of a message. Listening is just as important as talking because it involves both inputs and outputs. When communicating effectively, and trying to develop positive relationships with their players, coaches can increase the chances of team success (Johnson et al., 2011).

Zourbanos et al. (2010) found that positive coaching environments can result in positive self-talk. Positive self-talk can boost confidence, anxiety control, and competency. Positive self-talk partnered with positive athlete–coach relationships can correlate with improved individual performance (Dahl, 2013). Great coaches also know that they are not in the game, and players will see things that they don't see, and listening to their players gives them eyes on the field. Having a player–coach relationship benefits coaches as well because they can adapt to things they can't see when athletes are able to communicate information about what is going on during a game. Whether it's in a game, during practice, in a meeting, or at an unrelated event to the team or sport, it is important that the coach creates an environment that prides itself on effective communication. "Effective communication is apparent when team members listen to one another and attempt to build on each other's contributions" (Sullivan, 1993, p. 79). Coaches should incorporate communication into every aspect of a sport because it is one of the most important fundamentals in the sports world. This should awaken a new area of application for instructional communication research and practice. Scholars are needed as helpful consultants to team operations and the provision of training health. They are also necessary as change agents in difficult conversations of inequity and social justice. Finally, team dynamics and player–coach relationships can improve with communication behaviors that are rooted in instructional communication work.

Corporate Training

Much like that of an instructor planning their course for the next semester, a trainer's preparation can impact relational trust, respect and influence (Mathis, 2020). In their work on attendees' reactions to training, it was noted that some attendees could tell when a trainer had not prepared. However, when a trainer did prepare, it was always appreciated, and interaction was higher. In fact, some fields (e.g., sales) noted that when trainees enjoyed a training session, they would join that trainer for social interaction outside of work, for example joining them for a meal after the training session or to an afterwork happy hour. The relational trust, respect, and influence become a product of the relationship between trainers and trainees. Trainers can approach their training sessions in the same way an instructor prepares for class. Materials, presentation outlines, visuals, and time for dialogue and questions are all contributing factors to success. While these aspects do not take place in the traditional classroom, the principles still apply.

When thinking about immediacy and modality, trainers must consider the importance of the learning atmosphere. Trainees noted a sense of appreciation for training sessions where they felt the environment was comfortable and friendly (Mathis, 2020). In relation to the modality, there was a strong appreciation for in-person experiences and a recognition for more online learning in the future. Trainers must take note of the importance of the use of immediacy, not for power use, but for relationship purposes. Trainees showed more appreciation for opportunities for interaction and dialogue than lecture-style training. This brings attention to the importance of communication and instructional design. It also highlights the connection between instructional communication behaviors and training effectiveness. Trainees were more satisfied when they felt more closeness between the trainers and other attendees. This can promote higher levels of organizational identification in the future.

Organizations realize that trainers and professionals can engage in effective training (Kraiger, 2014). However, trainees have provided insight into how trainers can develop and maintain instructional effectiveness as organizational leaders (Mathis, 2020). The relationship between both provides an important look into the social construction of learning in professional workspaces. In order for trainees and trainers to reach their desired outcomes, they must work together and shape a learning experience that's rooted in relationship and not power. Therefore, relational dynamics between trainers and trainees should be explored to look at how both roles influence the learning process withing training programs.

Developing a social construction within organizations, can be a challenge. Although research shows the potential for effective training and outcomes, the relationship aspect can be impeded by misunderstandings.

Whiteley et al. (2013) discussed the need for structure when adapting or changing organizational culture. This refers to the processes that help create and re-create the way an organization interacts. Cultural change is something that will impact various parts of the organization, including stories, traditions, norms, and roles. Managers and leaders are always important in these processes, but nonleader employees must also be a part of the process. This is where organizations with hierarchies can struggle. The relationships, and subsequent power dynamics, have an impact on how individuals construct their organizations. The culture of an organization will also impact the learning environment. Trainers have influence on how the trainee learns the information of the training program but also the aspects of the organizational culture. More research in this area should look at how instructional communication processes influence perceptions of organizational identification, or even retention of new employees.

Legal System

When a person commits a crime, they are charged (sometime go on trial), and if found guilty must pay a debt to society. However, when this debt is paid, how can that person reenter society and move forward with their life? Through their punishment, what have they learned? What does our current legal system teach us about criminals and our ability to forgive? Let's look at the possibilities of work in this area.

Griffith et al. (2019) note that in the United States managers are highly sensitive to social expectations surrounding people with criminal records, which leads to a higher level of discrimination for those persons who have a criminal history. Our nation has often looked at a criminal history as a reflection of an individual's ability to be and do good, leading our society to stigmatize criminal pasts regardless of whether a person has completed sentencing and been deemed ready to reenter society. This stigma not only impacts the way the dominant group of society views criminal pasts, but also the nondominant group: those who have criminal records. What, and how, we perceive individuals with criminal backgrounds shapes the behaviors we use. This reinforces any stigmas and hidden curriculum to the legal system, which should warrant more research. Scholars should investigate how messages from parole officers and legal representatives reinforce or counter negative perceptions of criminals.

Much of what society believes about ex-offenders has been socially constructed and socialized to be the truth (Hinck et al., 2019). In this construction, those who are formerly incarcerated are seen as less than their peers in society, especially in the workplace. Interactions between the two communities show how those constructs can be reshaped, which is necessary in comprehending the power of communication.

Over the last few decades, society has seen a shift in attitudes toward individuals with criminal backgrounds and America's criminal justice system as a whole. This alludes to the majority of Americans feeling as if our past views on how we look at crime and people with criminal records is outdated and not effective in serving and supporting those individuals. In other words, members of society want to see criminals reform and progress, but lack the communication messages to do so. This is where instructional communication research is essential. Scholars should look for individuals who can reconstruct narratives and shift perceptions to an improved work of actual change and reform.

When looking for employment within organizations, people with criminal histories generally face more challenges than their peers, often due to the fact that the presence of a criminal record negatively impact's an employer's views of those candidates (Mikkelson & Schweitzer, 2019). Society has communicated such a negative idea of ex-offenders: that they are immediately considered immoral individuals who should not be considered for employment. These views create a rather unique difficulty for those trying to find employment, or those required to find employment as a term to their rehabilitation or probation. In turn, this can often lead to a higher chance of recidivism or returning to incarceration.

Just as important as finding employment, many people with criminal pasts have unique experiences once they have successfully gained employment. Blessett and Pryor (2013) address diversity initiatives in business practices that covertly leave out ex-offenders when discussing diversity management. This literature examines public administration as well as individual practices of organizations in regard to diversity initiatives within organizations. The authors find that in almost all instances of diversity management, ex-offenders are the "invisible" community, usually never mentioned as an underrepresented population that can contribute to an organization. It is argued that no special treatment or considerations should be given to those who are formerly incarcerated, but more awareness of this population of jobseekers is necessary for their inclusion in the workplace.

Discussions of criminal background and reformation should include all voices, employers too. Some view these widespread discussions as charity, while others understand the need to create genuine and tangible support for these qualified individuals who have a considerably harder time navigating the workplace (Goodstein & Petrich, 2019). Organizations often find themselves in the position of meeting diversity quotas or "checking a box" of inclusion by hiring employees with previous criminal convictions instead of valuing the qualifications and abilities of those individuals. Instructional scholarship can address these errors by applying approaches to teach managers and leaders how to bring criminals back into the workforce successfully. Once these conversations take place, organizations can develop policies as artifacts, which can contribute to changing the organizational culture.

As you can see, the reach of instructional communication research is vast. Scholars are not limited to educational organizations but can apply their knowledge to many fields of interest, across various disciplines. This speaks to Witt's (2017) challenge to ask new questions, deeper questions, and look beyond traditional contexts. Scholars should look for fields where instructional communication principles can be applied. While instructional communication began with an understanding of classroom interactions, it can expand far beyond the classroom, bringing effective instructional practices to many fields across disciplines.

We've seen many examples of how instructional communication can and will be applied in the future. However, it's important to think about these suggestions for the future. After reading a number of new future directions for instructional communication, Witt (2017) is not convinced that many will follow. He notes that far too often scholars consider new directions but settle for the same habits and lines of research that do not produce nuances. Instead, he challenges the field with a question that's just as pivotal as Sprague's (1992) six questions from the past. Will we follow these recommendations?

If we choose to go into these recommended areas, the field of instructional communication will see new life. The areas call for new forms of research, interdisciplinary collaboration, and expansion of application. The opportunities for scholars and practitioners show promise for the field's true reach across professions. Instructors should also encourage their students to pursue areas beyond classroom connections. One may think that instructional communication is related only to classroom environments and professor–student relationships. This chapter has hopefully changed that perception. The teacher and learner dynamic are found in so many areas across organizations, and the same instructional principles can be found. However, if we don't follow these recommendations, we run the risk of seeing a field-wide reinvention of the wheel. Scholars should be cautions to take instructional communication to new heights, opening new doors.

This is not to say that current research agendas and lines of research do not work. Instead, this is a reminder that scholars who are not going into new areas should consider refreshing their work and seeking replications with updates relevant to new advancements in society (Witt, 2017). By engaging in these ways, we will bring longevity to instructional communication by highlighting the importance of messages for instruction within professional contexts. It will also continue conversations that need attention in new ways. Everyone will benefit from these recommendations, and the field of instructional communication will grow stronger.

PART III

Health

CHAPTER 5

Background

Teresa L. Thompson, Nichole Egbert,
Heather J. Carmack, and Yan Tian

The relevance of communication in all professional contexts is apparent in the focus of this book. In this and the subsequent chapter we focus on instructional communication as it relates to health and health care delivery. This chapter overviews what we already know about instructional health communication; the following chapter offers future directions for work and application of the study and teaching of health communication.

The importance of teaching about communicative processes should be evident to all humans. We hope that the fact that you are reading this book means that it is evident to you. Relationships, groups, organizations, and cultures are created through communication. Later in this chapter we will mention some of the unique aspects of communication as it relates to health and health care delivery. We begin with a discussion of health communication in the traditional classroom context. This is followed by a discussion of instructional communication in clinical contexts; this is an issue that is more relevant to health communication than it is to most other areas of instructional communication, so the focus is rather exceptional. This second section highlights communication training for health care providers. Our third major section emphasizes the complement of the second section: communication training/education for patients. Whereas communication education for providers is relevant to only some readers, it is likely that all of us will operate in the patient role at times in our lives. Thus, the third section has wide applicability. That is also the case with the fourth and final major section: a focus on instructional aspects of communication technology as it is used in health care. The breadth and importance of technology in today's world are undeniable. We begin, then, with a focus on the traditional educational context: the classroom.

Health Communication in the Classroom

Health communication has steadily become a mainstay in communication and health curricula in the United States. In the 1970s, health communication was hailed as an "emerging and exciting subfield of communication" (Nash, 1977, p. 70) because of its important connection to people's everyday lives as well as the ease of its integration with other major subfields, including interpersonal, organizational, and mediated communication. Today, health communication is no longer an "up-and-coming" subfield, but a robust and growing area of study that has become part of communication departments, including as standalone majors, minors, and certificates (McKeever, 2014; Robson et al., 2013). Moreover, health communication curricula has been incorporated into preprofessional health curricula at the undergraduate, graduate, and professional levels. Communication is valued as an important skill and included in standardized patient training for future health providers.

Health communication curricula offered by communication departments must balance theory and application and meet the demands required of knowing communication concepts as well as health issues. This is often accomplished by offering two different types of health communication courses: the introductory health communication course and specialty health communication courses.

The introductory health communication course is often a survey course covering the major areas of health communication: patient and provider experiences, health interactions, risk and crisis, health campaigns, media and technology, and organizational and team communication. Departments interested in health communication, or who offer health communication majors, minors, or certificates, also offer more advanced, specialized, or niche health communication courses. These courses allow students to delve deeply into an area of health communication, such as health campaigns (Booth-Butterfield, 2003), or explore important health experiences, such as dying and death (Pagano, 2016).

Common specialty courses include health campaigns, health communication and culture, mediated health communication, patient–provider communication, and health organizing. Health communication courses have also been added to general education curriculum, as exemplified by Landau and Johnson Thorton's (2015) general education courses about rhetoric and medicine, designed to introduce students to complex health topics and communication concepts and show how health communication is part of their everyday lives.

Health communication curricula integrate innovative and forward-thinking topics and approaches to help students see and approach health from different perspectives. Like other communication subfields, health communication is grounded in theory and uses those theories is highly applicable ways. It is very common for health communication courses to integrate an experiential learning component into the curriculum, be it working with clients to create health campaign materials (Neuberger, 2017), drafting communication plans for health care organizations, or creating digital health manuals (Cooke-Jackson, 2013). Health communication educators also turn to medical education, creative writing, and performance studies to help students engage health topics in different ways and address pressing social justice issues related to health (e.g., Ho et al., 2009; Kerr et al., 2020; Tullis & Ryalls, 2019).

Health communication is not relegated to communication courses only; it is often included in preprofessional health curriculum through communication in the discipline's (CID) curricula (Dannels, 2001). CID positions traditional speech communication concepts, such as public speaking, small group communication, and listening, as important for all disciplines, and no-communication disciplines incorporate communication concepts in ways that are appropriate for their disciplines (Dannels, 2001). Nursing educators and students have identified several communication concepts they find valuable, including interpersonal communication, written and online communication, and public speaking (Boschma et al., 2010). Similarly, dietetics students and faculty believe public speaking and interpersonal communication are important (Vrchota, 2011); however, they also believe conflict management and organizational communication concepts like power and supervisor–subordinate relationships are even more important in their daily practice.

These studies highlight the major struggle of integrating CID curriculum into preprofessional health programs. Because the emphasis in CID is on public speaking and oral competency, noncommunication students often struggle with CID curricula because they do not see the importance of communication training beyond public speaking (Dannels, 2002). This is especially troubling for health communication educators, who would like to see health communication concepts included in CID curricula. Additionally, communication components are often integrated into preprofessional health courses without the guidance or knowledge of health communication educators, meaning preprofessional health students may not receive proper or correct communication education. Carmack and Harville (2020) found that, although fundamental nursing textbooks included communication into their coursework, often devoting entire chapters to communication, these chapters were cursory and lacked the depth of knowledge expected from communication educators (as the chapters were written by nursing faculty). Boschma et al. (2010) identified a similar problem with the inclusion of communication in preprofessional health curricula; although "communication" was discussed, it was often not explicitly focused on communication concepts and was just generally discussed. Preprofessional health students may learn those basic communication concepts in their health classes, but unless they take communication courses, they are not likely to explore the depth of communication theories, concepts, and interactions.

Where preprofessional health students often encounter health communication is during standardized patient and clinical trainings (discussed in more detail later). Students can begin to develop their communication skills during these trainings, and depending on the program, they have 3 to 4 years of practice. Standardized patient training involves the use of human actors presenting certain illness symptoms to students as a way for them to practice their diagnostic skills. Simulated patient training involves the use of a full or partial body mannequin on which students to practice clinical skills, such as intubation, gynecological examinations, and cardiopulmonary resuscitation. Standardized patient trainings typically focus on the traditional medical interview experience but can also focus on helping diagnose in unique health settings, such as during emergent visits or during oncology treatments. Although they are framed as diagnostic training, standardized patient training is inherently a communication training as future providers learn how to best listen, ask questions, and talk with patients about their health issues.

Feeley et al. (2010) found that 1st-year medical students engaging in standardized patient communication training about organ donation learned new information about the topic, enabling them to engage in more thoughtful conversations with patients. As students near the end of their education, they enter clinicals, where, under the guidance of a preceptor or mentor, they interact with and care for real patients in hospitals and clinics. Although the focus of standardized patient training and clinicals is the improvement of diagnostic ability, some programs may focus directly on communication training. Students who are exposed to communication training curricula during their clinical year reported an improvement in overall communication skills, such as information giving and nonverbal communication (Suojanen et al., 2018). Preprofessional health students transitioning into their professional careers are required to complete assessments of their clinical and diagnostic skills, such as Objective Structural Clinical Examinations (OSCE) and Clinical Nurse Leader Exams (CNLs). Nursing students who received communication training received higher communication evaluation scores in their OSCE simulations (Hsu et al., 2015). The inclusion of communication curriculum in standardized patient training also helps future providers critically engage in self-reflection about their knowledge, attitudes, and beliefs about salient issues and vulnerable groups, helping students consider their positionality and what prejudices they may bring into the clinical space (Duggan et al., 2009).

Whether it is in the communication classroom or in a standardized patient lab room, health communication contributes to the education and training of future health providers as well as provides a vocabulary for everyone to be a thoughtful and critical consumer and creator of health communication. In the next section, we will discuss how health communication education continues past the traditional classroom learning space and is also part of health professionals' clinical practice.

Communication Skill Training

Programs that emphasize instructional communication for health care providers are typically called CSPs, the acronym for communication skills programs. They include both specific interventions designed to develop skills in a particular context and broader educational aspects of the training of health care professionals. Only a small number of CSPs have focused on improving patient communication skills. Our overview in this second section will primarily focus on those CSPs that are geared to care providers; those directed toward patients will be discussed in the next (third) section of this chapter. As we move through this chapter, please also keep in mind the "hidden curriculum" that is a part of medical- and health-related instruction. Students and other professionals model what they see when on rounds or otherwise interacting with more senior health care professionals.

The need for such programs is apparent when one examines the lack of communication skills evident in most care providers, the absence of training until recent years, and the outcomes of communication in health contexts. Readers of this volume are likely already aware of limited com- municative competency in many health care providers based on personal experiences with health care. Few of us go through life experiencing only health care encounters characterized by shared meaning creation and understanding. More frequently, we encounter a lack of sharing needed information, poorly delivered messages, unclear information, and many other communication-related problems. The voluminous amount of research that is available substantiates the common nature of such nega- tive experiences. Although many people are ultimately satisfied with the care that they receive from providers, there is less satisfaction with the communication accompanying that care.

In light of such dissatisfaction, many researchers, practitioners, and educators have begun developing CSPs to improve communicative pro- cesses in health care. These CSPs go beyond the traditional classroom. Communication is now generally seen as an essential and important component of the training of health care providers. The outcomes of communication make the need for improvement even more evident. The volume of which this chapter is a part makes clear the importance of com- munication in all professional contexts, but, as noted in our introduction, there are some unique aspects of health care that lead to special concerns. Communication between health care providers and patients and among health care providers impacts such issues as the likelihood of malpractice litigation, quickness of recovery, need for reliance on medication, patient adherence to treatment and medication regimens, safety concerns, medical errors, accuracy of diagnosis, and many important health outcomes.

Based on our knowledge of the dyadic nature of all communication, it should be obvious that both care providers and patients impact the health care context, but reaching patients is more difficult than connecting with and providing training to care providers. Thus, most communication skills programs are geared toward health care professionals. That should not lead us to believe, however, that care providers contribute to communication problems more than do patients. We do know that most care providers dominate communication, and counter-acting such domination is one of the issues addressed by some CSPs. It is also true, however, that patients may play a role in allowing communicative control by providers; we as patients are responsible for speaking up and preventing domination. Some experts refer to this as moving from the rhetoric of passivity to the rhetoric of agency. Examination of health care interactions does not indicate that patients do a great job of describing their health care problems; even those patients who attempt to be more assertive are not always effective. Patients frequently do not provide full information, ask important questions, or provide helpful feedback to care providers.

Returning to what we do know about CSPs, however, it is important to note some recurring problems in health care interactions that have been addressed in past work. Soliciting the patient's concerns, demonstrating empathy, becoming more patient or relationship centered, asking questions, having difficult conversations, communicating about end-of-life issues, bad news delivery, discussions of mental health and sexuality, adapting to varying health literacy levels, and avoiding unclear jargon are some of the common foci of CSPs for providers. Historically, nursing educators have been more concerned about communication issues than have other health professionals. Nurses also typically spend more time with patients than do most other care providers.

As medical and other health educators have become more aware of the importance of communication skills training, we have seen growth in the emphasis on CSPs in medicine, nursing, and allied health programs as well as inclusion of testing communicative proficiency in many areas of health education and licensing. Such testing frequently includes reliance on simulated or standardized patients. Simulated or standardized patients are also frequently a part of CSPs. The data indicate that CSPs can indeed have an impact on short-term and simulated interactions, but there is less evidence of the transfer of those skills to ongoing clinical health care (Cusanno et al., 2021).

Communication skills programs may be enacted during medical rounds, through one-on-one didactic training, remotely, in the classroom or workshop, based on readings or role-plays, or through other electronic modes of communication such as video. Most CSPs are group activities, but some are targeted at the individual level. Experiential dimensions to CSPs are important aspects of effective training. Many CSPs are not based on sound communication theory; they are more likely to reflect the experiences of care providers than more generalizable findings from rigorous research. Indeed, the area of health communication that is least likely to be strongly based in theory is work that focuses on provider–patient interaction (Schulz & Jiang, 2021). It is not unusual to see formulaic recommendations in health-care related CSPs. These involve teaching students an acronym on which they can rely when interacting with patients. An oft-cited example is the acronym SPIKES (setting up, perception, invitation, knowledge, emotions with empathy, and strategy or summary; Rosensweig, 2012), which is focused on bad news delivery. Although there are examples of such work that are strongly based on sound communication theory, such as the work on COMFORT (communication, orientation/

opportunity, mindfulness, family, oversight, reiterative/radically adaptive messages, team; Wittenberg & Goldsmith, 2021), most are not. Programs such as SPIKES are generally referred to as "tool kit" training (Cusanno et al., 2021) as opposed to those that are based on a more humanistic "lens-based" approach to looking at communication. This second, broader approach focuses on understanding how communication constructs relationships and realities and is strongly influenced by a more qualitative, cultural conceptualization of health communication. The notion of cultural humility is central to some of these CSPs, as is understanding the various structural/cultural (rather than individual) influences on health and health-related behaviors. Additionally, one must think about both formative and summative assessment as CSPs are developed and the evaluation of them as they progress.

Instructional Communication for Patients

As discussed earlier, health provider CSPs only address half of the potential breakdown in patient–provider communication. Historically, the patient side of the equation has received much less attention (Cegala, 2003). Patient education in general has been seen in a very limited way, such as pamphlets on display in a doctor's office or a video package where a stoic professional in a white coat explains a medical procedure or treatment. More recently, researchers and practitioners have developed a wider range of strategies to educate patients about important health topics. For example, some of the education interventions linked to improved health outcomes include responding to emotions, managing uncertainty, enabling self-management, and making quality decisions (Street et al., 2008).

Educating patients requires more than providing information; it means actively influencing patients' knowledge, beliefs, and behaviors (Vahabi, 2006). Focusing only on providing information may lead to uninformed health decisions and behaviors that can prove costly and dangerous if patients do not attend to or understand that information. One strategy to improve safety instruction is to present information in a narrative or anecdotal format (Ricketts et al., 2010). Another widely accepted approach is to develop patient-centered communication that alters the format, language, and visual components of the instructional message (Morrow et al., 2005).

The ways that instructions for taking medication are presented on prescription and nonprescription labels provide a good example of the importance of communication. If a medication label states that the medicine is to be taken "twice daily," or "PRN," there is a good chance the patient may take two or more doses at one time, exceed the maximum daily dose, or wait fewer than 4 hours between doses (McCarthy et al., 2013). A more patient-centered message, such as "Take 1 or 2 pills; then wait 4 hours before taking again," is clearer and closer to the way most patients speak.

According to physicians, one of the most pressing problems in educating patients is discovering when patients have knowledge gaps or other types of uncertainty (Arnold et al., 2012). Patients often fail to ask questions, disclose potential barriers to treatment, and provide incomplete medical histories. Cegala et al. (2000) built a communication skills training program to increase patient participation in medical interviews. The program consisted mainly of a training booklet provided to patients prior to their medical visit. The booklet prompted patients to consider their medical condition, why they had scheduled their appointment, and their goals for the appointment. Patients were also instructed to write out their symptoms and questions for the provider before their medical visit. In their research, trained patients asked more questions, elicited more information from physicians, and were more likely to experience a patient-centered visit. Notably, training patients before their medical visits did not significantly increase visit length (Post et al., 2002).

Patients can be educated to manage their chronic illnesses through training that provides information, empowers them, and increases their participation in their own health care. Self-care management education programs are delivered by physicians, nurses, and other clinical staff, and even by peers or other laypersons (Lillyman & Farquaharson, 2013). Although peer facilitators are less qualified to answer technical or medical questions, they can help patients by sharing experiences and social support. Patient training programs can be delivered virtually through the internet, although there are concerns about patients' ability to engage some online programs due to lack of experience, interest, and access, especially patients who are older or members of some racial and ethnic minority groups (Gordon & Hornbrook, 2018). Self-care interventions that enhance health literacy also show potential for improved outcomes.

Addressing patient low health literacy has been a high priority in the past 30 years. Health literacy is the degree to which individuals have the capacity to obtain, process, and understand basic health information and services needed to make appropriate health decisions. In the United States, only 12% of patients are proficient in health literacy, which is why improving patient health literacy has been a major goal of Healthy People 2020 and 2030. The financial impact of low health literacy is between $100 and $200 billion annually in the United States (Vernon et al., 2007). There are two major approaches for dealing with the population's low health literacy: assessing and instructing at-risk patients to improve their health literacy and developing patient-centered, approachable messages that reduce health literacy demand for everyone. Both approaches rely on health communication research and education to succeed.

Much of the early health literacy was focused on developing assessments for health literacy to identify at-risk patients. At first the skills associated with low health literacy involved basic reading and literacy skills. Patients might be asked to pronounce and/or recognize health-related words in a list provided by their clinician. However, the scope of skills related to health literacy has broadened considerably to include "knowledge and skills that include reading, writing, numeracy, listening, oral, and visual communication, problem solving and decision making" (Helitzer et al., 2012, p. 161). Modern health literacy skills often include the ability to navigate and locate health information on the internet and via mobile devices and social media (Aldoory, 2017). A wide range of instruments continue to be developed to assess this wide range of skills in patients via written, oral, and digital tests (Haun et al., 2014) These tools vary in length and specificity and generally require patients to be tested in person.

Assessments of low health literacy have allowed researchers to describe the parameters of the problem of low health literacy but have been limited in their ability to improve it. Many studies assess health literacy using one of these instruments before and after an educational intervention. Interventions often occur in small groups of patients but can also be carried out through cell phones, social media, and one-on-one education (Walters et al., 2020). Although some interventions have been shown to improve both patient health literacy as well as targeted health behaviors, they are not always successful, can be very expensive, and may be difficult to deliver to many marginalized patient groups. More systematic approaches are needed to address this complicated and widespread problem. For example, integrating health literacy education in medical education for clinical staff can improve their knowledge, communication skills, and confidence in addressing low health literacy in their patients (Toronto & Weatherford, 2015).

An alternative to the somewhat limited approach of patient assessment and intervention is the "universal precautions" approach that instead focuses on making health messages clearer to everyone, regardless of their level of health literacy (Brega et al., 2015). Aside from the often-prohibitive cost of delivering patient education interventions, the universal precautions approach protects patients' dignity and privacy, as patients are not undergoing potentially embarrassing tests of their knowledge and understanding (Killian & Coletti, 2017). In addition, providing health information in clear and easily accessible formats improves the likelihood that all patients are making more informed choices and actively participating in their health care.

The basics of improving patient understanding of health messages begin with reducing the literacy demand of the material by avoiding medical jargon, complex sentence structure, and using plain language. Patients can more readily understand terms that they encounter in everyday life such as heart instead of cardiac and stop instead of discontinue. Sometimes replacing potentially confusing medical terms with everyday words may require more words. For example, benign could be replaced with is not cancer. The terminology should be easily understood and represent what the health care provider needs to convey. However, not every patient uses the same everyday language, so the diversity of the target audience's cultural and linguistic needs must be considered carefully (Neuhauser & Kreps, 2008). Multiple patient- and culture-centered versions of health messages may need to be developed and pretested with members of the target audience. In the end, attending to both cultural differences and limited health literacy has been found to "reduce medical errors, improve adherence, patient-provider-family communication, and outcomes of care at both individual and population levels" (Lie et al., 2012, p. 14).

Two other tools that health care providers can utilize to improve patient understanding include infographics and teach-back methods. The use of carefully designed graphics in print and online health messages can substantially improve patient comprehension and recall in general, but especially among patients with low health literacy. Visual images also have the capacity to stimulate emotional responses that support motivation and adherence, as well as create opportunities to promote inclusion and connection to the target audience (Houts et al., 2006). For maximum benefit, graphic representations should include simple captions, remain uncluttered, and be pretested with both health professionals and patients. Teach-back is a procedure typically used in primary care, inpatient, and emergency medicine contexts (Yen & Leasure, 2019). In a nutshell, after receiving information verbally from their health care provider, patients are asked to paraphrase what the provider told them in their own words. In so doing, the health care provider can check the accuracy of the patients' recall and understanding. This procedure is recommended by the Agency for Healthcare Research and Quality as well as the Institute for Healthcare Improvement.

Technology in Health Communication Instruction

Technology plays an increasingly important role in instructional communication for health care. From traditional alphabet boards, picture boards, speech generation devices, and pagers to telemedicine systems, cell phones, tablets, and social media, health students and professionals need knowledge and skills in various types of technologies to communicate with patients as well as to communicate with each other. On a global scale, 4.66 billion people, or 59.5% of the population, are using the internet, 5.22 billion, or 66.6% of the population, are unique mobile phone users, and 4.2 billion, or 53.6% of the population, are actively using social media (Kemp, 2021). With the ever-growing trend of technology adoption, it is important to train health students and professionals to take advantage of the new technologies to improve efficiency and quality of health communication and to eventually improve psychological and physical outcomes of health care. The Association of American Medical Colleges' (AAMC) Institute for Improving Medial Education (2007) published the "Effective Use of Educational Technology in Medial Education" report, which categorized medical education technology applications into three areas: computer-aided instruction, virtual patients, and human patient simulation. Based on this framework, we discuss the current education and research in computer-aided instruction and virtual reality, virtual patients, and human patient simulations. We also discuss education and training related to telemedicine, which is extremely important during the COVID-19 pandemic, and electronic health records (EHR), which is an important component of digital health education.

DIGITAL EDUCATION

Computer-aided instruction is an essential format of digital education. Digital education is teaching and learning though digital technologies, with modalities ranging from basic transformation of media format (e.g., converting a book into a PDF file) to development and use of complicated digital technologies (e.g., serious games, virtual reality; Car et al., 2019). New communication technologies are providing exciting opportunities for us in health classrooms and health professional training. Just as is the case with general digital education, digital health education can use technology-based tools such as discussion boards, blogs, wikis, and video meetings to promote interactions, engagement, and critical thinking (Foronda et al., 2013). For instance, an online clinical discussion board, which allowed medical students in a university's rural medicine rotation program at different clinical sites to communicate with each other, helped students share their rural clinical experience, develop peer-based reflective learning, and build interpersonal relationships, professional networks, and support systems (Baker et al., 2005). Similarly, podcasts have been found to be useful and beneficial in supplementary learning by medical students (Prakash et al., 2017) and nursing students (Mostyn et al., 2013).

VIRTUAL INSTRUCTION

Virtual reality, virtual patients, and human patient simulations are innovative tools in digital health education and communication. Virtual reality for health education refers to "a technology that allows the user to explore and manipulate computer-generated real or artificial three-dimensional multimedia sensory environments in real time to gain practical knowledge that can be used in clinical practice" (Kyaw et al., 2019, p. 1). For example, in a simulated virtual world, nursing students can have live communication with instructors, colleagues, and patients, while using the virtual system to learn knowledge and skills in areas such as fluid calculation and lab result checking (Foronda et al., 2013). Learners use virtual patients, which are computer programs that simulate real-life scenarios, to imitate what health care providers would do, including obtaining patient history, conducting physical exams, and making medical decisions (AAMC, Institute for Improving Medial Education, 2007).

As noted, simulated patients are frequently used in clinical training. In recent years some training programs have moved to the use of virtual patient simulators. A systematic review of virtual patient simulators for medical communication training indicated that virtual patients are used to teach communication skills associated with patient information gathering, skills to explain and plan treatment for patients, and skills to build relationships with patients using emphatic communication in clinical interactions (Lee et al., 2020). Empirical evidence suggests that medical students who were trained by computer simulation, featuring virtual humans, successfully learned how to improve their intercultural and interprofessional communication skills; they also scored significantly higher in the objective structured clinical examination and had more positive attitudes and evaluation of the training experience than the medical students who were trained through multimedia computer-based learning (Kron et al., 2017). Meta-analysis of studies on virtual reality and health professions education also suggested that, compared to traditional education (e.g., using two-dimensional images or textbooks) or other types of digital education (e.g., online or offline digital education), virtual reality led to improvement in knowledge and skills for health profession learners (Kyaw et al., 2019).

TELEMEDICINE

Similar to virtual reality and virtual simulations, telemedicine is gaining increasing attention among health professionals and health educators. Telemedicine delivers health care and provides health services from a distance (Hyder & Razzak, 2020). It was traditionally known for expanding health care access to rural areas and underserved populations, but it has gained new meaning during the COVID-19 pandemic (Smith et al., 2020). Telemedicine helps decrease the risk of infectious disease transmission, reduce travel cost, and save time, and it can lead to health outcomes similar to what are achieved through in-person visits (Smith et al., 2020). Staff training, patient education, and audiovisual communication platforms are key elements for telemedicine systems to work (Smith et al., 2020). Researchers have developed curricula to train medical students for telemedicine competency, with communication being an important component of the training. For example, in the curriculum developed by Sharma et al. (2019), digital communication and website manner is the first domain of core competencies for virtual health care, which includes items such as reducing communication speed to clear enunciation, avoiding colloquial speech, minimizing body motion and gestures, and looking at the camera to maintain eye contact. With medical school training shifting to online mode in response to the COVID-19 and other future pandemics, communication skills and rapport building continue to be important aspects for telemedicine curricular activities (Iancu et al., 2020).

ELECTRONIC HEALTH RECORDS

Digital health education also involves teaching communication skills related to the use of EHR, which refers to "a means a comprehensive medical record or similar documentation of the past and present physical and mental state of health of an individual in electronic form," and EHR provides "ready availability of these data for medical treatment and other closely related purposes" (Kierkegaard, 2011, p. 505). EHR use, however, may disrupt patient–provider communication, because when health care providers spend more time looking at the computer, they may look at the patients less and provide less information to the patients (Noordman et al., 2010). Therefore, it is important to teach health students and professionals not only the technical skills, but also the communication skills of using EHR. Palumbo et al. (2016) developed a 10-point checklist for EHR communication skills, which includes items such as asking open-ended questions and giving patients adequate time to answer, educating patients on the use of computers, setting up computers in a way for patients to be able to see the screens, explaining long duration of typing, and maintaining good eye contact. Data from nurse practitioner students showed that students benefitted from instruction on such communication skills for EHR use (Palumbo et al., 2016). Similarly, researchers developed a patient-centered curriculum embedding training in communication skills into EHR onboarding and taught medical school students communication tips (e.g., maximizing patient interaction; letting the patient look on for EHR use); the approach has been found to be effective and successful (Alkureishi et al., 2018).

The list of technologies reviewed in this section is by no means exhaustive. Other technologies such as mobile apps and serious gaming/gamification are also widely used in digital health education (Aungst & Patel, 2020; Gentry et al., 2019). Similar to general online education, digital health education takes advantage of new technologies' capacity in providing multimedia information and in allowing interactivity between instructor and students and interactivity among peers. Digital health education is also unique in that it covers clinical training and one of its key goals is to improve patient–provider communication. It is imperative for health educators to find innovative ways to capitalize on the strength of new technologies and minimize the limitations that new technologies present to have effective and efficient health communication and to eventually improve health outcomes.

Conclusion

We hope that this overview makes evident the fascinating and significant role that communication education plays in one important professional context—health and health care delivery. Our understanding of the context of health requires continual expansion and adaptation due to the aging of the population and the advent of new health problems. The numbers of health professionals are also consistently increasing. Thus, educating these health professionals about effective communication becomes even more important than it has been in the past. In the next chapter we move beyond what we already know about instructional communication as it relates to health and speculate about future directions in practice and research.

CHAPTER 6

Current Trends and Future Directions

Heather J. Carmack, Angela Cooke-Jackson, Yan Tian, Michael Mackert, and Teresa L. Thompson

As we build on the previous chapter and move to a discussion of new directions and exciting avenues to explore in relation to instructional communication in professional health contexts, there are several important themes that we must address. We noted in the previous chapter the ever-increasing importance of health professionals in what we hope will soon be a post-pandemic world. We will return to this issue in the present chapter as we identify opportunities for further development within the classroom. We will also discuss broadening our understanding of instructional health communication as we rely even more on health literacy education and improvement. We will focus on the need to expand our work; it must more appropriately incorporate an understanding of the role of culture, race, and ethnicity in effective and ethical health communication education. Cultural intelligence, appreciation, and humility are important parts of this. Finally, we will return to a discussion of technology and how it must be studied and applied in professional instructional health communication contexts. We begin with the context with which most of us are most familiar: the classroom.

Health Communication in the Classroom

One major area for the future of health communication in instructional contexts is the systematic integration of health communication into university communication across the curriculum (CXC)/communication in the disciplines (CID) programs. Current CXC/CID programs focus primarily on designing communication courses or adding communication components to curricula to help students develop their communication competency skills (through public speaking, small group communication, and conflict management) and competencies in engaging in disciplinarily discussions, critically analyzing research, and speaking knowledgeably about topics (Dannels, 2001). CXC/CID curricula relies heavily on public speaking, interpersonal communication, and argumentation courses to help students develop these competencies. However, the COVID-19 pandemic underscored that health communication competencies are just as important to help students become thoughtful and well-rounded citizens. Students need to learn about how to be effective and ethical health communication consumers and creators, and these skills are fostered in health communication courses. The purposeful integration of health communication courses into CXC/CID programs, especially in nursing and allied health profession majors, can help students see the importance of health communication and develop their health communication skills.

Adding health communication to CXC/CID courses can be accomplished in several ways. They can be added to university general education curricula, similar to the inclusion of public speaking, critical decision-making, and interpersonal communication courses. Many universities offer students the option of taking introductory communication courses to meet general education requirements, and health communication could be offered as an option to meet those requirements. Landau and Johnson

Thorton (2015) each taught health rhetoric courses designed as general education courses to help cultivate informed health citizens and inter-disciplinarity in students early in their university programs. Hill and Griswold (2013) worked together to combine written communication skills and health science in a collaborative service-learning course; they reported their students developed a higher level of written communication skills. Health communication educators should be called on to develop or teach introductory health communication courses for general education programs. Communication departments could also work with other academic departments to integrate health communication concepts, units, or courses into their disciplinary curricula. The increased presence of COVID-19 health information and health disinformation/misinformation shows the importance of health communication, and we hope to see more universities creating health communication courses, curricula, and degrees.

We believe health communication also has the potential to become a mainstay in nursing, allied health, and premed students' programs of study as ways to help them meet Interprofessional Education Collaborative (IPEC) and Medical College Admission Test (MCAT) requirements. In 2009, the Association of American Medical Colleges, American Association of Colleges of Nursing, American Association of Colleges of Pharmacy, American Association of Colleges of Osteopathic Medicine, American Dental Education Association, and Association of Schools of Public Health formed an education collaborative with the goal of creating a unifying curriculum to help future professionals develop important collaboration skills (Schmitt et al., 2011). Starting in 2011, university preprofessional health programs associated or accredited by the six educational associations required curricula that incorporated four core competencies (values/ethics, roles/responsibilities, interprofessional communication, teams and teamwork; IPEC, 2011). In 2015, the Association of American Medical Colleges (AAMC) added two sections to the MCAT focused on psychological, social, and behavior determinants of health and critical reasoning skills (American Psychological Association [APA], 2013). AAMC recommended premed students take social science and humanities courses to help prepare them for these new sections. Communication concepts are already integrated into nursing curricula through communication chapters in nursing foundational textbooks and skills training; however, as we noted in the previous chapter, these learning materials and lectures often do not explicitly teach communication concepts or cover communication concepts in depth. Health communication curricula can help preprofessional health students learn and practice the four IPEC competencies and teach premed students social and behavioral determinants of health as well as reasoning and analytical skills. This can be accomplished by hiring health communication educators to teach communication-focused classes in the preexisting curriculum or by integrating health communication courses into preprofessional health programs. Introductory health communication, patient–provider communication, health campaigns, communicating in health organizations, health and media, and health communication and culture courses are all courses where preprofessional students can learn about these determinants and skills. This is also an opportunity for communication departments to develop and promote health communication minors for preprofessional health students, ensuring they are able to spend time digging deeply into health communication issues.

Health communication educators can also contribute to creating collaborative health provider education. Integrating IPEC into preprofessional health curricula is designed to teach future providers how to work together effectively to care for patients. However, the implementation of IPEC curricula makes it difficult for health educators to design true interprofessional educational opportunities. Health communication can be the glue to bind the health professions together by showing how communication connects their fields through team communication, team simulations, information seeking and information giving, collaborative decision-making, and patient-centered communication. The integration of health communication courses and curricula into preprofessional health students' programs of study creates opportunities to learn and practice communication skills related to traditional dyadic patient–provider interactions, as well as the communication skills needed to communicate and work in teams and supervisors. Additionally, the inclusion of health communication in health curricula helps students learn and practice communicating about care issues, such as disclosing medical errors, breaking bad news, and working through ethical care situations. As communication skills training moves more into the forefront of preprofessional training, designing communication training to account for the diversity of communication experiences providers may encounter is needed. Although communication training for dyadic patient–provider interactions is common in preprofessional and professional programs through the use of standardized patients and simulations, medical and nursing students report receiving uneven communication education and training about unique communication instances, such as reporting medical errors to supervisors (e.g., Noland, 2014; Noland & Carmack, 2015) or telling families their loved one has died (Ombres et al., 2017). Additionally, these trainings are usually reserved for students' final years of undergraduate study or in professional programs (i.e., medical school), instead of incorporated at the beginning of programs so that students can practice early and often. Integrating health communication training focused on unique and mundane communication interactions early in students' education and training will help them develop the skills necessary to communicate effectively with patients.

Finally, health communication training and education can explore the positive and negative impacts of technology on patient care, using standardized and simulated patient trainings to train future providers on communicating in telehealth visits. Health communication scholars have long discussed the importance of training health providers on how to effectively communicate on online platforms (e.g., Matusitz & Breen, 2007), and the explosion of telehealth appointments during COVID highlighted the communication promises and perils providers will encounter. Verbal and nonverbal communication expectations and practices are different for telehealth appointments (Faucett et al., 2017), and future providers can work on developing their nonverbal competency in both displaying positive nonverbals and reading their patients' nonverbals. Additionally, the inclusion of telehealth communication training will help future providers learn how to deliver difficult news, such as death notifications, using telehealth platforms. Focusing on telehealth communication training for providers during their undergraduate, graduate, and professional programs will help future providers transition successfully into the new health care delivery landscape.

Moving beyond explicit health communication training and curricula, instructors at every level and in every discipline will need to determine how to negotiate students' communication about their health issues. Students turn to professors to disclose and talk about health issues, ranging from explaining they have a common cold to disclosing mental health issues that may impact their performance in class. Students disclose to their college instructors for a variety of reasons (Zengaro et al., 2020), and instructors must determine how to use that information appropriately in order to maintain the student–instructor relationship (Price et al., 2021). Although students do not have to disclose their health issues to instructors, faculty are finding that students are more open to communicating about their health issues than in previous years. Students are also disclosing their health issues in their classes, openly talking about their mental health and chronic health. The COVID-19 pandemic introduced a new long-term health issue for students and instructors to find the best way to talk about and potentially disclose their health status. COVID, in particular, created a unique disclosure event as many universities require students to disclose positive test results to their instructors while prohibiting instructors from talking to their classes about being exposed and getting tested. Moving forward, instructional health communication researchers must explore these new disclosure events and how they impact the way we study student–instructor communication and use disclosure theories, such as communication privacy management theory (Petronio, 2002) and the disclosure decision-making model (Greene et al., 2012).

The COVID-19 pandemic created massive upheaval for college students across the globe, forcing students and instructors to adapt to online instruction, and for students, finding ways to learn without the social support of their classmates. Along with exploring COVID student–instructor disclosures, health issues related to mental health, trauma, stress, burnout, and resilience are likely to become mainstays in the instructional health communication literature. Understanding how these health concepts are experienced, enacted, and communicated by students and instructors in the classroom as well as how they impact learning experiences is desperately needed and should provide instructional and health communication educators ways to help students when navigating pandemic impacts on education. We want to emphasize, however, that students are not the only ones impacted by this. Understanding instructor and staff experiences with mental health, trauma, stress, burnout, and resilience is equally important. We all have a part in the college experience and impact how we each experience and thrive in learning spaces.

Health communication educators have the opportunity to help preprofessional health and communication students learn and practice health communication skills as well as come together in interprofessional groups to work together for the betterment of patients and their families. Additionally, adding more complex communication interactions to students' training will help them more successfully navigate the unique interactions they will have with their patients. Ultimately, we hope to see health communication curricula infused across communication, general education, and university curricula as more educators and administrators see the importance and contribution of health communication in everyday lives. An important outcome of this increased health communication infusion is patient health literacy.

Patient Education and Literacy

Health literacy is an essential component in determining health decisions and outcomes. Through recognition that those with lower health literacy are less likely engage in preventive health behaviors (Fernandez et al., 2016) and often have worse health outcomes for myriad reasons (Berkman et at., 2011), there is a substantial opportunity to consider how education programs can help address the disparities that impact those with lower health literacy. Although training programs exist to help build skills for health care providers (e.g., Kripalani et al., 2006), there is also notable opportunity to explore how different education programs can build important health literacy skills among the public to support personal health as patients and improve public health more broadly. This is essential given the argument that health literacy is a product of multiple cognitive and social factors and can change over time (Paasche-Orlow & Wolf, 2007). Additionally, researchers studying health literacy as a field have long understood the potential for the education system to contribute in a meaningful way to individuals' health literacy (Nielsen-Bohlman et al., 2004).

One prime opportunity to build health literacy skills, particularly given some of the factors associated with risk for lower health literacy, is building this kind of training in adult literacy programs. This might include general educational development (GED) preparation classes, adult basic literacy tutoring, and English as a second language (ESL) instruction. One study of such programs found that while the majority were already providing health information in their classes, there was a recognized need for training in particular skills; interacting with doctors was the most common need (Mackert & Poag, 2011). The programs also reported that their students expressed frustration with navigating the health care system, filling out insurance paperwork, and not knowing where to go for treatment (e.g., how to search for the appropriate provider for a particular medical issue). A more recent survey of adult literacy programs found themes consistent with those just mentioned, as well as evidence that the those running the programs prefer more general resources and skills than a focus on particular diseases (Champlin et al., 2020). There is already literature on how to design resources for integration into these kinds of programs (Soricone et al., 2007), and evaluations of such programs have demonstrated positive results (Chervin et al., 2012; Soto Mas et al., 2015).

Although a focus on adults at risk for lower health literacy provides an important opportunity to build health literacy skills via educational programs, it is also true that programs focused on youth can build these skills that will serve them over the course of their entire lives. Interventions designed to develop health literacy skills among elementary school students have shown meaningful improvements, including a study by Knisel et al. (2020) that pilot-tested a program to build health literacy skills in students aged 6–12. Similarly, a focus on health literacy and digital literacy skills helped students build health literacy skills that could translate into healthy decisions and behaviors (Hyman et al., 2020). It is important to appreciate that programs focused on health literacy and improving children's health can often exclude the children themselves and focus only on their caregivers, but programs that take a more holistic approach can benefit the skills and outcomes of children and their caregivers (Aghazadeh et al., 2020).

Finally, another critical intervention point for building health literacy skills could be college and university students, who are emerging adults with increased responsibility for their health decisions. Research about college students' health literacy is mixed, but more recent findings support the idea that college students cannot be assumed to have adequate health literacy (Ickes & Cottrell, 2010; Rababah et al., 2019). As an additional consideration, we should note that international students are navigating the U.S. health care system for the first time, and thus might suffer from the same lack of skills as domestic students taking ownership of their health for the first time; international students, too, would benefit from programs designed to build skills regarding the health care system (Mackert et al., 2017). Patil et al. (2021) have advocated for health literacy and digital health literacy to be incorporated into all college curricula given the potential benefits to students. Many of the approaches and topics developed for use in the adult basic education setting would have utility for faculty in colleges and universities, eliminating the demand on individual faculty to develop such materials for every new class on their own.

In considering all programs designed to build health literacy skills in the context of other educational programs, it is essential to recognize the distinction between knowledge about a health issue (e.g., end-of-life care) and skills related to finding, understanding, using, and communicating about health information (Mackert et al., 2015). A focus on general health literacy skills can help individuals build capacity to deal with new health information regardless of the context, which could be particularly useful when dealing with a new health issue; any focus on general health literacy skills must be tempered by the recognition that some health issues are unique and present particular issues related to the role of health information, such as mental health and illness (Jorm, 2015). As an example, the public response to COVID-19 could have been improved if members of the public were more sophisticated in their abilities to find credible health information, understand how the science and knowledge about a novel virus might change over time, and understand the links between personal and public health. Personal and public health are also impacted by other systemic health and well-being issues, such as mis/disinformation, mistrust, and historical and contemporary racism. Our next section focuses on communication education and training to address these systemic issues.

Communication Training for Misinformation, Mistrust, and Historical Racism

Receiving additional educational training continues to be an important avenue for advancing the career of health providers and for the provision of innovative support by communication specialists who work for health care facilities. The COVID pandemic made apparent the need for more immersive and continual education training to attend to new communicative concerns and unaddressed issues and topics. At least a few unique issues emerged regarding information flow and access surrounding the pandemic. Some issues surfaced during the early COVID-19 outbreak. Other issues have been a part of the ongoing dialogue surrounding the impact of the pandemic. Most prominent among these issues have been (1) the lack of clear information and the breakdown of communication and information provision during the early days of the pandemic; (2) miscommunication of the impact of COVID-19 and mistrust of vaccine information among different sectors of society; and (3) communication distrust among various racial and ethnic groups because of historical injustices. Each is important to address as we understand the value and important role of communication training for professionals.

First, future training must help professionals understand how communication breakdowns can happen and the importance of creating and disseminating clear, concise, and consistent information to the public. To date, the Centers for Disease Control and Prevention (CDC) has put the training of health care professionals and educators at the top of their list of recommendations. This is significant given the critical role health care professionals have been given during the pandemic as first responders in the administration of vaccines and information on COVID-19 as well as in their customary roles providing care (CDC, 2021). The CDC recommendations acknowledge that this training needs to move beyond traditional health care professionals and take place within medical support teams, administrative support teams, and even experienced vaccinators. The rationale for this is to provide a training mandate and protocol that is robust and fluid across different administrative roles and infrastructures. The CDC also acknowledges that partners and community clinics should create audience-specific tool kits and planning guides that "build confidence in COVID-19 vaccination, educate patients and answer COVID-19 vaccine-related questions and learn proper COVID-19 vaccine storage and handling guidance" (Planning Guides and Toolkits for Partners and Community Clinics, 2021, para. 1).

Second, inconsistent communication of information and mistrust regarding COVID-19 and vaccine information has amplified local and governmental agencies' understanding of the rate at which different communities share and receive information and whether they act on it. For instance, at the time this chapter was written there were still numerous messages on social media and some news outlets of misinformation from individuals who mistrust vaccine protocols and treatment. Even during the pandemic, we saw and still see an outpouring of fact-based information from primary health care providers, the Food and Drug Administration, the CDC, as well from Dr. Anthony Fauci, the director of the U.S. National Institute of Allergy and Infectious Diseases, as they move quickly to address misinformation, provide trustworthy data, and restore confidence in medical facilities across the country.

Mistrust of health information does not exist in a vacuum, and we must understand the impact of centuries of racism and mistreatment at the hands of medical professionals as they continue to affect African American and Native populations. Decades of racism, abuse, and mistreatment have resulted in a deep distrust of the health care system, whereby many people are wary to take the COVID-19 vaccine. This historical divide highlights why communication training for professionals must include comprehensive programs that actively dismantle mistrust and focus on improving communication with increased transparency for populations of color. There are some models within which researchers bring community members into the conversations to cocreate and participate in collaborative research with the objective that their role as stakeholders is inclusive and adaptive for any community health initiative (Jaiswal, 2019). There are other models of sharing information, particularly in Native and Latino/a/x communities, whereby those with membership in the specific race play a key role in the dissemination of information. Even with this realization it is important to understand that mechanisms (advisory boards, Navajo Nation institutional review board) for community consent and collaboration must be central to ensure no harm (Wallerstein & Duran, 2006).

Across many Indian countries, a variety of factors are important to consider, specifically but not exclusively as they relate to the pandemic. First, multigenerational households made social distancing challenging. Additionally, difficulties accessing water, basic utilities like electricity, and adequate transportation made the pandemic a more serious problem for these communities. These issues as well as the historical mistrust of the federal government and centuries of failure to honor treaty agreements with American Indian and Alaskan Native tribes means there are multiple challenges for many communities (Hostetter & Klein, 2020). The dissemination of information that comes from members of the community is far more impactful than those that come from government entities, and community members are more receptive to those they trust. Hence, training must include Indigenous individuals who speak the native languages as well as include culturally relevant information. One report shows that the Dine Nation, which is the largest Native nation in the United States, had the most dynamic frontline health care workers and the best rollout of information and precautions within and across the reservation communities. The Dine Nation experienced early success with vaccinations because of their aggressive steps using drive-through clinics, strict shelter-in-place mandates, and multisite access to testing in reservation communities (Sanchez & Foxworth, 2021). All of these actions came from those who were members of and lived in the community. The approach taken by the Dine Nation was more effective than that taken by most non-Indigenous groups, as well.

The Los Angeles County Department of Public Health, which is one of the largest county public health facilities in the country, initiated a Latino/a/x community health workers (CWH) outreach program whereby they mobilized public health teams to educate different communities (Community Health Worker Outreach Initiative Extended, 2021). The CHW was made up of trusted community members who shared ethnicity and language with the people they served, often in their own neighborhoods. The success of this communication training was its commitment to closing the gap and dispelling myths and rumors to make sure residents in respective communities had accurate information, understood basic safety protocols, and had easy access to testing to prevent further break-outs. Other larger agencies have instituted community training modules that have been culturally specific and provided multilingual information to make sure community members have access to content in their language.

Third, diversity and inclusion training emerged in the 1980s to "help businesses turn diversity into an asset and to combat the racism, sexism, intergroup conflict being experienced in the workplace" (Paige & Martin, 1996, p. 42). Training that unpacks concepts of culture, race and ethnicity can be challenging because people arrive with their own set of perspectives and experiences; however, the subtlety and depth of culture influences how many marginalized groups move through society. For instance, an African American family living in a rural southern region might experience subtle cultural differences or ways of being that are different from an African American family living in a metropolitan northern region of the country. Considering this, educational training is improved when it acknowledges and addresses historical injustices that are systemic among African American, Asian, Native/Indigenous and Latino/a/x populations/individuals while also considering the cultural nuances that emerge because of place and location. Recent scholarship notes the importance of intensive diversity, equity, and inclusion training and orientation for medical students who are often unprepared to address health inequities in their interactions with patients (Davis et al., 2021). Creating a space whereby medical students can build relationships among themselves and with faculty that seeks to address rather than ignore race and differences serves to enrich communication skills and dynamics while locating these skills as foundational to promoting equity in health care and practicing medical safety and effectiveness.

Finally, as we understand the implications of COVID-19 on vulnerable populations we have seen the emergence of communication training for professionals on trauma-informed or resilience training.

The body of research is extensive as more dialogue about mental health, sexual assault, and other trauma is being discussed in mainstream outlets. The pandemic amplifies the importance and need for training to support the public as they move through traumas they experience on personal, societal, racial, and economic levels. For instance, K–12 teachers are being trained to address multiple needs among the children in their classrooms. Currently, states like Oklahoma, Arkansas, and New Mexico are being encouraged to engage in statewide training for trauma-informed instruction to address academic, behavioral, and mental health needs among children (Oklahoma State Department of Education, 2021). Even more unique is trauma-informed training for immigrant populations to the United States, specifically women. One study noted that Central American immigrants living in the United States have a high prevalence of trauma and posttraumatic stress disorder because of their exposure to political violence and instability in their countries of origin (i.e., Argentina, Chile, Columbia, and Peru) and the unknown and unforeseeable future in the United States (Kaltman et al., 2011). These are just two areas in which trauma-informed training for medical professionals, public health workers, and health communication experts can be valuable and should become a standard practice.

Health communication education and instruction will rely on a variety of channels and messengers to train, educate, and guide patients, students, and the general public to make more thoughtful health decisions. These channels will be interpersonal, mass mediated, and personal to help maximize instructional effectiveness. So far, we have emphasized the interpersonal channels, but technology will obviously be a part of this. Thus, we now move our discussion to this important topic.

Technology in Health Communication Instruction

Communication technologies are widely used in health education and practice. As reviewed in the previous chapter, digital health education involves technologies as basic as converting a hardcopy document into an electronic file and as sophisticated as using virtual simulation in health classrooms and clinical trainings (Car et al., 2019). Electronic health records (EHR), computer-aided instruction, virtual reality, virtual patients, virtual simulation, and telemedicine are some of the most frequently used technologies in health communication and health education. With the constant evolution of technologies and the increasing importance of technology use in health education and practice, it is imperative to investigate future directions of instructional communication for optimized education and clinical outcomes. In this section, we discuss future directions in curriculum development, instructional design, education outcome measurement, and research methodology, all in the context of technology-mediated health communication and digital health education.

Skill training in technology-mediated communication should be an integral part of a regular curriculum in health education. Health organizations need to recognize the importance of communication skills in using technology-mediated systems and include training in such skills as a core component of digital health education programs (McConnochie, 2019; Sharma et al., 2019). For example, training in use of EHR systems needs to include not only technical skills but also communication skills, because without appropriate communication skills, use of EHR could compromise the quality of patient–provider communication (Palumbo et al., 2016). A systematic analysis of 31 studies on virtual reality for health profession education, published between 2005 and 2017, indicated that the majority of the training programs were not part of a regular curriculum; in addition, the programs mainly focused on doctors, nurses, and medical school students, while seldomly targeting other health professional such as dentists and pharmacists (Kyaw et al., 2019). Future curriculum development on health education needs to include skill training in technology-mediated communication as a key component, targeting health students and professionals in various fields.

With the recognition of the importance of communication training in health education curriculum, instructional design of technology-based training programs needs to be informed by communication theories and research. Adopting technology by itself does not lead to successful learning, and scientific instructional design can help guide how and when a specific technology should be used to optimize learning outcomes (Lee et al., 2020). For instance, based on our understanding of communication theories, we know that nonverbal communication is as important as verbal communication. Technology-mediated communication, however, presents challenges to nonverbal communication training, as virtual patients or mannequins do not communicate nonverbal cues as real human beings (Lee et al., 2020). Unsurprisingly, communication training programs using virtual patients focus on verbal communication skills but do not pay sufficient attention to nonverbal communication skills (Lee et al., 2020). Furthermore, there seems to be a lack of use of learning theories in designing health profession education programs using virtual reality (Kyaw et al., 2019). Communication theories such as kinesics, media equation, hyper-personal communication, and supportive communication can provide insights into how to design effective technology-based training programs to improve the quality of health communication. For example, based on understandings of kinesics, instructional designers can have virtual patients programed to adjust eye contact, gesture, posture, and facial expression for better-quality interactions (Concannon et al., 2020). In the same vein, with the theory of social support, finding an optimal match between the support a patient needs and the support a health professional provides may contribute to positive health outcomes of telemedicine use (Turner et al., 2013), and instructional designers can incorporate the process of learning how to identify such an optimal match for supportive communication into education and training programs.

Once an education program is designed and delivered, we need to evaluate effectiveness of the program. Education outcomes need to be measured in rigorous and comprehensive ways. Current practices in evaluation on technology-based communication health training are limited, and health educators need valid instruments to evaluate training effectiveness (Lee et al., 2020). Evaluations of effectiveness of virtual reality–based training programs typically measure learners' knowledge, skills, attitudes, and satisfaction as outcome variables, while not addressing patient-related outcome variables, changes in behavioral variables, or unintended effects of the training programs on the patients or the learners (Kyaw et al., 2019). As important as it is to measure impacts of technology-mediated instruction and communication on health students and health professionals, understanding how the technology-based training affects patient–provider communication through patient-related variables is necessary to patient-centered health care. Clinical outcome data are as essential as, if not more than, data on learner attitude or performance in simulated virtual environments (Lee et al., 2020). Future education and training programs should include patient-related psychological, behavioral, and physical variables as key outcome variables for program evaluation.

Future instructional communication should also address innovation in research methodology based on technology-mediated health communication. Computer-aided instruction, virtual reality, virtual simulation, and telemedicine all result in natural communication data, from communication between instructors and learners and between patients and providers to communication among peers. Researchers can use qualitative and/or quantitative approaches to analyze the data. For instance, a researcher can conduct digital ethnography in virtual patient–based training sessions, observing how learners interact with the virtual patients in a "natural" but also mediated environment. Similarly, researchers can conduct quantitative content analysis or qualitative text analysis on messages communicated between providers and patients in a telemedicine system to identify patterns and problems of communication. Big data approaches, text mining, and sentimental analysis are also important tools for analyzing data generated through technology-mediated health communication. Nevertheless, these new methods should not replace traditional research methods (e.g., experiments, surveys, interviews, focus groups); instead, researchers should choose the appropriate research method(s) based on the research questions and hypotheses, and traditional and new research methods can be used complementarily for better understandings of technology-mediated health communication and education. Teaching health students and professionals how to use these research methods can help improve both research and practice in technology-mediated health communication.

As beneficial and pervasive as technology is, it does not work as a panacea. How to use technology effectively in health care is influenced by many factors, among which communication is a vital one. Health educators need to embed skill training for technology-mediated communication as a core component into regular health education curricula, design theory-informed education programs, evaluate program effectiveness with both learner-related and patient-related outcome variables, and take advantage of new research methods enabled by new communication technologies. Given that technologies can increase access to health care and aggravate health disparity at the same time (Bakhtiar et al., 2020), health researchers and educators should also work on programs and initiatives that can help bridge the digital divide and improve health equity.

Conclusion

We remind the reader once again of the ever-increasing importance of health, health care, and health communication in the world into which we will move as the world continues to expand. We hope that this chapter has made clear some of the interesting and important directions in which we may move in terms of professional instructional health communication. The COVID-19 pandemic has made apparent to all of us the interdependent nature of health and health care delivery in our world. Communication is central for mitigating health consequences and preventing future pandemics. We know all too well what happens when rumors, misinformation, and unclear communication about health concerns abound. Health communication educators have a responsibility to their communities and publics to ethically confront and engage current and future health issues and crises, providing learning spaces for everyone to become more informed consumers and decision-makers. Instructional health communication in professional contexts is a fundamental part of this responsibility.

PART IV

Technology

CHAPTER 7

Background

Nicholas D. Bowman, Kyle R. Vareberg,
Kenneth T. Rocker, Stephanie Kelly, and David Westerman

An often-circulated anecdote about the presumed corrosive influence of instructional technology in the classroom is attributed to a nameless "school principal" from the 1800s. Several versions of the quote exist, but they generally take the following form:

> Students today depend on paper too much. They don't know how to write on a slate without getting chalk dust all over themselves. They can't clean a slate properly. What will they do when they run out of paper?

One can replace "paper" with "ballpoint pens" (circa 1950), and even "treebark" (from 1703; see *Quote Investigator*, 2012), and the general argument remains the same: Newer technologies *de facto* disrupt mainstream and established modes of teaching. Although intended as satire (see Zirkel, 1978), the question echoes an ongoing tension: How do we understand and implement instructional technologies in ways that leverage their affordances while minimizing their distractions, all while coping with a rapid rate of change among the technologies themselves? In part, answering this question for contemporary technologies requires us to first understand the roots of instructional technology. Doing so reveals a pattern: Instructors often (1) engage in moral panics over "new-fangled" technologies that fundamentally alter their instruction, (2) grow with, adopt, and even embrace these technologies as they learn over time that it is possible to effectively communicate material through these new technologies, and then (3) engage in moral panics over the next technology(ies) that emerge later. This chapter reviews the historical development and implementation of technology in education—broadly and through the lens of instructional communication scholarship—concluding that (1) technology has always been "normal" in the classroom, (2) it can be used well or not, and (3) we have always debated (and will probably always debate) this use.

Technologies as Natural to Education

Technologies of some form have always been at the center of the educational setting. Slates and chalk evolved into pens and paper, which evolved into word processors and laptops. For many students, the instructional space—be it a primary school classroom, a community computer lab, or a college laboratory—provides access to technologies not found in a typical home setting. The authors of this chapter remember fondly the excitement of looking through microfiche in their local library, booting up the Apple II to play *Oregon Trail* only to die of dysentery (again!), punching out the earliest lines of computer code, or rushing into the computer lab to pick the best-colored Macintosh (iMac) computer (the blue one!).

The earliest instructional technologies predate the formal study of instructional communication—at least the 1972 origin of *instructional communication* as a discipline (see Myers, 2010 for a history of the field). Perhaps the best example of technology in an educational setting is the use of language itself, most apparent during the age of rhetoric and argumentation (e.g., the Socratic method of teaching; Brogan & Brogan, 1995). Ancient schools in Greece were outdoor spaces where students could speak and debate current events, politics, and other topics, and through this discussion, learn, and thrive. Any good argument requires a fair amount of audience analysis and customization toward that audience's unique needs and goals; and likewise, knowledge was best understood when it could be tailored to those *listening*—listening being an important word, as some of these philosophers (such as Socrates) rejected the emergence of the written word as deleterious to knowledge (it would weaken memory and allow thoughts to exist outside of the thinkers [argued in Plato's *Phaedrus*]).

Beyond the spoken word, the written word also represents an early instructional technology. Around the Middle Ages, the hornbook found its way into widespread adoption that lasted into the early 20th century (Plimpton, 1916). Hornbooks were single-sided printed documents protected by a thin layer of animal horn that students—usually elementary-aged students—would use to practice basic literacy skills (Bailey, 2013). The presence of hornbooks increased the standardization of teaching and learning and provided teachers with a fast and efficient way to teach reading, writing, and arithmetic.

Another early instructional technology is the chalkboard. Documents from early 1850s teachers reveal chalkboards and blackboards were among the first technologies adopted in classrooms, and anecdotally we often think of the green or black chalkboard when we think of the classroom (in a recent renovation of a schoolhouse in Oklahoma, chalkboards from nearly a century ago were uncovered and chock full of illustrations and lessons of the day; Izadi, 2015). Similar to the hornbook, chalkboards increased the number of pupils per teacher, but with technologies such as the blackboard and hornbook, instruction could be mass delivered (Krause, 2000). Later on, overhead projectors performed a similar task. These technologies, popularized in post–World War II military schools, further expanded the teacher-to-student ratio (Perlberg & Resh, 1967). The projectors likewise rectified some issues related to blackboards: Instructors could prepare materials in advance and avoid having to "write-erase-write-repeat" on the chalkboard. Not only did projectors stretch the teacher's reach, but they also made more efficient use of instructional time.

Chalkboards and projectors, along with other technologies, including classroom lighting systems, calculators, and microphones, and others, reflect historical trends to place technologies into learning spaces (Beckwith et al., 1949; Pomerantz, 1997). Other technologies (e.g., mimeograph, filmstrips) phased out as the new phased in (e.g., photocopying machines, videocassettes), and technological convergence ushered in devices capable of handling all these features and more, such as tablet computers and built-in class projection and presentation systems. These technologies are commonplace today, though they faced initial backlash, as we'll discuss later in this chapter. More than being devices of initial debate and skepticism, what these technologies had in common was clear: a proclivity for personalized learning and the ability to reach more students. Both trends would persist through the decades.

Mass and Mediated Technologies for Distance Learning

The global COVID-19 pandemic might have brought distance learning to the forefront, but the concept is hardly new. Since the late 1800s, students have engaged in correspondence or distance learning—the first distance course having been released in 1892 (Casey, 2008). Keegan (1980) synthesized several definitions of distance learning and derived six key provisions of distance education, most of which still apply today:

1. the separation of teacher and learner which distinguishes it from face-to-face lecturing
2. the influence of an educational organization which distinguishes it from private study

3. the use of technical media, usually print, to unite teacher and learner and carry the educational content of the course
4. the provision of two-way communication so that the student may benefit from or even initiate dialogue
5. the possibility of occasional meetings for both didactic and socialization purposes
6. the participation in an industrialized form of education (p. 42)

These systems mostly resembled an instructional pen pal: Instructors prepared readings and assignments, packaged them, and mailed materials to students who, upon completing their assignment, mailed them back for assessment. Entire courses occurred this way. The early goals regarding distance education were simple: Reach students and provide formal learning opportunities without the confines of a classroom. Early users of distance learning opportunities were often learners who were kept from the classroom by some societal or geographical barrier (e.g., women and minorities as well as rural Americans). Some correspondence courses were often marketed toward older adolescents, adults, and other "rank and file of an industry" (Jones & Powrie, 1971, p. 463) looking for advanced training and education but outside of (often inaccessible) formal college or university programs. Distance learning seemed to benefit both learner and teacher. By engaging in distance learning, students received personalized attention while instructors reached more students—exchanging lessons and feedback through the postal system. Such a system might seem antiquated to today's learners, but much of this process can also be seen in the learning management systems (LMSs; e.g., Blackboard) that students and instructors use today: Classroom content is posted to a central online location, and interactions take place within that system (and perhaps through additional email and other communication). In a real sense, these processes are another iteration of a more than centuries-old distance learning model that reinforces learning's potential to extend the boundaries of education.

In between the original "class by mail" and the online LMSs commonly in use today, we see other advances leveraging the technology of their times. As explained by Kelly and Westerman (2016), interactive video networks (IVN) shifted education spaces by allowing for both distance *and* synchronous interactions (Swan & Brehmer, 1994)—schools could offer real-time instruction to people at different physical locations. Through IVN, remote and distance students connected with instructors in other classrooms (typically with their own students) through several television screens. Cameras captured multiple angles in the classrooms so that distance students could feel physically present despite clear geographical separations. Importantly because this technology allowed for synchronous interactions, students could receive personalized feedback from their instructors. These benefits, coupled with demonstrated effectiveness in early research, popularized IVN prior to a time in which widespread internet access was more common (Smith, 1987).

Mass technologies greatly expanded the opportunities for distance or correspondence learning. Broadcast systems in the 1930s and instructional television in the 1950s expanded learning into otherwise far-to-reach locations (Blakely, 1979; Fritz, 1960; Helwig & Friend, 1985) and provided programming targeted at specific ages and ability levels (Hew, 2014; Saettler, 1968). In 1952, the National Education Television (NET) launched as an educational television distribution service (funded by a grant from the Ford Foundation). In 1970, the NET merged and became what we know today as the Public Broadcasting Service (PBS). Beyond specific instructional television, others began experimenting with edutainment programming (a portmanteau of education and entertainment). One of the most familiar is *Sesame Street* (first aired in 1969), which was created in collaboration with educational advisors and television producers to provide entertaining programming with specific pedagogical goals to children after school (Lesser, 1974). With these programs, instructors who long had a "desire" to use the technology available to overcome space and time limitations for education had a stable and engaging medium through which to teach. Likewise, learners were able to incorporate educational materials into their daily media diets, with programs such as *Sesame Street* setting the foundation for more educational developmental-focused content (we call this cognitive learning). However, programs such as *Mr. Roger's Neighborhood* (first aired in 1968) helped children develop socioemotional skills (we call this affective learning), and various other television programs released over the years continue the success of at-home education programming. *Mr. Roger's Neighborhood* is notable for two other very compelling reasons. First, it was among the very earliest programs distributed by NET (in February 1968). Second, the program was incredibly inexpensive to produce—in an impassioned testimony in May 1969, Fred Rogers (the eponymous Mr. Rogers) explained that the production budget for his show was a mere $6,000 (about $46,000, adjusted for inflation to 2021). The show still airs in reruns today and alongside other programs (*Sesame Street* has a production budget that can top $800,000 per episode; see Whitaker, 2021); its resilience suggests that the quality of an instructional technology is as much about the quality of the content itself and the communication skill with which that content is delivered as it is about the production value of the technology itself.

Digital Media and Classroom Instruction

It can be easy to think of computers as a common and stable feature of the modern classroom, as one might be hard-pressed not to see computing devices being used by students and instructors throughout the learning process. However, it was not always so widely accepted that computers had a place in traditional instructional models and settings. Cuban (1994) wrote that "introduction of film and radio into schools in the 1920s and 1930s and instructional television in the 1950s and 1960s saw a similar pattern of blue-sky promises" (p. 50). In an editorial for *USA Today*, Stoll (1995) opined that "no CD-ROM can take the place of a competent teacher," and while we are inclined to agree with him as teachers, we would also not presume that technologies replace instructors but, rather, supplement instruction (just as the book in front of you supplements the class you're currently taking).

Of course, unlike film and radio, which mostly existed as entertainment and information technologies, a flaw in these early critiques was that they overlooked the increased role of computing technologies in the modern workplace. Many early classroom computer labs—especially those in higher education—were mostly developed for use in the STEM fields (science, technology, engineering, and mathematics), as those fields were developing and actively using computer technologies. By the 1970s, computer science and engineering programs were already forecasting a growth in demand for computer professionals entering the 1980s (Ramamoorthy, 1976), with others concerned that students were not learning more advanced programming techniques required of the modernizing workplace (Dodd & Gluckson, 1974). Gaede and Singletary (1979) wrote more broadly about the use of computer applications and simulations for science education:

> We see the computer as a very powerful tool that the science teacher can use—but it is only one of many tools available. Teachers should not use a computer just to be using a computer. Rather, they first should establish good learning objectives. If those objectives can best be met by using a computer in the curriculum, then by all means, use one. This is a discussion of how to use computers as a teaching tool. (p. 4)

One application that educators of the time saw as particularly useful for computers was for simulations—learning exercises that allowed students to engage a concept or process that might be difficult, dangerous, or even impossible to experience firsthand. Computer-based simulations had been used in military training since at least the 1940s (Valverde, 1968) and in various vocational applications (Gagné, 1954). Gredler (1986) provided a useful taxonomy of simulations that differ depending on learning outcomes. From basic demonstrations of math problems to detailed and high-fidelity flight simulators, computers had already begun to establish themselves as powerful tools for education.

Another type of computer simulation? Video games, which found their way into the classroom as early as the 1970s (Smith, 1976).[1] Among those early games still available to learners today? *Oregon Trail,* developed by the Minnesota Educational Computing Consortium (MECC). An online exhibit offered by the Strong Museum of Play explores the game's critical, cultural, and educational history.[2] From an early 1971 prototype in a Minnesota state history course, it is difficult (at least, in the United States) to find anyone having gone to school since who has not loaded a wagon train, forded a river, hunted for food, or died of dysentery while traversing the Oregon Train on computer screen (for overview, see Hoelscher, 1985; Yarwood, 2015). Unfortunately, some versions of *Oregon Trail* also contained problematic cultural biases and views—for example, in early versions of the game players could only choose to play as White males (Bigelow, 1997). Still, the private nature of play afforded students personalized opportunities for learning, and educational video games are commonplace in formal and informal education today, from *Mathblaster* to *Typing of the Dead* (a zombie shooter designed to teach typing skills by replacing guns with keyboards, challenging players to type as quickly and accurately as possible to defeat on-screen monsters). Gamification efforts

---

1 Notably, the very first video game, *SpaceWar!,* was invented in an academic setting—by research scientists at the Massachusetts Institute of Technology in 1961 writing programs to test the limits of their PDP-1 mainframe computer (Graetz, 1981).

2 The Strong Museum of Play curates an online exhibit detailing *Oregon Trail's* history and development: https://artsandculture.google.com/exhibit/the-oregon-trail-mecc-and-the-rise-of-computer-learning-the-strong/TAICA3oJZQm2Kw?hl=en.

in which common workplace activities—including training simulations and other vocational skills—are turned into competitions are increasingly commonplace across a broad spectrum of industries (Deterding et al., 2011). Beyond the common usage of simulations for training pilots and physicians, interactive technologies are starting to be used in a wide variety of careers, including the use of virtual reality to teach hotel employees a variety of encounters (Condon, 2020) and using similar technologies to introduce social workers to new environments (Lanzieri et al., 2021).

Personal Computing for Personalized Learning

If mass technologies successfully extended an instructor's reach, digital technologies simplified and expedited personalized learning. This was seen in several early initiatives, especially in primary schools, that strove to put devices into students' hands. In the early 1980s, computers were *slowly* integrated into schools by way of computer labs, although integration into actual classrooms was slow as the computer faced significant pushback. Unlike earlier technologies such as projectors and lighting systems, which were mostly accepted at face value, computers were met with resistance—in part because they meant that teachers had to *de facto* relinquish at least some control of learning to their students, which was seen as pushing back against formal education practices (in which the teacher is the sage on the stage; see King, 1993). For example, Earle (2002) reported paradoxical critiques from educators in that computers were being integrated both too fast and not fast enough; digital technologies could not guarantee increased student learning and had been shown to increase student learning; money was best spent on increasing students' access and on increasing instructors' training; computers both mass-produced standardized instruction and increased learner personalization.

Despite those initial critiques, a trend to increase learner access is seen in 3 decades of initiatives and programs. By the mid-1990s, many classrooms had a computer for instructional delivery, though teachers did not always have access for preparation (or the proper training on the device itself, as is discussed later in the chapter). School administrators debated whether to invest money in training (of teachers) or to buy more devices (for students). What occurred? An increase in school-owned devices used most often for skill-and-drill practice as these required little additional training. For better or worse, the focus was on access for students to mirror the demand of computer-based applications in the *real world* (Earle, 2002). Presumed links between technology access and intrinsic motivation to play with and use only exacerbated this, as there was a prevailing presumption that if students have access to a computer, benefits should follow.

It may have been this drive for access that sparked the bring-your-own-device (BYOD) initiative in the 2000s and 1:1 device (one student, one device) programs shortly after. The premise was simple: Teachers could leverage learning opportunities from the devices students already carried in their bags. For BYOD, students originally relied on mobile devices such as laptops and tablets. Since BYOD assumed students use their own personal devices, instructors could then shift their attention to crafting engaging learning experiences in multiple learning spaces (Nowell, 2014). Unfortunately, inequities between users introduced complications; device ownership was not consistent, so in-class activities suffered proportionally (Vareberg & Platt, 2019). Partly in response to the inequities of BYOD programs, 1:1 device programs shifted the responsibility of securing personal learning technologies to the schools. Early research on the impacts of 1:1 device access on learning revealed students had more opportunities to learn in creative or autonomous ways, but that device use, or overreliance on device use, was equally possible (Storz & Hoffman, 2013; Zheng et al., 2014).

However, the outcome of increased student learning was coupled with another issue—distractions—and teachers questioned again whether instructional technologies were effective. After all, digital personal devices bring with them *extreme personalization* in the sense that the same tablet or mobile phone that a student is practicing their in-class lessons on also allows them ready access to social media and live-streaming television. Taneja et al. (2015) found that so-called cyber-slacking in the classroom was not so much attributed to the technologies themselves as it was a byproduct of students feeling apathetic to course content and lacking motivation to engage content. Unfortunately, when students begin cyber-slacking, teachers feel increasingly frustrated with their students, which has an overall negative influence on the classroom environment (Flanigan & Babchuk, 2020). Of course, even instructors might not be above digital distractions such as checking personal email or text messages during class—broadly understood as instructor misbehaviors (Goodboy & Myers, 2015). In these debates and examples, we are reminded of an enduring truth that permeates and drives instructional technologies. Technologies are tools with features that afford myriad uses and outcomes, but their mere presence alone is not enough to ensure pedagogical success.

Early Research Into the Effectiveness of Instructional Technologies

Just as the integration of technologies has been central to formal education, research on the relative effectiveness of those technologies has generally shown positive effects on the educational process, as well as some associated anxiety with their adoption (on behalf of instructors and students). Although technologies such as hornbooks and chalkboard were not subjected to empirical research—in part because their invention and implementation mostly predated social scientific approaches to instructional technology—we did see research throughout the 20th century into several classroom innovations. Likewise, this research saw the contributions of instructional communication scholars, although much of the research discussed predated the formal study of instructional communication (i.e., pre-1970s; see Myers, 2010).

Researchers discovered early promise when integrating technologies into classrooms. Classroom lighting systems (Hopkinson, 1949) and early overhead projects (Krasker, 1943; Reynolds, 1975) were quickly identified as aids for student learning. Implementing these technologies allowed students to perform *at least* similarly, if not better, than they did without the technology. Projectors, for instance, offered a richer medium of content delivery without increasing costs. Film strips, stereographs, and transparencies optimized the classroom environment. As much as you might giggle when your instructors pull out yellowed acetone transparencies during class lecture, Boswell (1980) found that transparencies paired with lecture materials resulted in higher student exam scores in a college-level psychology course. In fact, an instructor's credibility at teaching has long been evaluated by students in tandem with their ability to effectively integrate presentation technologies (Myers, 2004; Schrodt & Witt, 2006).

Much of early integration of mass communication technologies into classroom was not based on empirical evidence; as Cuban (1986) noted, it mattered less that the technologies resulted in increased learning and more that the technologies were *believed* to result in increases. Minimal correlations between instructional radio, instructional television, or computer-assisted learning, and learning demonstrated these instructional technologies were about as effective as traditional instruction when used as supplements to already existing teaching practices (Jamison et al., 1974). Rarely was technology integrated in ways that leveraged their unique qualities; and when devices were integrated in novel ways, findings from empirical research were less conclusive (Coley et al., 1996). Again, the push was toward student access, so much of what mass technologies provided was mass production. Education, already industrialized, could be packaged and shipped faster and with less expense.

This is not to say research into personal devices and technology did not show promise; the opposite, in fact, is true. For instance, despite concerns that calculators are detrimental to mathematics education, research has established the opposite—for example, Suydam (1981) reported in meta-analysis of 75 studies that only 3% found that calculator access was detrimental to learning, while 35% showed student improvements in learning various basic skills: counting, arithmetic, estimation, and basic trigonometry, among others. By the late 1980s, nearly half of all U.S. states had policies supporting the use of and providing for calculators to be used in mathematics education (Kansky, 1987). At least one reason calculators are so effective is that they require the operator to understand the basics of arithmetic to be used in the first place. Personal devices are especially critical for students with disabilities. For example, Horton et al. (1992) found that calculator usage closed academic achievement gaps between students with educable mental handicaps and their peers in basic arithmetic instruction of the course of 1 month's time. Likewise, newer technologies based on digital media use alternative text descriptors for learners who are vision impaired or automated annotations for learners who are hearing impaired, and many of these technologies are critical to making educational content broadly accessible—especially in an age where technologies are increasingly multimodal and, thus, there are presumptions that learners (and teachers alike) can access these modalities equally.

Early Debates About Instructional Technologies in Instructional Communication

Already alluded to elsewhere in this chapter, there have been debates around the appropriate and effective use of technology in the classroom for almost as long as we have had formalized classrooms of any sort. We close our chapter by highlighting a few of those debates around power imbalances, moral panics, the perceived "impersonalness" of instructional technologies, and teacher training.

THE MYTH OF THE DIGITAL NATIVE

Instructors have not only concerned about their efficacy at using technology, but also that they might be woefully inadequate compared to their students. These concerns were fanned by scholars such as Prensky (2001), who coined the term *digital natives to* describe students seemingly born into a screen-based technological society and thus, possessing of innate skills for those technologies. Unfortunately, this impression that students naturally knew more than their instructors when it came to technology eventually backfired on the education system. The first generation of children who grew up with computers in their homes needed to truly understand computers to entertain themselves (Brown et al., 2020). For example, some basic DOS programming was required to get Oregon Trail running in the 1980s—and after internet came into the classroom, failure to delete temporary internet files from the directory or manually defragment the computer became basic computer maintenance needed to keep the entertainment seamlessly running.

Computers became increasingly more user friendly though, eliminating the need to understand how computers ran in order to play on computers, especially after the need to program was completely eliminated with the introduction of point-and-click graphic user interfaces. This meant that by the late 2010s many public school systems had completely eliminated computer education from the curriculum, assuming that students would learn it naturally when their entertainment devices no longer required such self-education. This has left education and technology in a precarious position, with many universities presuming that their students have stronger technological skills than they really do. Nielsen (2006) refers to this as the empowerment divide, or the extent to which we can "make full use of the opportunities that such technology affords" (para. 9). Lacking an understanding of how to send effective mails or use computers to secure credible information continues to be a concern, despite learners and future employees who seem to be highly experienced with digital and social media (at least, for personal use). Ng (2012) found that careful instructor guidance and instruction can help students better understand the use of digital media for both formal and informal education, developing literacies that transcend the classroom.

MORAL PANICS AND CLASSROOM TECHNOLOGY

A closer read of the critiques offered is also reflected in other parts of this chapter, and it suggests something of a misdirection. For many, fears and frustrations are often less about the technologies themselves and more about a general lack of guidance as to how to use them as purposeful and functional tools toward a pedagogical goal. In the 1960s, scholars had already begun developing training materials to help teachers better understand how to synchronize their general teaching objectives with basic media technologies such as classroom transparencies and other audiovisual media materials (Pula, 1968). While some of these older technologies might have been easier to grasp or at least existed in such a way that it was unlikely that students would have any more experience with them than the teachers themselves (most families do not have overhead projectors and transparencies in their homes), the scenario changed a bit with computing technologies—most of which were already being rolled out for personal home usage at about the same time they were being integrated into classrooms. In the early 1980s, Stevens (1982) reported that while teachers were supportive of teaching computer literacy in high schools, they also felt inadequate in teaching the courses (somewhat related to digital natives' arguments). A similar note was shared by Gordon (1980) who noted that "the organization of the traditional 'school' or the distribution of resources within it [do not] help teachers cope with the change thrusting at them" (p. 40).

THE COLD, MECHANICAL CLASSROOM

Yet another common historical fear of instructional technology is that the classroom experience will become impersonal and mechanical—owning to a common myth about the inherently impersonal nature of communication technologies. Such fears were noted by Kvaraceus (1961) in writing about technology-assisted teaching: "When the novelty of levers, lights, and pushbuttons wears off, auto-instructional devices may have difficulty in attracting, interesting, and especially exciting the student to greater effort" (p. 291). In these critiques, a common note is that while machines are probably pretty good at executing automated tasks, they fail to offer a competent replacement for authentic and meaningful human interaction—that machines cannot inspire students in the same way that qualified and effective flesh-and-blood teachers can. Similar concerns were noted by Selfe (1988), who expressed that with the rapid adoption of computers in the English classroom, "we have allowed ourselves to forget what we know about literacy ... in exchange for acquiring knowledge about technology" (p. 69) and suggesting that computers both complicate literacy and threaten to replace humans as the center of communication. This notion of inherent pedagogical loss was also shared by Risser (2011) in their review of common fears expressed by mathematics teachers in articles, opinions, and published journals about concerns that technological skills had become more central than subject matter skills. In response, administrators such as Burke (1994) suggested that technologies can be leveraged precisely to be more personal and tailored for individual students. In writing about technology in the humanities—in particular, writing courses—Kerr (1978) explained that the pedagogical goal of teaching how to clearly communicate is central "regardless of the message or the media" (p. 74). They continued by discussing the inherently mixed-modal nature of technologies as effective for communication, nothing that "technology's blend of words and illustrations may require a minor adjustment, but it is definitely not an insurmountable obstacle" (p. 75). Modern approaches to teacher immediacy (a perception of how close students feel to their instructors; Gorham, 1988; Liu, 2021) generally agree that teaching through technologies can foster student–instructor immediacy (McArthur, 2021).

TEACHER TRAINING AND TECHNOLOGY

Somewhat related to the previous section, we can look at historical concerns about the asymmetrical relationship between teacher training (which tends to evolve logarithmically) and technological innovation (which tends to evolve exponentially). Simply put, teachers were already concerned that technologies were entering their teaching spaces more quickly than the teachers could learn how to use each one. Finn et al. (1960) argued that some of the struggle toward instructional technology training could be attributed to what they noted as a "poor culture" perspective on education—that modern teacher training approached teachers more as public servants than as pedagogical experts in their own right. Others were seemingly recalcitrant to the influence of technology in the classroom, concerned that "teachers were now confronted with the need to redefine and reconstruct their roles and functions in the enterprise" (Fritz, 1960, p. 298) despite, "with monotonous regularity, the literature [reporting] no real differences in learning achievements" (p. 268) attributable to instructional technologies. Already cited elsewhere in this chapter, Cuban (2006) was especially critical of 1:1 personal device programs as an extension of a common critique echoed by many—computers *in and of themselves* are not a solution for pedagogical challenges. The critiques here were often focused on two opposing concerns: a general appreciation for the pedagogical potential of instructional technologies, but trepidation at using an unfamiliar technology. That said, and as again reinforced by McArthur (2021), there are as many strategies for engaging students through technologies as there are engaging them through classroom instruction. In this vein, scholars such as Witmer (1998) have made available published guides for teaching courses focused on communication technologies, and associations such as the United Nations Educational, Scientific, and Cultural Organization (UNESCO) have offered guides for incorporating information and communication technologies into educational systems, recognizing them as "one of the basic building blocks of modern society" (Anderson et al., 2002).

Conclusion

Our chapter opened with an enduring critique of technology in the classroom, wherein instructors often critique emerging technologies as *de facto* challenges to established teaching methods. To some degree, these critiques are not unfounded given that technologies have an inherently disruptive influence on various systems (Verdoux, 2009). At the same time, our retrospective highlights two critical themes central to instructional technologies. The first is that we must understand technologies as tools with various features that might or might not afford desired or undesired pedagogical outcomes. This might sound like a complicated thought (it is certainly a complicated sentence), but the implications for instructional communication are simple: Users (both instructors and learners) must learn when and how to use technologies for maximum effect. The second theme, and one that will be unpacked in the following chapter, is that technologies have great potential to allow instructors and learners to share and learn in ways impossible prior to their invention. Hornbooks and chalkboards provided the opportunity to standardize content and thus allowed instructors and learners to spend more time engaging each other, and broadcast and digital technologies expanded the space-time available for instructor–student interactions. Debates around technology's influence on the classroom—broadly and specifically on the instructor–student relationship—have always existed (and will likely always exist), but the enterprise of learning has consistently benefited from these debates.

CHAPTER 8

Current Trends and Future Directions

David Westerman, Stephanie Kelly, Kyle R. Vareberg,
Kenneth T. Rocker, and Nicholas D. Bowman

The previous chapter shows us a few things. First, technology has always been a part of education. Second, there have always been promises and fears around the use of that technology. Third, the actual use of that technology likely lies somewhere between utopia and dystopia. This chapter will keep those ideas in mind as we draw on them to outline some ideas about current technologies in instructional communication and speculate about the "new normal" that the future might bring. (Spoiler alert: It may look a lot like the "old normal.")

The idea of "normal" in education is a bit oxymoronic in that education will never have a permanent normal—at least, we hope not (wouldn't it be sad to think that one day education will stop improving?). Education will continue to evolve as new technologies emerge and new generations of learners with their unique methods of interacting with the world enter the classroom. Those students (and perhaps those teachers) best suited for online education are those who can search for and leverage the perils of technology while also objectively and critically understand the pearls of the same. We'll unpack that idea throughout this chapter. Others might think that teaching and learning are *de facto* better done face-to-face. Indeed, a push to return to "normal" in the face of the global COVID-19 pandemic—"normal" in this case referring to being face-to-face and physically present in the classroom—suggests such a framing, which is often how communication and technology are thought of, in which we presume face-to-face to be the gold standard and technology as flawed somehow (i.e., always inferior to face-to-face). We focus on what is lacking from technology compared to face-to-face communication (Hollan & Stornella, 1992) rather than focus on goals of communication and consider how to build and use systems to accomplish those goals, possibly even better than we can face-to-face. Indeed, students report learning about the negatives of technology use (social media in this case) from teachers and parents (i.e., authority figures) or from friends and personal experience; they learned about the potential downsides of face-to-face communication from no one (Westerman et al., 2016).

On this backdrop, our chapter presents updated scholarship on the effectiveness (or not) of modern instructional technologies informed by instructional communication scholarship and prognosticates about the future of instructional communication for a variety of learning contexts.

Social Presence and Instructional Technology

There is no shortage of places to go for advice on how to teach online and or use technology for education in any setting. For example, in *Small Teaching Online*, Darby and Lang (2019) offer a volume of research-backed suggestions for how to do small things that can make a big difference in the use of technology in teaching—they devoted entire chapters to "Building Community" (Chapter 4) and "Making Connections" (Chapter 8). Of course, both are crucial to most any learning environment, and we would add that research on computer-mediated communication (CMC) broadly and social presence specifically can help expand this discussion.

Early theorizing in CMC suggested that communication would be poor online and that relationships would not be formed well, or possibly at all. One of the earliest theories applied to computer-mediated communication is known as social presence theory (Short et al., 1976). In general, social presence theory seems to suggest that bandwidth, or the number of cue systems a technology can convey (i.e., text, audio, pictures), is positively related to the social presence of that technology: More cues equal more social presence. This perspective does seem typical of the way that communication, education, and technology are discussed today—technology cannot be used in place of in-person communication (the "cold, mechanical classroom" fears from the previous chapter).

However, the perspective is somewhat outdated. As Kelly and Westerman (2016) point out, modern approaches to social presence theory suggest two general categories of thought, each that define the concept in different ways. The first considers social presence as how similar a technology is at replicating the face-to-face interactions—more similar means more social presence. In this way, technology is always going to be at best equal to face-to-face and most likely slightly worse. This perspective of social presence seems more in line with theories like media richness theory (Daft & Lengel, 1986, discussed later in the chapter), and it generally focuses on what technology lacks in comparison to the "gold standard" of face-to-face communication. As noted at the start of this chapter, calls to return to the "normal" classroom somewhat echo this approach. In a very real sense, if educators consider technology in the classroom in this way, then *de facto* technology will always be considered poor replications of the "normal" face-to-face environment.

The second perspective on social presence defines the concept as a sense of psychological connection or closeness with someone *regardless of the technology (or channel) used* (Kelly & Westerman, 2016). Rather than focusing on how similar a channel is to another, or how similar or dissimilar technologies are to face-to-face interaction, it instead starts with the end goal of communication and asks about how well the goal is accomplished.

From this perspective, sometimes the technologies are useful at facilitating that goal, and other times, they might be disruptive—just like sometimes we talk face-to-face for a goal and other times we might send a text message or use some other channel. This latter take is more in line with theories like social information processing theory (SIPT) and the hyper-personal model of communication (both discussed later; Walther, 2007) in which human communication and connectedness goals are possible online, but under certain conditions. If educators consider technology in education this way, it highlights attention on the goal to achieve (rather than the "limits" of the technology) and asks us how we might use a technology, any technology (including face-to-face), to better accomplish that goal.

Yet another approach to social presence is the community of inquiry model, in which social presence in the classroom (however that is defined) is highest when learners and teachers engage in affective, interactive, and cohesive communication (Garrison et al., 1999, 2010). Affective communication involves the sharing of opinions, personal insights, and feelings and is often a door to insight into someone's life outside of the virtual environment. Sharing information about one's physical location such as the current weather or sharing a personal story that illustrates course content are both examples of affective communication. Interactive communication includes communication that attempts to keep conversation active. Responding to virtual messages promptly and inviting further communication (e.g., ending an email with "If you have any questions, let me know") are examples of interactive communication. Finally, cohesive communication involves the use of inclusive language, such as referring to the learning community as "our" class or what "we" are doing. The more these cues are used, the stronger the sense of community that is built.

Regardless of the definition or approach, developing adequate social presence in the classroom is key to ensuring students have a positive learning experience. How much social presence students perceive will dictate how much they believe they have learned and how satisfied they were with their learning experience (Richardson et al., 2017). Yet, students and faculty are unlikely to exhibit the keys to conveying social presence if they do not know what social presence is or how to cultivate it—or if they make the "fatal flaw" of presuming that social presence is an inherent property of a technology (or even worse, something that can only be felt in face-to-face interaction). Anyone new to distance learning, whether they be student or teacher, in formal education or industry training, needs fundamental training on social presence and other effective CMC skills before diving into their learning experiences. Otherwise, they will not only be a barrier to their own learning, but they will also detract from the community of learning they are engaging with.

CMC Theories and Learning Implications

For many, and as noted earlier, media richness theory (Daft & Lengel, 1986) was interpreted as a theoretical approach suggesting that technologies can never really meet the "gold standard" of face-to-face communication. However, a deeper read of the theory reveals a slightly different story— that some tasks might be *more efficiently accomplished* through technologies. How so? It depends on the complexity of message being delivered. In particular, when a message is highly equivocal (i.e., it has numerous possible interpretations), then technologies with more communication cues are more useful for efficient communication, called "cue rich technologies." Likewise, when equivocality is low (it has very little room for misinterpretation), fewer communication cues are more efficient, called "cue lean technologies," as additional information can simply clutter a message. Think for a moment about ordering a pizza: A menu with prices (asynchronous text) is more than sufficient for ordering a basic cheese pizza through a food delivery app, but you might need to call the pizzeria (synchronous voice) to get detailed information about the freshness of ingredients or make special requests.

If we expand this idea to education and instructional communication, we run into potential complications. For example, if we presume that learning is *implicitly equivocal* (certainly, not every learner interprets every lesson plan in the same way, no more than we all agree to the lyrics of our favorite songs), then we might naturally assume that cue rich technologies as face-to-face interaction are necessary. That said, such an assumption is flawed. While education as an enterprise is highly equivocal, it is unlikely that all academic lessons share this equivocality. Imagine for a moment the different pedagogical needs (and thus, different communication technology needs) when distance learning basic computer code compared to building a complex computing device. Programming is a text-based activity that can likely be learned using cue-lean (textual) technologies found in a printed textbook or online course module. Conversely, building a computer is a delicate and physical activity, and learning here might require access to highly tactile and immersive media such as virtual reality that could provide a gamut of sensorimotor inputs for the learner to engage. A complex VR simulation is probably not needed to learn how to operate Windows 10 (although updates to Facebook or Instagram's interfaces commonly send at least a few of your authors into a slight rage).[1] In other words, just as not all conversations need to be had face-to-face, not all instruction needs to be done through cue-rich technologies (Limperos et al., 2015).

Other theories of CMC would support this claim, such as the aforementioned SIPT (Walther, 1992). SIPT does not concern itself with the

---

1 Notably, Walther and Parks (2002) pointed out that MRT had yet to be truly tested fully (and seems to remain so). Also, what is a rich channel? That idea is certainly far different today than it was in 2002—and more so different than in 1984. Essentially, early connotations of MRT implied that humans were meant to interact face-to-face, so to be social in a mediated channel, technology would have to be as rich as face-to-face. But then a funny thing happened: Scholars began to find that people used computers not just for work. Even as MRT was being developed. A mid-80s study found that even in the workplace, people used computer-mediated communication for social purposes (Steinfeld, 1986). Thus, people were using technology to seemingly do things that they were supposedly not able to do.

extent to which CMC and face-to-face are equal but rather suggests that both present different ways to accomplish shared goals. For example, some forms of online communication might take longer—typing can take longer to write out and then be read, processed, and responded by conversational partners, but typing also draws focus away from nonverbal communication and instead encourages all involved to focus on the messages in front of them, similar to the notion of disentrainment from hyperpersonal model (Walther, 1996). In this way, SIPT and hyperpersonal model might also help understand how we might come to feel *more* social presence online (Westerman & Skalski, 2010).

Focusing a bit more on cue-lean media for a bit, these technologies also expand the boundaries for *where* we communicate and learn. With the increased number of computer-mediated channels, students have less need to meet with instructors in person (to the extent that they ever did frequent in-person office hours). Vareberg et al. (2020) found that students overwhelmingly use technologically mediated out-of-class communication with instructors, and those tended to be cue-lean technologies such as emails and other text-based messages. Some might see this as "laziness" on behalf of the students, but such a perspective does not recognize the effectiveness of this communication.

Indeed, supposedly cue-lean channels can be useful in personalizing education and making education more accessible. One prominent potential is the emoticon— ;-) —and more recently, the emoji— —that are used by more than 60% of U.S. employees in the workplace according to the Adobe Emoji Trend Report of 2019. Emojis help add social and emotional information into messages in ways that can feel more personal. Indeed, Vareberg and Westerman (2020) discovered a smiley face emoji influences learners to feel their instructor *cares* about them, but this comes at the expense of the instructor's *competence* (which could be a sign that the messages are seen as less professional). That said, Clark-Gordon et al. (2018) found no influence of emojis on how students interpreted assignment feedback, even though anecdotally they seem to enjoy seeing a bit of the instructor's personality shine through.

These discussions suggest that CMC can be useful under some conditions, but still seem to implicitly suggest technology to be mostly inferior to face-to-face interaction. However, Walther (1996) introduced the idea of hyper-personal communication to explain those times in which we feel *even closer* when communicating online compared to face-to-face—perhaps one reason those emoji messages led students to feel closer to their instructors. The hyper-personal model argues that a certain combination of sender, receiver, channel, and feedback characteristics are critical. First, senders tend to have an increased ability to selectively self-present online (Bargh et al., 2002) and likewise, receivers might be more likely to idealize these selective self-presentations, especially if they value the relationship. Mediated channels can foster interactions that can be somewhat asynchronous—imagine if you took long pauses before verbal responses during a job interview, only to delete and retype answers before posting them. In all of this, the constant feedback loops between sender and receiver can further reinforce the self-presentations being given in ways that benefit the relationship. Returning to our emoji-laden emails, a student respects their instructor and asks a question about their homework, and the instructor responds in a polite and intelligent way with an encouraging and friendly emoji, which in turn reinforces the student's admiration of the instructor. Research into the use of emojis and other technology-based nonverbals between students and learners is limited, especially in nonacademic contexts (e.g., corporate training or vocational preparation) in which there are not always expectations for strong interpersonal connections between trainers and learners.

Yet another concept from CMC useful for instructional communication is that of electronic propinquity, defined as "electronic presence" (Korzenny, 1978, p. 7) or "the psychological feeling of nearness that communicators experience using different communication channels" (Walther & Bazarova, 2008, p. 624). These definitions sound very similar to social presence as a feeling of connection to someone, using electronic technologies. Although this theory predates the internet as we know it today, Walther and Bazarova (2008) later found evidence that it could apply to online interactions.[2] In particular, the research found that electronic propinquity was influence by two key variables: user skill and available alternatives for communication. Those with greater skills at a given technology are more likely to experience electronic propinquity, and when there is no face-to-face alternative, we are also more likely to experience electronic propinquity. During the COVID-19 pandemic, we already see the value of this approach: Those more skilled with computers tended to thrive (or at least maintain) when learning through computers, while those without lower skills struggled—which is particularly problematic when we presume digital natives implicitly skilled at using their computers for learning (as noted in chapter 7). Notably during the pandemic, face-to-face communication was not possible.

Futurecasting Instructional Technology

As noted in the previous chapter, online education is not a trend but rather an enduring part of the educational landscape. Part of embracing online education is taking stock of what we know works well in online learning while also recognizing when those effective practices differ from what is effective practice in the face-to-face environments that we may be more accustomed to. Only when teachers and learners effectively adapt their communication to the online environment can optimal learning take place. As such, the review of what we do know about effective online learning and communication is critical for ensuring that all participants who engage in online learning are armed with the knowledge of most effective practices to facilitate their experiences. Yet, taking stock in what we do know

---

2 The theory was even (albeit prematurely) empirically discredited by its own author (Korzenny & Bauer, 1981)!

is a critical step in identifying what we do not know (Smith, 2019). Only by recognizing our ascertained knowledge of online education and communication can we begin the process of discovering what we have only presumed to be true about interactions in these environments because those things are true in the face-to-face environment. Revealing that presumed knowledge provides the foundation of new discoveries for bettering the online classroom. In that spirit, we see a few areas of emerging technology and, thus, emerging questions.

UNPACKING ZOOM FATIGUE

One of the big complaints on online communication recently has been explained as a sort of sluggishness and lack of energy and engagement during and following videoconferencing calls—coined by several as "Zoom fatigue" in referencing a popular videoconferencing technology. Bailenson (2021) suggests that at least one reason for this fatigue is that users experience a nonverbal overload of so many different faces with their own cue-rich messages to send, and that Zoom fatigue is the direct result of a combination of excessive amounts of close-up eye gaze with others, cognitive load in attending to so much information, increased self-evaluations from staring at video of one's self for long periods of time, and a general constraint on physical mobility. Indeed, many classrooms and work-from-home environments mandated that learner and employees leave their camera on at all times so that they could compel constant attention during the given lesson or work task. Ironically, Bailenson would argue that these mandates had the exact opposite effect: They fed Zoom fatigue! Indeed, forcing all users to be online and on camera all of the time seems like exactly what Hollan and Stornetta (1992) would have discussed if they were writing today—using tech as a crutch (which poorly represents walking) rather than a shoe (which helps go beyond walking). Conversely, allowing people to turn off cameras when necessary and/or possible may be a part of using the channel to filter out unnecessary cues (focusing too much on one's self-presentation and seeing everyone else as well), and focus more on the things that are needed, like listening to others. Likewise, from SIPT we already know that verbal communication (which does not require live video feed) can be used to foster relationships and thus compel a sense of social presence, as does the use of text-based chat functions and other tools in most videoconferencing software. Unfortunately, the discourse around these technologies seems to lean toward "cameras on, eyes up," and as result we can only wonder about the short- and long-term determinants of these interactions.

MACHINE TEACHERS

Machine teachers are artificial intelligence (AI) systems that assist instructors in delivering content and managing course organization (Kim et al., 2021). Typically, the current machine teacher looks like a live chat feature embedded in the course management system, which may or may not have an accompanying avatar. Some machine teachers can respond in text only, while others can respond verbally to questions. Although it might sound impossible, machine teachers can develop social presence in ways similar to a human teacher (Kim et al., 2021). Yet little is currently known about how to optimize the effectiveness of machine teachers. Students are very much aware when working with machine teachers that they are not speaking to a human. So far, it is established that if students do not perceive the machine teacher to be very helpful or easy to communicate with, they do not want to work with it—although we would suggest that the same is true for a "flesh-and-blood" teacher. Further, when machine teachers use a voice function to review course material, students prefer machine teachers who use relational cues, such as asking students how they are before diving into the material.

Machine teachers are useful for answering student questions about class content and about course policies that students may have missed in the syllabus. Machine teachers are available 24/7 to answer student questions, which means that when learners are ready to focus on class material, the machine teacher is guaranteed to be available to assist them at that very second. Some machine teachers can also provide short lectures on course material to review topics students have struggled to comprehend. Machine teachers can save organizations (both education and industry) a lot of time and manpower. Having machine teachers answer student questions, in college courses or internal company trainings, through an automated chat system means that the instructor is only needed to answer complicated questions outside of the classroom. Reallocating the time-consuming practice of responding to emails answering basic questions, and often questions to which students already have the answer, means that the instructor can either devote more time to individual students or, as is often the case, take on larger class sizes while still having time to attend to each student's needs.

All of this said, many questions remain about the functionality of machine teachers, such as how tone and pace of vocal AI affect learners and if there could be such a thing as too much social presence with these AI. Students are more engaged in class and perceive that they learn more when they can develop a rapport with their instructor (Frisby & Martin, 2010). Whether it is possible to develop a rapport with a machine teacher and what effect that would have on student learning is yet unknown. Like all new instructional technology, machine teachers present learning with a variety of opportunities, but only if instructors and scholars learn how to use this technology well.

Online Learning as a New Normal

A hard-learned lesson for many first-time online instructors is that to teach a concept well online means adapting to that environment, not simply uploading the in-class materials into the online classroom format (as one author's first mentor states, putting a worksheet online is still just a worksheet.) Adaptations must be made in online course delivery to accommodate for the instructor not being able to physically interact with students one-on-one when additional assistance is needed. Professors must also adapt their communication skillfully to the mediated environment, recognizing that students have different communicative needs in the online channel versus face-to-face. For example, instructors have long relied on the use of immediate behaviors and content clarity to alleviate students' writing apprehension in the face-to-face classroom, but those same instructional communicative behaviors have no effect on students' writing apprehension when they are learning online (Gaytan et al., 2021). Further, online instructors must recognize that students have a variety of anxieties and skills in relation to the technologies of the learning platform. Simply forcing students to take a class online when they are uncomfortable with that learning platform will change their comfort with interacting with the instructor, and the instructor will need to be much more intentional in reaching out to individual students to start one-on-one interactions to achieve the same level of rapport and out-of-class communication than would naturally happen with the same student in class (Goke et al., 2021).

That said, technology is not bad, nor is it a poor substitute for face-to-face learning. It is simply different. Teachers and parents are often the individuals voicing the idea that more technology is a bad idea, perpetuating the misnomers that technology-mediated communication is lesser and more addictive than face-to-face communication (Westerman et al., 2016). The prevalence of technology in socializing and learning has certainly changed the concept of normal, but shifting the primary channel of communication to technology-mediated rather than face-to-face poses no more threats to one's effectiveness or mental health than face-to-face communication does. Rather, technology can offer more opportunities for learning than traditional face-to-face classrooms because it can seamlessly incorporate informal social communities (e.g., YouTube, Facebook, Twitter) into their platforms to create crossover learning experiences (Panke, 2017; Vareberg, 2021).

That said, online education can offer *superior* communication techniques when compared to face-to-face instruction. For example, eye contact has been consistently shown to increase students' motivation to learn and affective learning in the classroom (Allen et al., 2006). In the face-to-face classroom, instructors can only give eye contact to one student at a time. However, in the online classroom, if instructors use the technology effectively by looking directly into their webcam while speaking, they simulate eye contact with every student in their class simultaneously, a phenomenon called "augmented gaze" (Bailenson et al., 2008). Augmented gaze can be established during live class using videoconferencing software or during recorded lectures. Likewise, online learning allows for more involvement. In the face-to-face classroom, direct student participant is contingent on the size of a class and how long it meets, and, for the most part, only one (or a few) students can speak at any given time. Through asynchronous discussion boards, however, these limitations disappear, allowing all students continuous involvement in class discussions—and to do so in unique ways. Understanding how learners utilize their already existing tools becomes as necessary as learning which new tools to integrate (Vareberg, 2021). In many cases, what students use is sophisticated enough to facilitate learning, albeit in ways we may not expect (e.g., TikTok).

There are many additional ways that online learning can be more effective than face-to-face learning if the instructor uses the technology to communicate skillfully. Goodboy and Myers (2015) have identified three primary typologies in which instructors can misbehave: being antagonistic toward students, presenting disorganized lectures, or failing to articulate content. We argue that these perceived misbehaviors can be mitigated when using technologies, especially if the instruction is happening asynchronously. Regarding antagonism, communication is mostly likely to take place via email or another text-based system, which can allow instructors to carefully think through how they want to word their messages, especially if their message will contain bad news, to carefully craft messages with the lowest probability of being seen as aggressive. Further, and as noted earlier, professors supplement the tone of their messages with emojis (Vareberg & Westerman, 2020). Lectures can be reviewed and potentially remastered to alleviate confusing elements, and subtitles can also be used to reinforce core content. Students can also be shown how to speed up or slow down lecture materials for review or, for example, if a professor's natural cadence is too slow or too fast—many of these latter suggestions can also help improve articulation.

Another advantage of distance learning is that it can create safe, anonymous spaces for discussing sensitive topics that cannot otherwise be achieved in the face-to-face classroom such as diversity and inclusion discussions. As suggested by Pain (2021), online classrooms provide unique opportunities to engage in anonymous discussion through discussion boards, which gives many students the opportunity to ask honest questions they would never ask in a face-to-face environment for fear of sounding ignorant or insensitive. Because of this, online learning can foster opportunities for deeper and more honest discussion of sensitive topics than the traditional face-to-face classroom.

ACCESSIBILITY AND ONLINE EDUCATION

Online learning also allows students who would otherwise be unable to attend school access to higher education. Students who are too far away from school to physically commute to campus especially benefit from online learning because of its anytime, anywhere availability. For example, the military makes up a large percentage of distance learners because students can attend class regardless of where they are deployed (Plein & Cassels, 2021). Students who have obligations during the day when courses are offered, such as taking care of small children or working a full-time job, can also benefit from online learning's flexibility. The great pivot of 2020—moving (most) all courses and degrees online—provided more opportunities for learners in these time-limited and geographically dispersed categories to pursue higher education than ever before. Hastily moving these courses and programs back to campus would limit the ability of many to complete their degrees.

Many of the features of online learning that make teaching more effective than face-to-face, such as the ability to caption videos with subtitles, were designed specifically to make learning accessible for students with disabilities. For example, in the face-to-face classroom, students with visual disabilities cannot work directly with the same handouts as their visual peers. Yet in the online classroom, visually impaired students can access the same documents and navigate the same learning management system with the use of keyboard navigation and a screen reader—presuming that instructors are following accessibility standards such as those posted by the U.S. Department of Education for technology accessibility (https://www2.ed.gov/about/offices/list/ocr/frontpage/pro-students/issues/dis-issue06.html).

Instructional Communication for Maximum Effect: A Few Tips

Pulling from the notes in the previous section, we can offer specific suggestions as to how to communicate for maximum effect. For example, it would be safe to say that most of the communication in online learning environments is asynchronous. That means that most of the communication between students and instructors is asynchronous, giving the instructor time to think through the most socially perfect responses to messages (thanks hyper-personal theory!), which avoids misbehaviors. This also develops an online persona for instructors (thanks social presence theory!), helping students feel as though they know the instructor well and can predict how they will respond to certain types of messages. An online instructor's ability to establish and maintain a clear personality in their communication that permeates through different channels of richness (e.g., a recorded video with sound and audio versus an email with only text) is a hallmark of effective online teaching (Robinson, 2019). Having a clear understanding of who the professor is takes away apprehension about writing messages and allows learners to focus on the actual learning. Cues like emoticons help to make messages and personalities clearer in text-based messages. One of the most important cues for establishing personality online is to have enough communication in which to establish a personality. It is critical that instructors respond to student messages as promptly as possible and invite further communication. The faster that an instructor responds to student emails, the more the student will perceive the instructor as liking, caring, and competent (Tatum et al., 2018). Students generally expect that a professor should respond to any email within 24 hours (Zhang et al., 2016).

The "anytime, anywhere" nature of online learning makes it available to students when they are ready and available for learning. However, it also means that when they are ready to look at course material or feedback and have a critical question, the professor may be asleep for the night or taking the day off. Waiting for a response and finding that it doesn't come until after a student no longer has time to focus on the course can be frustrating. Therefore, it's critical that instructors always let students know if their communication patterns will change, for example, if they will be taking a vacation day or need extra time to give feedback on an assignment that is particularly time-consuming to grade. It is equally important to have interaction policies clearly laid out in their syllabus. Students should know how long they can reasonably expect to wait before seeing feedback on an assignment or hearing a response to email. They should also have clearly laid out instructions on what to do should they not hear from their professor within the set amount of time. For example, it could be laid out in a syllabus that "Students will receive responses to email within 24 hours. If a student has not received a response within this timeframe, they should resend their message because it would have received a response by that point if the message had arrived." Setting up these clear expectations and procedures will help to minimize frustration. It also sets up important citizenship behaviors for students.

In fact, the reality is that there is only so much that an instructor can do to make a class beneficial if students are not good classroom citizens (Garland & Violanti, 2019). Students have to walk into the classroom with the mind-set to be engaged, or even the best instructor in the world will have a hard time winning them over. Student engagement in a course is necessary for having interesting peer interactions, saving everyone from the dreaded "post once and reply to two peers" discussions.

Students also must take responsibility for thinking through their communication in online classes (Garland & Violanti, 2019). Unclear communication is not just unhelpful, it's time-consuming. Consider the point from earlier that explains that students can get frustrated waiting for professors to reply to their emails. That frustration can be compounded if instead of getting actual help when the professor replies, the professor instead has to ask for the student to clarify the assistance they are seeking and then wait another 24 hours for actual assistance. In order to get the most out of their online experiences, students must carefully think through the messages they send in the class. For example, an email to the instructor which says, "I am having trouble with the content in Module 2" is not a helpful message in and of itself. For the professor to know how to help the student, they also need to know where in Module 2 the information became confusing and what, if any, resources the student has been able to access to move forward. They also need to know if the student has any specific questions about the content. Otherwise, the professor and student are going to waste quite a bit of time reviewing information that should have been provided upfront. Clear communication makes better use of everyone's time.

Time management is overall the key to success in an online course (Onuka & Ajayi, 2012). Just as professors have to be dedicated to giving quick feedback and closely monitoring their email, so too do students. Students also have to manage their own time to ensure that they start on modules early enough to finish them, anticipating that they may need assistance from the instructor that will not come immediately. They also have to be responsible for setting up their working environment for using that time wisely, minimizing distractions so that the time that they do dedicate is productive.

Conclusion

No doubt, technology is a powerful force for education. Yet, we don't want any of our readers coming to this last passage of the chapter with the idea that technology is a magic wand that can perfect any learning environment. Technology is only useful when used skillfully and purposefully. Consider the role of gamification in online learning, which is currently very popular in workplace training. Gamification is the notion of adding game-like components to activities that are not games (Eickhoff et al. 2012). Gamification of learning primarily means the incorporation of competition for highest score, most units completed, or the earning of badges in the digital environment. Gamification is highly effective at increasing engagement with content, but any increase in engagement will be very short-term if the gamification is not designed well. Van Roy (2019) uses the analogy of *chocolate covered broccoli* to describe poor gamification. By this, he means that one cannot simply throw gamification elements into learning that is poorly designed and expect that learners will like it. The gamification elements, the chocolate, will only look appealing for that brief moment until learners bite into the concoction and realize that what's under it is still broccoli. This is the case with all education technology. To effectively use technology to deliver education, technology must be chosen carefully to meet the learning objectives and be accompanied by strategic instructional communication tailored to the specific CMC channel and technologies being used. Yet all of the most skillful design in the world is still useless if the learners do not arrive ready to engage. Active learning requires activity—actively engaging with the technology, the course material, and other members of the learning environment. But it can be done, as it has been in the past. Thus, we predict a new normal that looks a lot like the old normal, where teachers and students alike continue using technology to communicate and experience class presence (or not), just as they always have.

PART V

Risk and Crisis

CHAPTER 9

Background

Jeffrey D. Brand

A s the communication discipline has matured and evolved, it has faced the need to address its role beyond the walls of academic institutions, and to engage publics as a place that can serve more than the student and educator. The evolution of applied communication research has identified reasons for expanding the boundaries of the discipline and the role of research within it. Four challenges, in particular, help to illustrate contemporary directions for communication studies. These include establishing respect for the field in academic and public arenas; the need to create a research-grounded body of knowledge; a desire to generate knowledge that contributes to solving social problems; and finally, promoting communication-based theory and practice for use and awareness by nonacademic publics (Cissna et al., 2009).

Recent years have demonstrated the fragility of our communities as a multitude of crises and disasters have upended people around the globe. Issues involving public health, the economy, race relations, public safety, and political violence, to identify just a few, have demonstrated the need for leadership and effective communication from government, private, and nonprofit organizations (Milligan, 2020). In a 6-month span after the start of the COVID-19 pandemic announcement in March 2020, more than 100 climate and weather-related disasters occurred worldwide, impacting more the 50 million people. The dangers represented by these hazards continue to involve more people, have increased in frequency and intensity, and have impacts that overlap and are intensified by many of the other challenges the world is confronting daily (International Federation of Red Cross and Red Crescent Societies [IFRC], 2020).

The vulnerabilities facing publics, the risks they face, and the crises they lead to, have accelerated the need for more information, communication, understanding, and action. Today's crises are often complex; they are compounded by each other as publics try to sort out how to make choices and decisions about difficult issues while facing uncertainty and stresses. If the communication discipline has a responsibility to share and contribute to solving social problems, our understanding of risk and crisis communication should extend outside our academic practices and be tasked to contribute to these serious challenges.

This chapter explores the role of instructional communication research (ICR) in the context of risk and crisis communication. It will explain the directions taken to use ICR to study and respond to risk and crisis issues in current scholarship and in partnership with nonacademic publics and to provide service to communities. This chapter will first explore the concepts of risk and crisis communication, their dynamics and needs. The field of instructional communication research will then be defined and explored for its capabilities to meet the requirements for successful risk and crisis communication efforts. Finally, existing research, theories, and models applying ICR will be explored to establish the current state of use of this body of research to respond to the demands of risk and crisis communication issues. The next chapter will identify new directions that might be taken to expand current understanding of IRC and to relate it to other theories and practices that can strengthen and grow the connections between the communication discipline and risk and crisis communication challenges the public confronts daily.

Risk and Crisis Communication

Treatments of risk and crisis communication traditionally identify both the unique qualities of each as well as their overlaps and influences on each other. By first defining each for their specific attributes and then exploring their confluences, a better understanding of how they may be addressed through ICR is possible.

In 1989, the National Research Council (NRC, 1989) established the need to consider risk communication more proactively and defined it as "an interactive process of exchange of information and opinion among individuals, groups, and institutions" (p. 21). Their work identified the variety of risk-based messages and determined that successful risk messages helped citizens to make better decisions in "order to reach a judgment, and to make decisions regarding risks, such as whether to protest, ignore, negotiate, or take protective action" (NRC, 1989, p. 27).

Defining risk or the variables that contribute to risk communication requirements includes issues such as "the nature, magnitude, significance, or control of a risk" (Covello, 1992, p. 359). Risk communication can be a "projection of what might happen," and it "tends to be focused within carefully planned media campaigns" (Seeger et al., 2003, p. 203). The public's capacity to accurately assess and understand risk is a frequent concern in the research. McComas (2006) explains that "public perceptions of risk frequently do not align with scientific assessments" (p. 78). Other issues cloud the public's ability to understand and process risk, mostly due to perceptual issues, that serve to inflate or deny the risks associated with personal safety and health. These perceptual problems include "a risk's voluntariness, controllability, catastrophic potential, scientific understanding, effects on future generations, and dread" (p. 78). How people feel about risk can also impair judgment, even to the extent of overcoming analytic reasoning and common sense. Because risk assessment is a complicated process, effective risk communication plays a vital role in relating risks and threats to audiences in meaningful ways.

Risk communication research is frequently used to inform public health campaigns, explanations of environmental hazards, and natural disaster prevention and warnings, among other issues. These campaigns often help change publics' understanding of risk by presenting the nature of the threats and identifying behavior changes that can lead to risk avoidance. As such, risk communication is often associated with "threat sensing and assessment" (Reynolds & Seeger, 2005, p. 45). Although the potential for effective risk communication exists to save lives and protect publics, getting nonscientific publics to take appropriate actions is a challenge (Sellnow-Richmond et al., 2018).

At the risk stage, messages are dialogic; they provide for interactive and multiple messages about the nature of the risks identified (NRC, 1989). As risk conditions transition to a crisis, messages become less interactive and more one-way, designed to reduce harm and to respond to the urgency and timeliness of the situation (Mayer, 2021; T. Sellnow & D. Sellnow, 2010).

An additional challenge to enacting effective risk and crisis communication messages are how the media portrays these issues and their lack of focus on efficacy or action. Dependency on media outlets for transmitting and sharing risk and crisis messages can potentially be counter-productive if efficacy issues are not properly addressed (Frisby et al., 2013; Wickline & Sellnow, 2013). There can be a tendency to overestimate the impact of the media on the public's perception of risk and the capability of mass media messages to accomplish risk communication goals. Research has suggested that "media primarily affect perceptions of risk to other people," and that these beliefs may "have little direct effect on individual health behavior" (Morton & Duck, 2001, p. 621).

Cultural issues are also important to creating effective risk messages, but a lack of cultural understanding and adaptation also have hampered successful risk messaging efforts (D. Sellnow & T. Sellnow, 2014; Littlefield

& Sellnow, 2015; Salazar, 2021; Salazar & Sellnow, D., 2021). Since much risk communication research is sender and message focused, the recipients do not always occupy enough attention. Because risk communication has the potential for a dialogical approach, engaging audiences more actively and carefully could be a useful technique. If risk communicators assumed a more culture-centered approach to messages rather than a culture-neutral or culturally sensitive one, they might have greater potential to enact changes. This might entail precrisis efforts to build relationships that are in place so that "the infrastructure and knowledge is available to be able to communicate effectively" (Littlefield, 2015).

The scholarship of risk communication demonstrates how challenging effective risk communication can be, but also its importance. Successful risk messages engage audiences appropriately based on a host of factors, including culture, perceptions of self and others, media influences, dialogue and decision-making, sender credibility, and message strategies. The potential for an instructional communication strategy to accommodate these issues will become evident.

Crises are situations that create different communication challenges than risk contexts. Coombs (2019) describes a crisis as a "breakdown in a system that creates shared stress" (p. 2). His work identifies different types of crises, such as disasters and organizational crises. His description of crisis elements include violations of stakeholder expectations and the fact the crises are perceptual in nature, engage organizational reputations, and can create harms to stakeholders (Coombs, 2019).

Organizational crises can also be defined as "a specific, unexpected, and nonroutine event or series of events that create high levels of uncertainty and simultaneously present an organization with both opportunities for and threats to its high-priority goals (Ulmer et al., 2019, p. 7). In addition to this definition, Reynolds and Seeger (2005) define crisis communication as it "seeks to explain the specific event, identify likely consequences and outcomes, and provide specific harm-reducing information to affected communities" (p. 46). Between these and other definitions of crisis communication, a variety of variables are revealed.

As opposed to risk situations, crises are often characterized by urgency, uncertainty, immediacy of threats, and stresses on publics that create vital communication demands. Chaos theory has been applied to explaining the breakdown or collapse that can accompany a crisis. Elements such as threats, surprise, and a rapid response expectation lead to emotional responses and confusion that require communication to restore understanding and sense making (D. Sellnow et al., 2017).

Crisis communication scholarship has also evolved to address both immediate crisis concerns and postcrisis issues by addressing the strategic goals behind crisis responses. Early crisis theory focused attention on issues such as blame, apology, and reputation recovery. More contemporary research and theory have begun to discuss opportunities that crises offer, such as narrative orientations for crises, organizational learning and growth, transformational leadership, and community and organizational renewal (Seeger & Sellnow, 2016; Sellnow & Seeger, 2013; Ulmer et al., 2019). These refinements for crisis communication theory offer potential for additional instructional communication research opportunities and applications.

At the intersection of risk and crisis communication are models that place the two on a continuum moving through stages. The CERC model, developed in conjunction with the Centers for Disease Control and Prevention (CDC, 2014), describes the communication life cycle and the communication needs for each, including precrisis, initial, maintenance, resolution, and evaluation. Fink (1986) uses a model developed using medical terminology to describe a crisis in terms of prodromal, acute, chronic, and resolution stages. Another common model identifies precrisis, crisis, and postcrisis communication challenges that then circle back to a new precrisis state (Seeger et al., 2003; T. Sellnow & D. Sellnow, 2010). Contemporary understanding of risk and crisis communication has identified and promoted the study and practice of the interaction of these two communication challenges and their evolution and influences on each other. As a situation arises, risk and then crisis communication efforts respond to address the needs of organizations and stakeholders to explain and resolve the issue and to prepare for future challenges.

The communication requirements of effective risk and crisis communication suggest that theories of communication practice are necessary that can accomplish the challenges posed by the presence of risk and crisis situations. The growing demands presented by a multitude of crises and potential risks in the world have created exigencies that require communication theory and models of communication that can respond effectively to these challenges. The adaptation of instructional communication research (ICR) to contribute to responding to these challenges is vital to educators and policy makers (Sprague, 2002).

Instructional Communication Research and Theory

Instructional communication research has a long tradition in the communication discipline. It is evolving and growing as it confronts both the internal dynamics of a transformed discipline of communication studies and the need to find ways to expand its scope and influence outside of discipline-based and academic foci to the larger role of contributing to the objectives of applied communication practices. Although past reviews of instructional communication research have emphasized limited effort beyond classroom and academic contexts, recent scholarship has been making inroads to applying instructional communication research to topics such as risk and crisis communication and other applications addressed in this book (Conley & Ah Yun, 2017; D. Sellnow & T. Sellnow, 2018; Valenzano & Wallace, 2017).

Coombs (2009) is usually referenced for his early assessment that "little research exists that explores ways to improve the development and delivery of instructing information" in risk and crisis situations (p. 106). Despite these misgivings, more contemporary efforts have been underway to apply instructional communication research to these challenges. These efforts include defining instructional communication's functions and matching them to the requirements of effective crisis and risk communication demands; applying instructional communication research models to risk and crisis contexts in both academic and applied environments; and developing specific models applying instructional communication to risk and crisis applications for applied use by governmental and other organizations where instructional communication would enhance their performance (D. Sellnow & T. Sellnow, 2014; D. Sellnow et al., 2017; D. Sellnow, Limperos et al., 2015; Frisby et al., 2013; Littlefield et al., 2014; T. Sellnow et. al, 2017).

Understanding why instructional communication is an appropriate extension to academic and applied practices in risk and crisis communication becomes evident when reviewing these contexts in light of instructional communication research understanding. Instructional communication research has been conducted as an interdisciplinary field, including educational psychology, pedagogy, and communication studies. These three disciplines have added to the depth and richness of instructional communication theory and research.

Educational psychology contributes to this area by exploring questions of how students learn and provides attention to psychological and intellectual processes that impact learning. It explores learning from perspectives of cognitive, affective, and behavioral processes.

Cognitive learning embraces the acquisition and understanding of knowledge. Affective learning involves how the receiver's attitudes, beliefs, values, and emotions are reflected in their knowledge acquisition. Behavioral learning extends these two learning approaches to refer to changes in learners' performance of the skills and actions the instructional messages are there to advocate for. The focus on cognitive, affective, and behavioral learning provides a means to identify instructional approaches that meet these needs and a means to evaluate their performance.

For instructional communication researchers, the identification of affective and cognitive learning functions is vital. Although the classroom might be an appropriate place to consider the cognitive realm of instruction and knowledge acquisition, "instructional communication researchers believe that affective learning is a more valid indicator of instructional effectiveness" (Mottet & Beebe, 2006, p. 18). This aspect of instructional communication research will be revealed as important in the context of risk and crisis communication challenges.

A focus on pedagogy has traditionally explored the study of teaching methods, philosophies of teaching, and assessment. Instructional communication research reveals the challenges of pedagogy as a look to how the content of instructional messages is shared with subjects and not just a focus on the best or most informed message content. The impact of instructional messages can be negated if the methods used to share them fail to accomplish their purposes. In educational terms, this issue might be referred to as teacher self-efficacy. From an instructional communication standpoint, a failed instructional message might be created due to a communicator's failure in the process of sharing content rather than the content alone. Training in pedagogy helps prepare teachers or other communicators to develop the appropriate instructional skills, not just a mastery of knowledge of content.

The communication discipline's contributions to this research area reflect the importance of the meaning of the messages created for recipients and are shared in effective ways. Communication functions from a process point of view and is viewed as a transactional process, engaging audience and speaker in the cocreation of shared meaning. Instructional communication research reinforces that view. Traditionally, variables that a communication theory orientation for instructional communication can benefit from are the basic rhetorical features of communication: persuasion, credibility, invention, organization, style, and delivery. Relational communication components also reflect the transactional approach to communication, incorporating feelings, emotions, and perception (Mottet & Beebe, 2006).

Advancement and refinements in instructional communication have addressed learning in any context as informed by a combination of factors, including knowledge acquisition, retention, and application (Frisby et al., 2013). Rather than focus on information communicated by the sender, instructional communication is measured by affective, cognitive, and behavioral learning by receivers (D. Sellnow, Lane et al., 2015). This research has applied instructional communication to the role of communication in teaching, training, and other contexts "across the entire life span" (Nussbaum & Friedrich, 2005, p. 578).

Instructional communication research has helped to design an approach that well suited for the communication challenges of risk and crisis contexts. Because risk and crisis communication situations must deal with a variety of variables that impact stakeholders and publics, instructional communication has been identified as "uniquely suited" to the tasks at hand (Edwards et al., 2021, p. 50). Characteristics of risk and crisis communication messages, such as uncertainty, dialogue, cultural adaptations, audience analysis, decision-making, safety, action, and message delivery, and other challenges are appropriately accommodated by instructional communication elements, including the need to demonstrate affective, cognitive, and behavioral learning outcomes.

Risk communication messages are designed to help publics make risk-informed decisions. These messages include announcements, warnings, instructions, information sources, connections to personal belief systems, feelings, institutional trust and attitudes, and a variety of formats that communicate from expert sources to nonexpert audiences directly and through journalists, public agencies, and private corporations (NRC, 1989).

In cases of crisis communication, important goals include minimizing harm or damage, maintaining operations, and reputation repair. As Coombs (2009) explains, information must be presented in ways that do not simply disseminate information to publics, but that stakeholders can act on and use to protect themselves and minimize harms.

Instructional Communication Research: Applications for Risk and Crisis Situations

Although instructional communication research has not been applied to risk and crisis communication until recently, the trajectory for this research to inform both academic and applied research is encouraging. Central to this challenge is the effort to find common definitions for ICR and to employ them in a way that builds on theory and scholarship. Seeger (2018) explains that there is confusion over "communication instruction and instructional communication," "that instructional communication is about the effect of communication in instructing," and that explaining "this distinction is important to creating a research agenda that can produce generalizable insights" (p. 492).

Seeger (2018) also identifies other requirements for moving instructional communication research forward. He explains that current research often depends on using theories from other disciplines and alternative areas within the communication discipline to study instructional communication. Although these theories are helpful, there is an absence of a body of theory specific to ICR. Seeger (2018) identifies two ways to build useful theories to apply to ICR that may take it beyond the classroom. The first type of theory would identify instructional requirements based on specific contexts such as crisis and risk communication. The second type of theory would describe the range of contexts appropriate for ICR and the related requirements this development of theory call for. A final concern that Seeger (2018) articulates, to be developed in the next chapter looking toward the future for ICR, is the question of ethics and those ethical principles that may help guide the use of instructional communication in ways that are responsible and appropriate.

For the remainder of this chapter, I intend to explore existing research in ICR on issues and topics related to risk and crisis. First, starting with those pulling existing communication theories into ICR applications; and second, looking at an existing model of instructional communication research, the IDEA model, that has been widely used outside of the classroom to respond to risk and crisis challenges in actual risk and crisis contexts.

One of the defining characteristics of risk communication is the opportunity it affords for dialogue between stakeholders and organizations and government agencies. The NRC (1989) affirmed that risk messages should serve as a dialogue among various groups and that it is a primary characteristic of risk messages. As T. Sellnow and D. Sellnow (2010) reveal, however, "crisis situations create an inherent constraint on dialogue" (p. 112). By exploring the differing requirements and challenges of risk versus crisis communication, they make a case for the "instructional dynamic of risk communication" (p. 113).

This article makes a strong case for the application of instructional communication in crisis situations to overcome the challenges of a crisis that hinder the capacity for dialogue to respond quickly and specifically enough to engage the crisis at hand. By advocating an instructional communication research approach to crisis communication, this essay supports the idea that learning must be measured by variables such as comprehension, retention, and action on the part of stakeholders. The understanding of audience and stakeholders built into an instructional communication approach is also highlighted in this justification for ICR's usefulness in addressing the dynamics of culture, audience understanding, preferences, and needs when designing crisis messages.

In another article extending instructional communication research into the areas of risk and crisis communication, researchers explore the role of chaos theory to explain the dynamics of a crisis situation and why an instructional communication approach would help address the difficulties to resolving a crisis that chaos theory reveals (T. Sellnow et al., 2012).

Chaos theory is used to describe the "bewildered sense of helplessness victims experience at the onset of an acute crisis and the urgent desire it instills to restore a sense of understanding and order" (p. 634). To restore the order that has been lost due to the crisis, the authors identify the importance of "sharing instructional messages that initiate self-protection and recovery" (p. 634). Instructional communication messages contain the necessary components (including comprehension, retention, and application) to help remedy the impacts of the crisis situation and provide a design that leaders and stakeholders can use to overcome the challenges created by crisis situations.

Other communication and education theories have been studied in the context of instructional communication research as applied to risk and crisis situations. Two theories, learning preferences and self-efficacy, were studied in the context of a test of instructional messages regarding a simulated food contamination and food-borne illness crisis (Frisby et al., 2013). Results of the study indicated that for individuals at risk from a crisis, "ways to increase efficacy should be considered" and a "message that appeals to all learning styles should be developed" (p. 264). In addition to these results, this study suggests finding ways to formulate instructional messages that can be successfully used by the media since existing efforts to get instructional messages into media coverage has often been a failure and even counter-productive at times.

In a related study, actual messages from an egg recall effort were used to identify instructional messages (Frisby et al., 2014). These were grouped into standard media messages or high instructional messages. After testing with subjects, the results indicated that the higher instructional messages resulted in greater knowledge by subjects and efficacy awareness. The study did not have the purpose to actually measure behavior changes, but recommends future testing. In the process of identifying actual instructional messages on the egg recall, the authors also identified the failure of media content to provide adequate instructional messages. These two studies help provide evidence for the use of instructional messages that provide needed information in a form that can lead to self-protection and learning during a crisis situation.

Efforts to identify expansions to the scope and application of instructional communication research have led to many new areas to be identified, including forensics education, technology, and digital games, along this focus on risk and crisis communication (D. Sellnow, Limperos et al., 2015). Other essays in this volume will address additional places where ICR can be applicable. A useful application of communication theory in the area of message design has been proposed as a complement to the work of instructional communication messages. Message design scholarship has also been growing in the discipline of public relations and will be discussed in the next chapter. Message design research has been supported by funding from the National Center for Food Protection and Defense and other government grant-funded research. It is also responsible for the development of the IDEA model, to be discussed in the coming pages. Understanding the nature of message design research and theory can help to promote success in instructional messaging.

Other communication theories have been used to explore how organizations and leaders might develop successful crisis or risk messages to mitigate potential harms. In a study of the 2013 Porcine Epidemic Diarrhea virus (PEDv), strategic message convergence theory was applied to identify successful "or effective persuasion that occurs when diverse viewpoints lead to a consistent conclusion" (D. Sellnow et al., 2019). Unlike many studies related to instructional communication, this one applied communication theory to explore how diverse communicators and messages can come together to provide for effective instructional messages to stakeholders in a strategic and intentional way. This study also reveals questions about the differences between message convergence in precrisis versus crisis situations and the potential for ethical problems that might be present if these communicators do not have the same interests of their stakeholders as a priority. This was a study in biosecurity practices that indicated how message convergence could improve the outcome of instructional messages.

Another study involving biosecurity issues examined the swine industry's response to a different disease, the African Swine Fever virus, and how the theory of communities of practice (CoP) can explain the successful use of instructional communication messages to combat the disease by stakeholders. The study included many useful conclusions about the nature of instructional communication to provide valuable messages in cases of risk and crisis situations and the incorporation of diverse communicators, messages, and audiences in the entire process of threat mitigation. The study also reinforced the necessity to apply instructional communication research to real-world contexts and to expand understanding of this body of research, and, finally, the potential for CoP and instructional research to address future biosecurity issues for both animals and humans (Edwards et al., 2021).

One of the limitations to some instructional communication research efforts has been the absence of the incorporation of recipient variables such as culture and even demographic differences that might impact the success of instructional communication efforts. In the case of Littlefield et al. (2014), attention is paid to the assessment of receiver message effectiveness on the bases of ethnicity and sex. This study is part of early research applying the IDEA model of instructional communication research, and the case is made for a receiver-oriented approach to the study of instructional communication messages rather than a sender approach.

The IDEA model has been developed and tested extensively since 2014. It was created using the objectives of instructional communication research and incorporates the scholarship of teaching, learning, and behavior change that ICR strives to integrate for use inside classroom contexts but also in applied, real-world contexts. Since then, it has been used in research for theoretical, case study-based, as well as qualitative and quantitatively designed, studies. It has been applied to a wide range of risk and crisis contexts, including disease outbreaks (animal and human), food contamination, mass shootings, terrorism, earthquake and early warning systems, among other situations. The research has been supported by grants and research contracts with a variety of organizations, including the World Health Organization (WHO), the U.S. Department of Agriculture (USDA), the CDC, the U.S. Geological Survey (USGS), and the Department of Homeland Security (DHS; D. Sellnow & T. Sellnow, 2020).

The model consists of four components: internalization, distribution, explanation, and action. These parts of the model are used to create and communicate messages to stakeholders, and it has been applied as a means to evaluate instructional messages surrounding risk and crisis situations.

The IDEA model suggests that instructional messages that account for all four components of the model are going to be more successful and that incorporation of these four elements can ensure that instructional messages can fulfill expectations.

Reviews of recent scholarship applying the IDEA model reveal the contemporary directions ICR is heading in risk and crisis communication and help point the way for future development of theory and application. In 2015, a study exploring messages incorporating the IDEA model, as opposed to traditional messages communicated by the press concerning a food contamination issue, were considered more effective (D. Sellnow, Lane et al., 2015). This study reinforced the importance of receiver-based scholarship rather than sender, and those instructional messages must accomplish more than explanation, but also incorporate internalization and action into message strategy. The study also acknowledged the importance of addressing a range of audience variables that this study did not, like gender, location and context, literacy, and other issues that create a diverse stakeholder pool that may need more tailored messages for them to be the most successful.

Biosecurity and the PEDv outbreak were the focus of another study that involved interviews with communicators generating instructional messages during the outbreak. The study revealed generalizable results that point to the need for flexibility in crisis communication planning;

the role of audience analysis and the adaptation of messages to them; the value of action steps in the instructional messages; and, finally, the benefits to using instructional messages for both risk and crisis situations (T. Sellnow et al., 2017).

The IDEA model is presented as a best practice for effective risk and crisis communication in a study of mediated messages about a real beef contamination case in 2011 (D. Sellnow, Lane et al., 2017). This study reinforced the importance of a complete instructional message incorporating the IDEA model components to have the greatest impact on both knowledge and action. The results of the study did not find significant individual differences based on sex or race in this research, although it was a controlled experiment with college students. The study also confirmed the value of extending instructional research beyond classroom contexts and the potential for instructional messages to still be valuable through mass media delivery systems.

The theory of exemplification receives treatment in a study of risk communication and the IDEA model concerning an Ebola outbreak in 2014. The study focuses on the goal to "instruct nonscientific publics to take appropriate actions for self-protection during risk and crisis events" using the IDEA model (Sellnow-Richmond et al., 2018, p. 140). Exemplification theory is used in this study to understand the effectiveness of the IDEA model in communicating about risk during the crisis. The theory suggests that examples can help people to understand complex situations and can provide "cognitive shortcuts to glean meaning about complex ideas or situations" (p. 141).

Exemplification is explained as operating in three ways. First, information is evaluated by audiences subjectively, not systematically. Exemplars can help alter risk understanding because they can function as subjective influences. Second, the frequency of exemplars can impact audience recall of the examples. And third, exemplars can be negative or positive, with both types having potential influence.

This research examined actual messages from multiple sources concerning an Ebola case in Dallas and evaluated them from the perspective of the IDEA model's framework and their use of exemplars. The study concluded that these messages "focused extensively on explanation over internalization and action" (Sellnow-Richmond et al., 2018, p. 152). In doing so they failed to adhere to the IDEA mode elements of internalization, explanation, and action. The resulting effects are they are not likely to be successful in providing the instructional communication objectives they need to respond to the crisis. The study also recommended use of positive exemplars to enhance the effectiveness of instructional messages.

Contemporary research, in addition to conducting research in risk and crisis communication through the IDEA model framework, has been applying the model to situations and roles facing communicators responsible for sharing instructional messages and addressing nonscientific publics. In the case of emergency managers and other spokespersons, the IDEA model has been presented as a method for designing instructional messages and to teach new professionals to prepare messages to their stakeholder publics (D. Sellnow & T. Sellnow, 2019).

In the case of the Flint water crisis, assessment of instructional messages by government agencies were studied for their balancing of explanation and action messages as a set of practices that demonstrate that the IDEA model can be applied successfully to crisis communication situations. In this study, Mayer (2021) identifies particular message characteristics during the crisis utilized by governmental agencies that might strengthen the success of instructional message components from the perspective of the IDEA framework. Techniques revealed by the study include coupling explanation with action messages, use of second-person tense to personalize content, sharing of content across agency websites, use of multiple languages to communicate content, use of specific sentence structure, and even visual images utilized by messages. This research looks closely at specific message techniques using the IDEA model framework to present recommendations based on actual instructional communication efforts during the Flint water crisis. Studies like this are bridging the gaps between academic and applied research efforts to recommend applications for models like IDEA to be implemented to fulfill risk and crisis communication situations and needs.

Finally, a pair of studies looked at how the IDEA model could be used to frame messages concerning COVID-19 directed toward Hispanic and Latinx audiences. The first study comparing risk and crisis communication messages by the CDC targeting Hispanics during COVID-19 revealed uneven coverage of components of the model that prioritized internalization and action over distribution and explanation. It also discovered that most information was simply a translation of the English versions of the message and did not actually create an appeal specifically to Hispanic audiences. It recommended that if authorities wish to appeal to vulnerable or unrepresented populations, more attention may need to focus on message content, not simply translation or distribution methods for the same content as others (Salazar, 2021).

The other study applied components of the IDEA model to test subjects who were Latinx and non-Latinx. Although it was a pilot study, it reinforced the recognition that populations respond to elements of the IDEA model in different ways and that finding an appropriate message type for ethnic and other groups that are tailored to them would enhance the effectiveness of the instructional communication. Messages of personal impact varied between the two groups, and recommendations for inclusion of more exemplars was recommended to improve the strength of these messages (Salazar & Sellnow, 2021).

Conclusions

This chapter has served as a review of efforts to apply an instructional communication research (ICR) agenda to issues related to risk and crisis communication. This agenda is consistent with efforts discipline wide in communication studies to expand the scope of academic scholarship to applied contexts and to make contributions to theory and practice in practical and valuable ways. The communication requirements of effective risk and crisis communication benefit from the perspective on human communication related to ICR, and the current trajectory of risk and crisis communication applying an ICR approach is growing. Multiple theories of communication are being brought to bear on the challenges of informing and motivating audiences to utilize risk and crisis communication messages effectively. Adaptations and variations of ICR, including the IDEA model, have proposed practical and working approaches to risk and crisis communication challenges. A growing body of research, including studies funded by government agencies, on a variety of risk and crisis situations are validating the benefits of ICR in the risk and crisis communication arena. The next chapter will explore extensions and new ways to apply ICR to risk and crisis communication challenges based on advances in current research, their recommendations, and shortcomings in current risk and crisis communication research efforts.

CHAPTER 10

Current Trends and Future Directions

Jeffery D. Brand

C ontemporary risk and crisis communication research incorporating instructional communication research (ICR) is an ongoing effort. As the last chapter demonstrated, the challenges of effectively communicating risk and crisis messages can be addressed by applying models of instructional communication to ensure successful learning by recipients. This can be studied and enhanced by recognition that learning is more than knowledge acquisition; it incorporates elements of cognitive, affective, and behavioral learning. These other dimensions of learning add richness to risk and crisis messages and ensure that important behaviors and actions taken by stakeholders have the potential for fulfillment.

Every day we are surrounded by very real challenges that impact the lives of people and institutions. There are risks and attending crises in everyday life that impact millions of people. In the lead up to such events, the risks need to be measured, considered, prepared for, and understood. Once a crisis erupts, communication is a key influence on how the crisis will evolve and whether anything can be done to protect stakeholders and to assist in the recovery process. The diversity of crisis contexts can be overwhelming, since each crisis is likely to have its own unique demands and challenges. During these situations, we still need models to follow, best practices to implement, and the training needed to address these events. In an applied communication sense, successful risk and crisis communication can protect organizations, communities, and institutions; limit losses to monetary resources; support better mental and physical health and, ultimately, lives.

In this chapter, existing research applying ICR to risk and crisis situations and calls for developing further applications will be explored. There are many ways ICR can be further studied and applied to risk and crisis environments. Theory and research in communication studies, psychology, and pedagogy may also be explored in greater depth for how they can help inform and detail instructional communication approaches. This chapter identifies some promising areas based on current research trends and by extrapolating this communication challenge to other elements of communication studies research.

Academic Settings

To begin, it is helpful to explore early speculation about the future for ICR generally, primarily from the academic setting perspective. These speculations dovetail into the more specific developments of risk and crisis instructional communication research initiatives. McCroskey and McCroskey (2006) were optimistic about the future for ICR research, recognizing the growth of quantitative social scientific study in the discipline and nature of the communication discipline to evolve and to connect with other disciplines as well. The six areas their essay identified for the future of instructional communication reflect what has happened up to now, which was reported in the last chapter. Their predictions help set a path for further speculation and recommendations. The first area identified the likely continued growth of IRC and its expansion both within and outside of the discipline. I have already explored some of the recent growth in ICR research projects and the fact that they are being shared and used outside of the academic communication discipline and have found utility in meeting risk and crisis challenges. Grant-funded study support from a wide variety of government agencies in areas including health and medicine (World Health Organization [WHO], Centers for Disease and Control and Prevention [CDC]); Agriculture (U.S. Department of Agriculture); warning systems (U.S. Geological Survey, and the Department of Homeland Security), among others, demonstrate the expansion and application of instructional communication research well beyond classroom pedagogy and academic theorizing. Instructional communication models, such as IDEA, are also being actively applied and shared by some of these agencies and are being explored for risk and crisis messaging and campaigns (D. Sellnow & T. Sellnow, 2019).

Technology and Mediated Communication

In 2006, the future of technology and mediated communication for instructional communication purposes could not have been fully imagined as resources and techniques have grown. Although ICR had focused in the past on a more interpersonal process of influence, the potential for mass-mediated communication and the dialogical features of social media channels has thrust the role of technology into the instructional communication equation. A significant part of this concern has centered around the fact that, during a crisis, communicators lack direct access to their audience and the need for immediate information places a premium on media coverage for rapid dissemination of instructional messages. Risk communication situations also frequently include large populations, making mass media and social media channels vital to instructional communication goals. This reliance on mediated platforms is vulnerable to how those sources frame risk and crisis communications. Current research had been critical about the mass media's failure to incorporate appropriate instructional communication content and format. This has led to reduced effectiveness in message reception by audiences, and even failure to promote safe behaviors and responses due to media outlets and reporting choices (Frisby et al., 2013). Future recommendations lead to the conclusion that the tendency for distribution sources to focus on explanation over internalization and action remain a critical limitation to instructional efforts (Sellnow-Richmond et al., 2018). To help reverse these limitations, it is understandable that many organizations are developing their own distribution systems in an effort to exert more control over message quality and type, by not relying on journalists and others to share and frame their messages for them. This research also demonstrates that instructional communication efforts might be a multiple stage process. First, communicators must train or teach media sources how to frame better messages; and then, with their participation, develop instructional communication content that may lead to behavioral change and action on the part of audiences faced with risk and crisis challenges.

Culture-Centered Approaches

A third area where growth and potential action for the improvement of instructional communication research is in culture-centered approaches. This started in ICR classroom contexts where recognition that international students, and even micro cultural differences in the United States, influenced instructional outcomes. Since good communication practice should always be centered on audiences or receivers, further development of this emphasis is becoming a critical aspect for future theory and practice. In order for instructional communication messages to be successful, they need to incorporate an awareness of and adaptation to cultural differences to help promote action and commitment by audiences. In the health area of the discipline, these trends are gaining strength, and calls for greater study are being answered (Dutta, 2008; Littlefield & Sellnow, 2015). Recent investigations of how COVID-19 information has been shared with Hispanic and Latinx individuals are good examples of this future direction in improving ICR research by incorporating a cultural perspective (Salazar, 2021; Salazar & Sellnow, 2021). Culture-centered approaches have great potential as communicators consider critical variables that can influence the success or failure of instructional communication campaigns. As part of this trend, greater recognition in the crisis literature is being placed on a variety of vulnerable populations (CDC, 2015). Groups who are medically, socially, economically, and at risk for other reasons are gaining recognition and incorporation into emergency planning. Additional research to identify how to successfully reach these groups is needed.

Measuring Learning

The fourth future direction for ICR involves improving and documenting measurements of learning and identifying the level and type of learning that is most important. In a classroom setting, pedagogy might explore ways to identify how to measure cognitive learning. But in the risk and crisis realm, learning takes on additional dimensions and areas of importance. Learning outcomes include other elements than ICR, as originally studied in the classroom, and did not prioritize. Learning for the purpose of risk and crisis communication also needs to identify techniques for promoting affective, cognitive, and behavioral outcomes. Behavioral learning outcomes may lead to the consideration of whether recipients are capable of engaging in self-protective actions or self-efficacy to avoid or respond to threats posed by risks or during a crisis (D. Sellnow et al., 2017). This learning process might also be influenced by other external variables, such a timing and speed. The demands of a crisis mean that behavioral changes have deadlines and restrictions. During the urgency of a crisis, learning is likely to occur under mediated, rushed, and chaotic times. These variables must be incorporated into decision-making on how to best warn or protect stakeholders. Therefore, choices made may not be ideal, but be the best in the context of the situation. Context may play a larger role in evaluating learning by placing constraints on both communicators and audiences (Seeger, 2018; Sellnow & Kaufmann, 2018).

Instruction and Audience Influence

The fifth area of future work to be done for instructional communication research is to improve and build models to understand the process of instruction and audience influence. McCroskey and McCroskey (2006) argue that many of the models of ICR have been borrowed or adapted from other disciplines such as psychology or education. They reiterate the importance of building models in the communication discipline and incorporating communication theory and models to explore the instructional communication dimension. The development of the IDEA model for instructional communication has been one important response to this call, and other applications of communication theories have also added to the knowledge we have about the instructional communication process and practice. The expansion of ICR to other contexts included in this book and in this chapter for the sake of risk and crisis communication practice has also led to greater fulfillment of the call for additional models and theory in ICR.

Communibiological Paradigm

The final focus of McCroskey and McCroskey's (2006) future speculation concerns a communibiological paradigm to explain communicator effectiveness. Research trends had suggested genetic traits that presume that some people are by their nature more effective communicators. This research approach has received limited development, perhaps because, even today, we still are learning much about the science of human behavior. From the risk and crisis perspective, this line of research has limited value, since the communicator is often not an individual but rather an organization, group, or mediated outlet. This approach might, however, eventually have a value if we can identify a communibiological relationship between audience learning styles and responsiveness to messages. Such work is far from done but worth further exploration.

Although early speculations about the general value of instructional communication research had marked useful directions for advancing scholarship, analysis of existing research projects point to other avenues for ICR development. Extending current research to other logical areas point to potentially new venues for understanding instructional communication needs in risk and crisis situations. Some of these developments may also be relevant to other areas where ICR is being studied and reflected in other chapters.

Risk vs. Crisis Communication Challenges

The first way to consider future applications for ICR is to identify unique aspects of risk versus crisis communication challenges and focus on these contexts as meaningful limitations and opportunities to instructional communication practices. When faced with risk considerations, the harm or danger is measured by its probability and magnitude (Bodemer & Gaissmaier, 2015). Messages in these cases are about minimizing and reducing risks facing individuals and communities (T. Sellnow, 2015). As such, they approach the cognitive, affective, and behavioral learning accomplished by audiences in particular ways. Harm is not certain, but probable in the absence of action or intervention. This presents communicators and audiences with more dialogic opportunities. The presence of a two-way process to communicate risk makes ICR in this area valuable, since dialogue as a process can lead to the learning goals the instructional communication should aspire to.

The risk environment is not only characterized by a measure of uncertainty about outcomes, but also by efforts to engage audiences to respond to risk situations, which may entail communication efforts that differ from instructional learning goals. For example, threats might be characterized using fear appeals to motivate audiences. The extended parallel process model, advanced by Witte (1992), has been a model focusing on fear appeals designed to promote change. Although the model has its limitations and critics, academic and applied communication settings continue to consider the merits and limitations of fear-based appeals as a persuasive tactic to motivate audience responses to risk messages designed to minimize harm (Popova, 2012). Fear appeals are just one form of persuasive appeal, and more ICR would be justified to identify persuasive techniques to meet the challenge of changing behaviors and call for action. Both psychology and communication disciplines have a long history of studying persuasion, and additional information and research concerning persuasion in risk and crisis environments would be helpful.

Risk is also an evolving variable. The more a situation is characterized by risk transitions into a crisis, the challenges of maintaining dialogue or using the same communication channels, messaging, and relationships become more pronounced (D. Sellnow et al., 2017). Two-way communication gives way to one-way instruction. The CERC model has been a unique and powerful way to bridge the risk and crisis communication environments to allow for the adaptive communication necessary as risk evolves and crises arise, and then back to future risks as the cycle might continue. The CERC manual produced by the CDC, offers six principles that are appropriate to all stages of a risk and crisis response. The CERC model has been useful in contributing to an instructional communication approach. Continued research and application of this model is called for and could continue to be used to develop campaigns based on instructional communication learning goals (CDC, 2014).

The primary reason an instructional communication model has been promoted for addressing risk and crisis situations is that it is an effective way to promote both knowledge acquisition, internalization, and action by audiences. Measurement of effective instructional communication is not focused on information created and shared by a sender; instead, it is a function of the affective, cognitive, and behavioral learning outcomes on behalf of the receivers (D. Sellnow, Lane et al., 2015). The messaging strategies for accomplishing this variety of learning outcomes are all vital areas for study, and there are interactions and implications behind these outcomes to receive further detailed study in the risk and crisis context. A discussion of some of the issues regarding messages designed to meet instructional communication outcomes illustrate some of the ways future scholarship should proceed.

One challenge when faced with a variety of learning outcomes to messages is finding a balance between them. Instructional communication messages must find a balance between explanation of the potential risks or harms from a crisis; identify ways to get audiences to internalize the value of the message; and then to promote action or behaviors to remedy the situation. These can be very different messages, making good instructional strategies complex and requiring multiple messages along with the practical and theoretical assumptions behind them. Internalization messages, for example, if not integrated into the message strategy, are likely to result in the failure to accomplish compliance by the recipients of the message campaign (Sellnow-Richmond et al., 2018).

In seeking a balanced strategy, individual learning outcomes must also be studied and enhanced. Efficacy is an important variable in the construction of risk and crisis messages. In psychology, the works of Bandura (1977) have been a useful starting point. His work studies self-efficacy and the cognitive processes that increase or diminish self-efficacy in people. Recent research in ICR has argued that efficacy should be identified as an outcome to be measured in instructional messages (Frisby et al., 2013). At least one study has concluded that the higher the instructional level of messages the higher the level of self-efficacy (Frisby et al., 2014). Due to the importance of action in many risk and crisis situations, individuals' belief in and willingness to actively respond can be critical. Self-efficacy and the variables that influence it are vital, and additional research is important.

There are additional variables that will impact the learning outcomes facing instructional communication efforts, such as questions of balance, efficacy, and characteristics of the message and source. Message design is one area of research with great potential. It is a focus in areas of public relations and for health campaigns. The strategic design of messages to accomplish learning goals has been the subject of recent scholarship. As more effort is placed into this research, more carefully crafted instructional messages are possible. Government-funded research, for example, has revealed "that instructional messages offering personal relevance, a brief explanation of the situation, and specific actions for self-protection result in a significant increase in (a) knowledge comprehension of the risk, (b) perceptions of self-efficacy, and (c) behavioral intentions to take appropriate protective action" (D. Sellnow, Limperos et al., 2015, p. 421). Efforts to study message design logics are a promising research focus to strengthen ICR, judging from recent scholarship (Sutton et al., 2015; Xu et al., 2021).

There are additional dynamics related to message strategies that invite further study and refinement. Message convergence research explores the strategic coordination of messages during a crisis. If audiences receive messages from diverse sources or viewpoints but support the same conclusion, this convergence or even coordination of messages can help lead to success. Recent scholarship has utilized the work of argumentation scholars Perelman and Olbrechts-Tyteca to study how message convergence occurs and how it might be intentionally used to improve outcomes (Anthony et al., 2013; D. Sellnow et al., 2019).

An additional area of research on messages prepared for instructional communication settings is exemplification theory. This theory suggests that "exemplars might serve as effective cognitive shortcuts to increase understanding of complex information" (Sellnow-Richmond et al., 2018, p. 141). Exemplars can be a variety of things; they serve as examples that audiences can relate to and internalize effectively (Mayer, 2021). Moreover, these research studies have suggested that exemplars can be positive or negative and impact audiences. As such, they can support or harm instructional communication efforts.

An additional variable that will impact the effectiveness of risk and crisis messages is the mental state and focus of potential recipients.

Chaos and sense-making theories have helped to improve the study of how audiences might respond during a crisis. Crises can cause a breakdown in an audience's understanding of their environment, and that confusion can prevent instructional messages from being fully understood (D. Sellnow, Lane et al., 2017). To be able to successfully address an audience's mental state during a risk or crisis can be helpful in accomplishing ICR goals. Further use of theories and the scholarship of crisis and psychology might make it possible to identify other ways people cope with and respond to a crisis.

Another theory that may prove useful is research is communities of practice (CoP). The construct of a community of practice continues to be studied, and its development has future potential for a variety of applications, including ICR (Iverson & McPhee, 2008). Because a CoP involves a group of individuals learning together, it might be valuable approach to orient learning responses during a crisis. "Moreover, a CoP focuses on knowledgeability of action" and "[is] particularly helpful in creating opportunities for learning in response to crises" (Edwards et al., 2021).

Although the IDEA model for instructional communication has generated a variety of research, it is still a vital area for future explorations. This model has been the subject of academic research as well as grant-funded efforts by a variety of government agencies and other organizations. The four components of the model are internalization, distribution, explanation, and action (Sellnow-Richmond et al., 2019). All of these components are appropriate variables for further research and refinement. Identifying contexts where the IDEA model is most effective is another way to extend this research approach. This theory has been an important development supporting McCroskey and McCroskey's (2006) goal of generating theory grounded in the communication discipline. A variety of studies incorporating IDEA were identified in the previous chapter, and this will continue to be a robust area for future research efforts.

Although there will be more innovations and approaches in the future to apply elements of ICR to risk and crisis situations, a final focus is vital for the future of this research trend. Instructional communication requires the inclusion of an ethical orientation, and additional research on the ethics of these practices has been repeated in multiple studies. A comprehensive review of ethical issues regarding ICR needs to be pursued, and the ethical requirements for ICR should be articulated. Seeger (2018) has called for future research to guide the ethical use of instructional communication. His call for ethical principles for the application of instructional communication in nontraditional contexts like risk and crisis situations is encouraged. These questions are not always asked or answered in contemporary studies. They are important because risk and crisis messages have tangible and real consequences, and their practice may help or do harm. For example, message convergence research recognizes that the goals for convergence could save lives but could also serve the competing interests of the communicators. How to reduce the potential for unethical message convergence efforts is critical as we explore message convergence as a technique (D. Sellnow et al., 2019). Since ICR has as an objective to impact behavior and actions on the part of audiences, any such campaign requires ethical consideration of audience, and in our concern for vulnerable audiences, and multiple audiences, ethical treatment is necessary.

There will be new directions and refinements to be made through future ICR scholarship. In the case of risk and crisis communication challenges, instructional communication practices can play a very practical and applied role. There can be much at stake in situations where publics are threatened by risks or experience crises. Communication scholarship can provide leadership that helps to protect publics, limit harms, and lead to better resolution of crises of all types. The continued study of these issues has real and tangible value and will continue to make vital contributions in the future.

About the Contributors

Nick D. Bowman (PhD, Michigan State University) is an associate professor of immersive and interactive media in the S. I. Newhouse School of Public Communications at Syracuse University. His research focuses broadly on the cognitive, emotional, physical, and social demands of emerging technologies, with a specific focus on social media, video games, and virtual reality. He has published more than 125 peer-reviewed manuscripts and presented more than 200 projects at regional, national, and international venues. He is the current editor of *Journal of Media Psychology* and an associate editor of registered reports with *Technology, Mind, and Behavior*. He teaches courses focused on media psychology and media uses and effects and has held teaching appointments in the United States, Taiwan, and Germany.

Jeffrey D. Brand (PhD, Indiana University) is an associate professor in the Department of Communication and Media at the University of Northern Iowa. He teaches courses in public relations cases, integrated communications, global public relations, and crisis communication. His research interests focus on crisis communication and organizational argumentation. His research has appeared in the *Journal of Applied Communication Research*; *Argumentation & Advocacy*; *Race, Gender & Class*; *Power and Public Relations*, edited by Courtright and Smudde; and the *Handbook of Financial Communication and Investor Relations, published by Wiley* (2017), edited by Laskin.

Heather J. Carmack (PhD, Ohio University) is an associate professor of health communication in the Department of Communication Studies at the University of Alabama. She is also the director of the Standardized Patient Communication Lab in the College of Communication and Information Sciences, which focuses on health care provider communication training and education through standardized interactions with community members. She teaches undergraduate and graduate courses in health communication, organizational communication, and research methods. Her research examines micro and macro communication practices surrounding patient safety and health care delivery.

Angela Cooke-Jackson (PhD, MPH, University of Kentucky) is a professor of health and behavioral science in the Communication Studies Department and an affiliate faculty in the Department of Public Health at California State University, Los Angeles. Her research centers around the nexus of health and behavioral science with an emphasis on sexual health, media literacy and community engagement. Her research seeks to address health disparities among high-risk urban youth, women, and gender minorities of color, along with other underserved or underrepresented populations.

Carly Densmore (MA, Central Michigan University) is a doctoral student in the School of Communication Studies at Ohio University. Her research interests are centered in instructional and interpersonal communication in the areas of family, memorable messages, social support, and identity.

Nichole Egbert (PhD, University of Georgia) is a professor in the School of Communication Studies at Kent State University. She has published over 45 academic articles and book chapters and recently coedited the book "Social Support and Health in the Digital Age" with Kevin Wright. Egbert was the recipient of the Outstanding Scholar Award from the Ohio Communication Association in 2021. Her research interests span health communication issues broadly, with specific foci on social support and health, health literacy, and communication at the end of life.

Angela M. Hosek (PhD, 2011, University of Nebraska, Lincoln) is associate professor and Fundamentals of Presentational Speaking course director in the School of Communication Studies at Ohio University. Her published research related to instructional communication focuses on student–teacher relationships as they relate to social identity, privacy and disclosure, social media, student success, and memorable messages. She researches issues and topics related to women and maternal health communication. Hosek was the recipient of the Ohio University School of Communication Studies Outstanding Mentor Award (2016, 2020) and is an Ohio University Bruning teaching faculty fellow.

Stephanie Kelly (PhD, The University of Tennessee) is a professor of communication in the Willie A. Deese College of Business and Economics at North Carolina A&T State University. She teaches several courses at the undergraduate and graduate levels, including computer-mediated communication, data visualization and communication, and introduction to data analytics. Her research is primarily focused on how presence variables mediate messages and information behavior in the instructional and organizational contexts.

Derek Lane (PhD, University of Oklahoma) is a professor of communication studies at the University of Kentucky. His research examines how specific message characteristics interact with individual differences and preferences to improve sustained attitude and behavior change in instructional, organizational, health, risk, and other applied contexts. His interdisciplinary research appears in both national and international journals and has been supported by several federal funding agencies including the Department of Health and Human Services, the U.S. Department of Education, the National Institute of Drug Abuse, the National Institute of Mental Health, and the National Science Foundation. He teaches graduate and undergraduate courses in instructional communication, communication training and consulting, quantitative research methods, group communication, negotiation, leadership, and communication theory.

Michael Mackert (PhD, Michigan State University) is the director of the University of Texas at Austin's Center for Health Communication and professor in the Stan Richards School of Advertising & Public Relations and Department of Population Health. His research focuses primarily on the strategies that can be used in traditional and new digital media to provide effective health communication to low-health literate audiences. He leads projects on a variety of public health issues, including tobacco cessation, opioid overdose prevention, and men's role in prenatal health, that generate evidence-based health communication strategies and contribute to health communication scholarship.

Kenneth T. Rocker Jr. (MBA, North Carolina A&T State University) is a doctoral student in communication at Massey University (Wellington, New Zealand). In addition, he also serves as an assistant lecturer in the School of Communication, Journalism, and Marketing at Massey. His research interests primarily focus on interpersonal and organizational communication contexts.

Grace O. Sikapokoo (MBA, University of Pretoria) is a 4th-year doctoral student in the School of Communication Studies at Ohio University. In addition, she is a former associate director for presentational skills program at Ohio University. Grace has trained graduate teacher assistants and has taught presentational speaking and interpersonal communication at the undergraduate level. Her research interests lie at the intersection of health and family communication as well as instructional communication.

Stephen A. Spates (PhD, The University of Tennessee) is an associate professor of communication at Missouri State University. In addition, Spates serves as the interim department head of communication. Courses taught at the undergraduate and graduate levels include communication in organizations, advanced public speaking, health communication, and research methods. His research is primarily focused on communication in professional, health care, and technology contexts.

Michael G. Strawser (PhD, University of Kentucky) is an assistant professor of communication in the Nicholson School of Communication and Media at the University of Central Florida. In addition, Strawser serves as the program coordinator for the Human Communication and Communication and Conflict programs at UCF. He teaches several courses at the undergraduate and graduate levels, including business and professional communication, advanced public speaking, and teaching communication. His research is primarily focused on matters relating to instructional communication and communication education.

Yan Tian (PhD, Temple University) is a professor in the Department of Communication and Media at the University of Missouri-St. Louis. Her research focuses on audience analysis and media effects. She studies how individuals use different media to understand and communicate various health issues, and how their health communication behaviors are related to cognitive and behavioral health outcomes. She teaches courses in communication theories, research methods, and global media.

Scott Titsworth (PhD, University of Nebraska) is a professor in and currently dean of the Scripps College of Communication at Ohio University. Titworth's research generally explores connections between classroom communication and learning, with particular emphases on teacher clarity, notetaking, and emotion.

Teresa L. Thompson (PhD, Temple University) is professor emeritus, University of Dayton. Thompson is the founding editor of the journal *Health Communication*; she has edited the journal since 1989. She has coedited all three editions of the *Routledge Handbook of Health Communication* and served as editor of the three-volume *SAGE Encyclopedia of Health Communication*. She has published 75-plus articles in such journals as *Human Communication Research, Communication Quarterly, Public Opinion Quarterly, the Journal of Nonverbal Behavior, Communication Education, Western Journal of Communication, Omega: Journal of Death and Dying,* and *Journal of Family Communication,* as well as numerous books. She has been honored by both the National Communication Association and the International Communication Association for her work in health communication. She received the annual Alumni Award in Teaching at the University of Dayton and the College of Arts and Sciences Scholar of the Year Award from the university. Her current work focuses on communication issues relevant to COVID-19 and ethics in health communication. She is also presently teaching for the University of Kansas.

Kyle R. Vareberg (PhD, North Dakota State University), is assistant professor of communication studies at Northeastern State University. Vareberg's research interests exist at the intersection of instructional and computer-mediated communication; he primarily researches how instructors can foster and maintain interpersonal relationships with students, how technology is used in the classroom to satisfy learning outcomes, and how learners use technology to engage in self-directed learning.

Shawn T. Wahl (PhD, University of Nebraska at Lincoln), is professor of communication and dean of the Reynolds College of Arts and Letters at Missouri State University (MSU). Wahl served as president of the Central States Communication Association (CSCA) in 2016. He has authored numerous books, including *Public Speaking: Essentials for Excellence* (2017), *published by Kendall Hunt, Nonverbal Communication for a Lifetime* (2019), *published by Kendall Hunt, The Communication Age: Connecting and Engaging* (2019), *published by SAGE, Business and Professional Communication: KEYS for Workplace Excellence* (2019), *published by SAGE, Persuasion in Your Life* (2017), *published by Routledge, Intercultural Communication In Your Life* (2018), *published by Kendall Hunt,* and *Public Relations Principles: Strategies for Professional Success* (2016), *published by Kendall Hunt.* Wahl has published numerous research articles in *Communication Education, Communication Research Reports, Communication Studies, Communication Teacher,* the *Journal of Family Communication,* and the *Basic Communication Course Annual.* Wahl earned the Distinguished Article Award: Instructional Development Division (IDD) National Communication Association (NCA) in 2021. In addition, Wahl has worked across the world as a corporate trainer, communication consultant, and leadership coach in a variety of industries.

David Westerman (PhD, Michigan State University) is an associate professor in the Department of Communication at North Dakota State University. He teaches classes across a variety of topics and levels. His research focuses broadly on how people communicate both through and with technology.

References

Aghazadeh, S. A., Aldoory, L., & Mills, T. (2020). Integrating health literacy into core curriculum: A teacher-driven pilot initiative for second graders. *The Journal of School Health, 90*(8), 585–593. https:/doi.org/10.0000/josh.12907

Alexander, A., & Reynard, L. (2008). Are you the next communication idol? Performing communication theories. *Communication Teacher, 22*(1), 14–17. https://doi.org/10.1080/17404620801914483

Alkureishi, M. A., Lee, W. W., Webb, S., & Arora, V. (2018). Integrating patient-centered electronic health record communication training into resident onboarding: Curriculum development and post-implementation survey among house staff. *JMIR Medical Education, 4*(1), e1. https://doi.org/10.2196/mededu.8976

Allen, I. E., & Seaman, J. (2015). *Grade level: Tracking online education in the United States, 2014.* Babson Survey Research Group. http://onlinelearningconsortium.org/read/ survey-reports-2014/

Allen, M., Witt, P. L., & Wheeless, L. R. (2006). The role of teacher immediacy as a motivational factor in student learning: Using meta-analysis to test a causal model. *Communication Education, 55*(1), 21–31. https://doi.org/10.1080/03634520500343368

American Psychological Association. (2013, May). New MCAT includes major sections on behavioral and social sciences. *Psychological Science Agenda*. https://www.apa.org/science/about/psa/2013/05/mcat-sections

Anderson, D. (1993). Cultural diversity on campus: A look at intercollegiate football coaches. *Journal of Sport and Social Issues, 17*, 61–66. https://doi.org/10.1177%2F019372359301700108

Anderson, J. (Ed.), van Weert, T. (Ed.), & Duchâteau, C. (2002). Information and communication technology in education: A curriculum for schools and programme of teacher development. UNESCO.

Anthony, K., Sellnow, T., & Millner, A. (2013). Message convergence as a message-centered approach to analyzing and improving risk communication. *Journal of Applied Communication Research, 41*(4), 346–364.

Arnold, J., Edwards, T., Hooley, N., & Williams, J. (2012). Conceptualising teacher education and research as "critical praxis". Critical Studies in Education, 53(3), 281–295. https://doi.org/10.1080/17508487.2012.703140

Association of American Medical Colleges, Institute for Improving Medical Education. (2007). Effective use of educational technology in medical education: Colloquium on educational technology: Recommendations and guidelines for medical educators. https://store.aamc.org/downloadable/download/sample/sample_id/111/

Aungst, T. D., & Patel, R. (2020). Integrating digital health into the curriculum—considerations on the current landscape and future developments. *Journal of Medical Education and Curricular Development, 7*, 1–7. https://doi.org/10.1177/2382120519901275

Bailenson, J. N. (2021). Nonverbal overload: A theoretical argument for the causes of Zoom fatigue. *Technology, Mind, & Behavior, 2*(1). https://doi.org/10.1037/tmb0000030

Bailenson, J. N., Yee, N., Blascovich, J., & Guadagno. R. E. (2008). Transformed social interaction in mediated interpersonal communication. In E. A. Konjin, S. Utz, M. Tanis, & S. B. Barnes (Eds.), *Mediated interpersonal communication* (pp. 77–99). Routledge.

Bailey, M. L. (2013). Hornbooks. *The Journal of the History of Childhood and Youth, 6*(1), 3–14. https://doi.org/10.1353/hcy.2013.0000

Baker, P. G., Eley, D. S., & Lasserre, K. E. (2005). Tradition and technology: Teaching rural medicine using an internet discussion board. *Rural and Remote Health, 5*(4), 435.

Bakhtiar, M., Elbuluk, N., & Lipoff, J. B. (2020). The digital divide: How Covid-19's telemedicine expansion could exacerbate disparities. *Journal of the American Academy of Dermatology, 83*(5), e345–e346. https://doi.org/10.1016/j.jaad.2020.07.043

Bandura, A. (1977). Self-efficacy: Toward a unifying theory of behavioral change. *Psychological Review, 84*(2), 191–215.

Bargh, J. A., McKenna, K. Y. A., & Fitzsimmons, G. M. (2002). Can you see the real me?: Activation and expression of the "true self" on the internet. *Journal of Social Issues, 58*(1), 33–48. https://doi.org/10.1111/1540-4560.00247

Barnum, C. (2011). Usability testing essentials: Ready, set … test! Morgan Kaufmann.

Becker, A. J., (2009). It's not what they do, it's how they do it: Athlete experiences of great coaching. *International Journal of Sports Science & Coaching, 4*(1), 93–119. https://doi.org/10.1260%2F1747-9541.4.1.93

Beckwith, H. L., Peterson, C. M. F., & Moon, P. (1949). Modern trends in room lighting. Electrical Engineering, 68(7), 577–580. https://doi.org/10.1109/EE.1949.6444868

Berkman, N. D., Sheridan, S. L., Donahue, K. E., Halpern, D. J., & Crotty, K. (2011). Low health literacy and health outcomes: An updated systematic review. *Annals of Internal Medicine, 155*(2), 97–107. https://doi.org/10.7326/0003-4819-155-2-201107190-00005

Bigelow, B. (1997). On the road to cultural bias: A critique of the Oregon Trail CD-ROM. *Language Arts, 74*(2), 84–93.

Blakely, R. J. (1979). *To serve the public interest: Educational broadcasting in the United States.* Syracuse University Press.

Blessett, B., & Pryor, M. (2013). The invisible job seeker: The absence of ex-offenders in discussions of diversity management. *Public Administration Quarterly, 37*(3), 433–455.

Bloom, B. S., Engelhart, M., Furst, E. J., Hill, W. H., & Krathwohl, D. R. (1956). *Taxonomy of educational objectives: The classification of educational goals.* David McKay Company.

Bodemer, N., & Gaissmaier, W. (2015). Risk perception. In H. Cho, T. Reimer, & K. McComas (Eds.), *The SAGE handbook of risk communication* (pp. 10–23). SAGE.

Booth-Butterfield, M. (2003). Integrating health communication pedagogy, social science, and health interventions. *Communication Quarterly, 51*(3), 332–350. https://doi.org/10.1080/01463370309370160

Boschma, G., Einboden, R., Groening, M., Jackson, C., MacPhee, M., Marshall, H., O'Flynn Magee, K., Simpson, P., Tognazzini, P., Haney, C., Crozen, H., & Roberts, E. (2010). Strengthening communication education in an undergraduate nursing curriculum. *International Journal of Nursing Education Scholarship, 7*(1), 1–15. https://doi.org/10.2202/1548-923x.2043

Boswell, D. A. (1980). Evaluation of transparencies for psychological instruction. *Teaching of Psychology, 7*(3), 171–173. https://doi.org/10.1207/s15328023top0703_12

Brandon, D. P., & Hollingshead, A. B. (1999). Collaborative learning and computer supported groups. *Communication Education, 48*(2), 109–126. https://doi.org/10.1080/03634529909379159

Brega, A. G., Freedman, M. A., LeBlanc, W. G., Barnard, J., Mabachi, N. M., Cifuentes, M., Weiss, B. D., Brach, C., & West, D. R. (2015). Using the health literacy universal precautions toolkit to improve the quality of patient materials. Journal of Health Communication, 20(sup2), 69–76. https://doi.org/10.1080/10810730.2015.1081997

Broeckelman-Post, M. A., & Pyle, A. S. (2017). Public speaking versus hybrid introductory communication courses: Exploring four outcomes. *Communication Education, 66*(2), 210–228. https://doi.org/10.1080/0363 4523.2016.1259485

Brooks, D. D., Althouse. R., & Tucker, D. (1996). African American male head coaches: In the "red zone," but can they score? *Journal of African American Men, 2*(2/3), 93–112. https://www.jstor.org/stable/41819306

Brown, G. T. (2002). Diversity grid lock. The NCAA News. http://www.ncaa.org/news/2002/20021028/active/3922n01.html

Brown, W., Drye, S., & Kelly, S. (2020). Tech tips for business students. *Business Education Forum, 74*(4), 14–16.

Burke, J. C. (1994). Education's new challenge and choice: Instructional technology—old byway or superhighway? *Leadership Abstracts, 7*(10), 3-4.

Burke, K. A. (1969). *A grammar of motives*. University of California Press.

Car, J., Carlstedt-Duke, J., Tudor Car, L., Posadzki, P., Whiting, P., Zary, N., Atun, R., Majeed, A., Campell, J., & The Digital Health Education Collaboration. (2019). Digital education for health professions: Methods for overarching evidence syntheses. *Journal of Medical Internet Research, 21*(2), e12913. https://doi.org/10.2196/12913

Carmack, H. J., & Harville, K. (2020). Including communication in the nursing classroom: A content analysis of communication competence and interprofessional communication in nursing fundamentals textbooks. *Health Communication, 35*(13), 1656–1665. https://doi.org/10.1080/10410 236.2019.1654179

Carrell, L. J., & Menzel, K. E. (2001) Variations in learning, motivation, and perceived immediacy between live and distance education classrooms. *Communication Education, 50*, 230–240. https://doi.org/10.1080/03634520109379250

Casey, D. M. (2008). A journey to legitimacy: The historical development of distance education through technology. *TechTrends, 52*(2), 45–51.

Cegala, D. J. (2003). Patient communication skills training: A review with implications for cancer patients. Patient Education and Counseling, 50(1), 91–94. https://doi.org/10.1016/S0738-3991(03)00087-9

Cegala, D. J., McClure, L., Marinelli, T. M., & Post, D. M. (2000). The effects of communication skills training on patients' participation during medical interviews. Patient Education and Counseling, 41(2), 209–222. https://doi.org/10.1016/S0738-3991(00)00093-8

Centers for Disease Control and Prevention. (2014). *Crisis and emergency risk communication.* Author.

Centers for Disease Control and Prevention. (2015). *Planning for an emergency: Strategies for identifying and engaging at-risk groups. A guidance document for emergency managers. Author.*

Centers for Disease Control and Prevention. (2021, April 6). A guide for community partners: Increasing COVID-19 vaccine uptake among members of racial and ethnic minority communities. US Department of Health and Human Services. https://www.cdc.gov/vaccines/covid-19/downloads/guide-community-partners.pdf

Centers for Disease Control and Prevention. (2021, November 1). *Training for healthcare professionals.* https://www.cdc.gov/coronavirus/2019-ncov/hcp/training.html

Champlin, S., Hoover, D. S., & Mackert, M. (2020). Health literacy in adult education centers: Exploring educator and staff needs. *Health Promotion Practice, 21*(2), 198–208. https://doi.org/10.1177/1524839918789690

Chatham-Carpenter, A. (2017). The future online: Instructional communication scholars taking the lead. *Communication Education, 66*(4), 492–494. https://doi.org/10.1080/03634523.2017.1349916

Chen, X., Hay, J. L., Waters, E. A., Kiviniemi, M. T., Biddle, C., Schofield, E., Li, Y., Kaphingst, K., & Orom, H. (2018). Health literacy and use and trust in health information. *Journal of Health Communication, 23*(8), 724–734. https://doi.org/10.1080/10810730.2018.1511658

Chervin, C., Clift, J., Woods, L., Krause, E., & Lee, K. (2012). Health literacy in adult education: A natural partnership for health equity. *Health Promotion Practice, 13*(6), 738–746. https://doi.org/10.1177/1524839912437367

Chesebro, J. L. (2003). Effects of teacher clarity and nonverbal immediacy on student learning, receiver apprehension, and affect. *Communication Education, 52*, 135–147. https://doi.org/10.1080/03634520302471

Cissna, K., Eadie, W., & Hickson, M. (2009). The development of applied communication research. In L. Frey & K. Cissna, (Eds.), *Routledge handbook of applied communication research* (pp. 3–25). Taylor & Francis.

Cohen, H. (1994). *The history of speech communication: The emergence of a discipline, 1914–1945.* Speech Communication Association.

Coley, R. J., Cradler, J., & Engel, P. K. (1996). Computers and classrooms: The status of technology in U.S. schools. *Policy Information Center.* https://eric.ed.gov/?id=ED412893

Common Core State Standards Initiative. (n.d.). College and career readiness anchor standards for speaking and listening. http://www.corestandards.org/ELA-Literacy/CCRA/SL/

County of Los Angeles. (2021). *Community health worker outreach initiative extended.* https://covid19.lacounty.gov/covid19-news/community-health-worker-outreach-initiative-extended/

Concannon, B. J., Esmail, S., & Roberts, M. R. (2020). Immersive virtual reality for the reduction of state anxiety in clinical interview exams: Prospective cohort study. *JMIR Serious Games, 8*(3), e18313. https://doi.org/10.2196/18313

Condon, S. (2020, March 21). Hilton uses VR to boost corporate employees' empathy for housekeeping staff. *ZDNet.com*. https://www.zdnet.com/article/hilton-uses-vr-to-boost-corporate-employees-empathy-for-house-keeping-staff/

Conley, N. A., & Ah Yun, K. (2017). A survey of instructional communication: 15 years of research in review. *Communication Education, 66*(4), 451–466. https://doi.org/10.1080/03634523.2017.1348611

Cooke-Jackson, A. F. (2013). Harnessing collective social media engagement in a health communication course. *Communication Teacher, 27*(3), 165–171. https://doi.org/10.1080/17404622.2013.782415

Coombs, T. W. (2009) Conceptualizing crisis communication. In R. L. Heath & H. D. O'Hair (Eds.), Handbook of Risk and Crisis Communication (pp. 100–120). https://doi.org/10.4324/9780203891629

Coombs, W. T. (2019). *Ongoing crisis communication: Planning, managing, and responding* (5th ed.). SAGE.

Corpuz, J. C. G. (2021). Adapting to the culture of "new normal": An emerging response to COVID-19. *Journal of Public Health, 43,* 344–345.

Covello, V. (1992). Risk communication: An emerging area of health communication research. In S. A. Deetz (Ed.), *Communication yearbook 15* (pp. 359–373). SAGE.

Cuban, L. (1986). *Teachers and machines: The classroom use of technology since 1920.* Teachers College Press.

Cuban, L. (1994). Computers meet classroom: Who wins? *The Education Digest, 57*(7), 50.

Cunningham, G. B. (2021). The under-representation of racial minorities in coaching and leadership positions in the United States. Routledge. https://doi.org/10.4324/9780367854287-1

Curtis, D. B., Beebe, S. A., & Brooks, D. M. (1986). A rationale for developing communication training programs. *Association for Communication Administration Bulletin, 55,* 55–58.

Cusanno, B. R., Ketheeswaran, N., & Bylund, C.L. (2021). Improving clinician and patient communication skills. In T. L. Thompson & N. Grant Harrington (Eds.), *The Routledge handbook of health communication* (3rd ed., pp. 194–212). Routledge.

Daft, R. L., & Lengel, R. H. (1986). Organizational information requirements, media richness and structural design. *Management Science, 32*(5), 554–571. https://doi.org/10.1287/mnsc.32.5.554

Dahl, K. D. (2013). External factors and athletic performance (no. 347) [Master's thesis, Liberty University]. *Senior Honors Theses.* https://digitalcommons. liberty.edu/honors/347

Dancer, D., & Kamvounias, P. (2005). Student involvement in assessment: A project designed to assess class participation fairly and reliably. *Assessment & Evaluation in Higher Education, 30*(4), 445–454. https://doi.org/10.1080/02602930500099235

Danells, D. P. (2000). Learning to be professional: Technical classroom discourse, practice, and professional identity construction. *Journal of Business and Technical Communication, 14*(1), 5–37. https://doi.org/10.1177 %2F105065190001400101

Dannels, D. P. (2001). Taking the pulse of communication across the curriculum: A view from the trenches. *Journal of the Association for Communication Administration, 30*(1), 50–70.

Darby, F., & Lang, J. M. (2019). *Small teaching online: Applying learning science in online classes.* Jossey-Bass.

Davis, D. L., Tran-Taylor, D., Imbert, E., Wong, J. O. & Chou, C. L. (2021). Start the way you want to finish: An intensive diversity, equity, inclusion orientation curriculum in undergraduate medical education. *Journal of Medical Education and Curricular Development, 8,* 1–6. https://doi. org/10.1177/23821205211000352

Deetz, S., & Mumby, D. K. (1990). Power, discourse, and the workplace: Reclaiming the critical tradition. *Annals of the International Communication Association, 13*(1), 18–47. https://doi.org/10.1080/23808985.1990.116787 43

Delia, J. G. (1987). Communication research: A history. In C. R. Berger & S. H. Chaffee (Eds.), *Handbook of communication science* (pp. 20–98). SAGE.

Deterding, S., Dixon, D., Khaled, R., & Nacke, L. (2011). From game design elements to gamefulness: Defining "gamification." *5th International Academic MindTrek Conference: Envisioning Future Media Environments. http://dx.doi. org/10.1145/2181037.2181040*

Dodd, G., & Gluckson, F. A. (1974). Industry reaction to computer science education. *Proceedings of 4th SIGCSE Technical Symposium on Computer Science Education*, 79–80. https://doi.org/10.1145/800183.810446

Donovan, E., Love, B., Mackert, M., Vangelisti, A., & Ring, D. (2017). Health communication: A future direction for instructional communication research. *Communication Education*, 66(4), 490–492. https://doi.org/10.1080/03634523.2017.1349917

Duggan, A., Bradshaw, Y. S., Carroll, S. E., Rattigan, S. H., & Altman, W. (2009). What can I learn from this interaction? A qualitative analysis of medical student self-reflection and learning in a standardized patient exercise about disability. *Journal of Health Communication*, 14(8), 797–811. https://doi.org/10.1080/10810730903295526

Dutta, M. (2008). *Communicating health: A culture-centered approach*. Polity Press.

Earle, R. S. (2002). The integration of instructional technology into public education: Promises and challenges. *Educational Technology*, 42(1), 5–13.

Edwards, A. A. H. (2021). From TED Talks to TikTok: Teaching digital communication to match student skills with employer desires. *Basic Communication Course Annual*, 33, 1–7.

Edwards, A., & Edwards, C. (2017). Human-machine communication in the classroom. In Handbook of Instructional Communication (pp. 184–194). Routledge.

Edwards, A., Edwards, C., Spence, P., Harris, C., & Gambino, A. (2016). Communicating with a robot in the classroom: Differences in perceptions of credibility and learning between "robot as teacher" and "teacher as robot." *Computers in Human Behavior*, 65, 627–634. https://doi.org/10.1016/j.chb.2016.06.005

Edwards, A., Sellnow, T., Sellnow, D., Iverson, J., Parrish, A., & Dritz, S. (2021). Communities of practice as purveyors of instructional communication during crises. *Communication Education*, 70(1), 49–70. https://doi.org/10.1080/03634523.2020.1802053

Edwards, C., Edwards, A., Spence, P. R., & Lin, X. (2018). I, teacher: Using artificial intelligence (AI) and social robots in communication and instruction. *Communication Education*, 67(4), 473–480. https://doi.org/10.1080/03634523.2018.1502459

Edwards, C., Edwards, A., Spence, P. R., & Westerman, D. (2016). Initial interaction expectations with robots: Testing the human-to-human interaction script. *Communication Studies, 67*, 227238. https://doi.org/10.1080/10510974.2015.1121899

Edwards, R., Watson, K. W., & Barker, L. L. (1988). Highly regarded doctoral programs in selected areas of communication: 1987. *Communication Education, 37*(4), 263.

Fassett. D. L. & Warren, J. T. (2007). Critical Communication Pedagogy. Thousand Oaks: Sage Publications.

Fassett, D. L. & Warren, J. T. (2010). The SAGE handbook of communication and instruction. SAGE.

Faucett, H. A., Lee, M. L., & Carter, S. (2017). "I should listen more": Real-time sensing and feedback on non-verbal communication in video telehealth. *Proceedings of the ACM on Human-Computer Interaction, 1*(44), 1–19. https://doi.org/10.1145/3134679

Feeley, T. H., Anker, A. E., Soriano, R., & Friedman, E. (2010). Using standardized patients to educate medical students about organ donation. *Communication Education, 59*(3), 249–262. https://doi.org/10.1080/03634521003628289

Feldman E. (2021). Virtual internships during the COVID 19 pandemic and beyond. *New Horizons in Adult Education and Human Resource Development, 33*(2), 46–51. https://doi.org/10.1002/nha3.20314

Fernandez, D. M., Larson, J. L., & Zikmund-Fisher, B. J. (2016). Associations between health literacy and preventive health behaviors among older adults: Findings from the health and retirement study. *BMC Public Health, 16*, 596.

Finn, J. D., Perrin, D. G., & Campion, L. E. (1960). The growth of instructional technology. *Teaching Aid News, 2*(15), 1–5. https://www.jstor.org/stable/44745116

Flanigan, A. E., & Babchuk, W. A. (2020). Digital distraction in the classroom: Exploring instructor perceptions and reactions. Teaching in Higher Education, 27(4), 352–370. https://doi.org/10.1080/13562517.2020.1724937

Foronda, C., Godsall, L., & Trybulski, J. A. (2013). Virtual clinical simulation: The state of the science. *Clinical Simulation in Nursing, 9*(8), e279–e286. https://doi.org/10.1016/j.ecns.2012.05.005

Frey, L. R., Pearce, W. B., Pollock, M. A., Artz, L., & Murphy, B. A. O. (1996). Looking for justice in all the wrong places: On a communication approach to social justice. *Communication Studies, 47*(1), 110–127. https://doi.org/10.1080/10510979609368467

Friedrich, G. W. (1987). Instructional communication research. *Journal of Thought, 22*(4), 4–10.

Freire, P. (1972). Education: domestication or liberation? Prospects, 2(2), 173–181. https://doi.org/10.1007/BF02195789

Frisby, B., Sellnow, D., Lane, R., Veil, S., & Sellnow, T. (2013). Instruction in crisis situations: Targeting learning preferences and self-efficacy. *Risk Management, 15*(4), 250–271.

Frisby, B., Veil, S., Sellnow, T. (2014). Instructional messages during health-related crises: Essential content for self-protection. *Health Communication, 29*(4), 347–354. http://doi.org/10.1080/10410236.2012.755604

Frisby, B. N., & Martin, M. M. (2010). Instructor–student and student–student rapport in the classroom. *Communication Education, 59*(2), 146–164. https://doi.org/10.1080/03634520903564362

Fritz, J. (1960). Educational technology: Boon or bane? *The School Review, 68*(3), 294–307. https://www.jstor.org/stable/1083927

Gaede, O. F., & Singletary, T. J. (1979). Computer applications in science education. The Illinois Series on Educational Application of Computers, No. 17e. Retrieved from https://eric.ed.gov/?id=ED183195

Gagné, R. M. (1954). Training devices and simulators: some research issues. *American Psychologist, 9*(3), 95–107. https://doi.org/10.1037/h0062991

Gallagher, V. J., Renner, M. M., & Glover-Rijkse, R. (2020) Public address as embodied experience: Using digital technologies to enhance communicative and civic engagement in the communication classroom. *Communication Education, 69*(3), 281–299. https://doi.org/10.1080/03634523.2020.1735642

Garland, M. E., & Violanti, M. T. (2019). Training time: Make the most of your experience. In S. Kelly (Ed.), *Computer-mediated communication for business: Theory to practice* (pp. 228–239). Cambridge Scholars Publishing.

Garrison, D. R., Anderson, T., & Archer, W. (1999). Critical inquiry in a text-based environment: Computer conferencing in higher education. *The Internet and Higher Education, 2*(2–3), 87–105. https://doi.org/10.1016/S1096-7516(00)00016-6

Garrison, D. R., Anderson, T., & Archer, W. (2010). The first decade of the community of inquiry framework: A retrospective. *The Internet and Higher Education, 13*(1–2), 5–9. https://doi.org/10.1016/j.iheduc.2009.10.003

Gaytan, J., Kelly, S., & Brown, W. (2021). Writing apprehension in the online classroom: The limits of instructor behaviors. *Business and Professional Communication Quarterly.* https://doi.org/10.1177%2F23294906211041088

Gentry, S. V., Gauthier, A., Ehrstrom, B. L. E., Wortley, D., Lilienthal, A., Car, L. T., Dauwels-Okutsu, S., Nikalaou, C. K., Zary, N., Campbell, J. & Car, J. (2019). Serious gaming and gamification education in health professions: Systematic review. *Journal of Medical Internet Research, 21*(3), e12994. https://doi.org/10.2196/12994

Giroux, H. A. (1988). Postmodernism and the discourse of educational criticism. Journal of education, 170(3), 5–30. https://doi.org/10.1177/002205748817000303

Goke, R., Berndt, M., & Rocker, K. (2021). Classroom culture when students are reluctant to learn online: Student dissent behaviors explained by their self-efficacy, control of learning, and intrinsic motivation. *Frontiers in Communication.* https://doi.org/10.3389/fcomm.2021.641956

Goodboy, A. K., & Myers, S. A. (2015). Revisiting instructor misbehaviors: A revised typology and development of a measure. *Communication Education, 64*(2), 133–153. https://doi.org/10.1080/03634523.2015.1041998

Goodstein, J. D., & Petrich, D. M. (2019). Hiring and retaining formerly incarcerated persons: An employer-based perspective. Journal of Offender Rehabilitation, 58(3), 155–177. https://doi.org/10.1080/10509674.2019.1582572

Gordon, N. P., & Hornbrook, M. C. (2018). Older adults' readiness to engage with eHealth patient education and self-care resources: A cross-sectional survey. BMC Health Services Research, 18(1), 1–13. https://doi.org/10.1186/s12913-018-2986-0

Gordon, R. M. (1980). Classrooms without chalkboards. *Educational Technology, 15*(4), 39–40. https://www.jstor.org/stable/44417962

Gorham, J. (1988). The relationship between verbal teacher immediacy behaviors and student learning. *Communication Education, 37*, 40–53. https://psycnet.apa.org/doi/10.1080/03634528809378702

Graetz, J. M. (1981). The origin of Spacewar. *Creative Computing, 7*(8). https://www.wheels.org/spacewar/creative/SpacewarOrigin.html

Graham, E. (2019). *Speaking and relating in the information age* (4th ed.). Fountainhead Press.

Graham, K. (2021). A culture of contribution—the hiring, training, and retaining of passionate employees: A Disney perspective [Senior thesis, Honors program]. Liberty University Digital Commons. https://digitalcommons.liberty.edu/cgi/viewcontent.cgi?article=2187&context=honors

Gredler, M. B. (1986). A taxonomy of computer simulations. *Educational Technology, 26*(4), 7–12. https://www.jstor.org/stable/44427369

Greene, K., Magsamen-Conrad, K., Venetis, M. K., Checton, M. G., Bagdasarov, Z., & Banerjee, S. C. (2012). Assessing health diagnosis disclosure decisions in relationships: Testing the disclosure decision-making model. Health Communication, 27(4), 356–368. https://doi.org/10.1080/10410236.2011.586988

Griffith, J. N., Rade, C. B., & Anazodo, K. S. (2019). Criminal history and employment: an interdisciplinary literature synthesis. Equality, Diversity and Inclusion: An International Journal. https://doi.org/10.1108/EDI-10-2018-0185

Harris, L. (2011). Secondary teachers' conceptions of student engagement: Engagement in learning or in schooling? *Teaching and Teacher Education, 27*(2), 376–386. https://doi.org/10.1016/j.tate.2010.09.006

Haun, J. N., Valerio, M. A., McCormack, L. A., Sørensen, K., & Paasche-Orlow, M. K. (2014). Health literacy measurement: An inventory and descriptive summary of 51 instruments. *Journal of Health Communication, 19*(2), 302–333. https://doi.org/10.1080/10810730.2014.936571

Helitzer, D., Hollis, C., Sanders, M., & Roybal, S. (2012). Addressing the "other" health literacy competencies—knowledge, dispositions, and oral/aural communication: Development of TALKDOC, an intervention assessment tool. Journal of Health Communication, 17(sup3), 160–175. https://doi.org/10.1080/10810730.2012.712613

Helwig, J. F., & Friend, J. (1985). Teaching where there are no schools. *Development Communication Report*, (49), 5, 12. https://pubmed.ncbi.nlm.nih.gov/12341672/

Hess, J. A., Taft, B., Bodary, S. R., Beebe, S. A., & Valenzano, J. M. (2015). *Forum: The common core. Communication Education*, 64(2), 241–260. https://doi.org/10.1080/03634523.2015.1014387

Hew, K. F. (2014). Past technologies, practice and applications: A discussion on how the major developments in instructional technology in the 20th century affect the following qualities—access, efficiency, effectiveness, and humaneness. Association for Educational Communications and Technology Annual Meeting. https://www.learntechlib.org/p/76902/

Hickson, M., & Stacks, D. W. (1993). Active prolific scholars in communication studies: Analysis of research productivity, ii. *Communication Education*, 42(3), 224.

Hickson, M., Turner, J., & Bodon, J. (2003). Research productivity in communication: An analysis, 1996–2001. *Communication Research Reports*, 20(4), 308–319.

Hill, S., & Griswold, P. (2013). Potential for collaborative writing in professional communication and health studies through service-learning. *Business Communication Quarterly*, 76(1), 54–71. https://doi.org/10.1177/1080569912470711

Hinck, E. A., Hinck, S. S., & Howell, A. (2019). Toward achieving the unthinkable: Transforming conversations about criminalized others through service-learning in correctional facilities. *Review of Communication*, 19(1), 19–37. https://doi.org/10.1080/15358593.2018.1554822

Ho, E. Y., Bylund, C. L., Rosenbaum, M. E., & Herwaldt, L. A. (2009). Teaching health communication through found poems created from patients' stories. *Communication Teacher*, 23(2), 93–98. https://doi.org/10.1080/17404620902779512

Hoelscher, K. (1985). The making of MECC. *Computers in the Schools: Interdisciplinary Journal of Practice, Theory, and Applied Research*, 2(1), 61–64. https://doi.org/10.1300/J025v02n01_08

Hollan, J., & Stornetta, S. (1992, June). Beyond being there. In R. Grinter, T. Rodden, P. Akoi (Eds.) *Proceedings of the SIGCHI conference on Human factors in computing systems* (pp. 119–125). https://dl.acm.org/doi/proceedings/10.1145/1124772

Hopkinson, R. G. (1949). Studies of lighting and vision in schools. *Lighting Research & Technology, 14*(8). 244–268. https://doi.org/10.1177/147715354901400802

Horton, S. V., Lovitt, T. C., & White, O. R. (1992). Teaching mathematics to adolescents classified as educable mentally handicapped: Using calculators to remove the computational onus. *Remedial and Special Education, 13*(3), 36–61. https://doi.org/10.1177/074193259201300304

Hosek, A. M., Munz, S., Bistodeau, K. C., Jama, Z., Frisbie, A., & Ivancic, S. (2017). Basic communication course students' perceptions of the purpose and their role in the peer feedback process. *Basic Communication Course Annual, 29*, 29–52. http://ecommons.udayton.edu/bcca/vol29/iss1/5

Hostetter, M., & Klein, S. (2020, September 30). Transforming care: Learning from pandemic responses across Indian country. The Common Wealth Fund. https://www.commonwealthfund.org/publications/2020/sep/learning-pandemic-responses-across-indian-country

Houser, M. L. & Hosek, A. (2018). Handbook of instructional communication: Rhetorical and relational perspectives (2nd ed.). Routledge.

Houts, P. S., Doak, C. C., Doak, L. G., & Loscalzo, M. J. (2006). The role of pictures in improving health communication: A review of research on attention, comprehension, recall, and adherence. *Patient Education and Counseling, 61*(2), 173–190. https://doi.org/10.1016/j.pec.2005.05.004

Hsu, L-L., Chang, W-H., & Hsieh, S-I. (2015). The effects of scenario-based simulation course training on nurses' communication competence and self-efficacy: A randomized controlled trial. *Journal of Professional Nursing, 31*(1), 37–49. https://doi.org/10.1016/j.profnurs.2014.05.007

Hyder, M. A., & Razzak, J. (2020). Telemedicine in the United States: An introduction for students and residents. *Journal of Medical Internet Research, 22*(11), e20839. https://doi.org/10.2196/20839

Ickes, M. J., & Cottrell, R. (2010). Health literacy in college students. *Journal of American College Health, 58*(5), 491–498. https://doi.org/10.1080/07448481003599104

Indeed Editorial Team. (2021, July). 8 top personality tests used in psychology (and by employers). *Indeed.* https://www.indeed.com/career-advice/career-development/types-of-personality-test

International Federation of Red Cross and Red Crescent Societies. (2020). *Come heat or high water.* https://media.ifrc.org/ifrc/world-disaster-report-2020

Interprofessional Education Collaborative. (2011). Core competencies for inter-professional collaborative practice: Report of an expert panel. Author.

Ismail, K. (2022, June 22). Assessing your team's digital workplace skills. CMS Wire. https://www.cmswire.com/digital-workplace/assessing-your-teams-digital-workplace-skills/

Iverson, J., & McPhee, R. (2008). Communicating knowing through communities of practice: Exploring internal communicative processes and differences among CoPs. *Journal of Applied Communication Research, 36*(2), 176–199.

Izadi, E. (2015, June 6). Haunting chalkboard drawings, frozen in time for 100 years, discovered in Oklahoma school. Washington Post. Retrieved from https://www.washingtonpost.com/news/morning-mix/wp/2015/06/06/eerie-chalkboard-drawings-frozen-in-time-for-100-years-discovered-in-oklahoma-school/

Jaiswal J. (2019). Whose responsibility is it to dismantle medical mistrust? Future directions for researchers and health care providers. *Behavioral Medicine, 45*(2), 188–196. https://doi.org/10.1080/08964289.2019.1630357

Johansson, B., Lane, D. R., Sellnow, D. D., & Sellnow, T. L. (2021). No heat, no electricity, no water, oh no!: an IDEA model experiment in instructional risk communication. Journal of Risk Research, 24(12), 1576–1588. https://doi.org/10.1080/13669877.2021.1894468

Johnson, S. R., Wojnar, P. J., Price, W. J., Foley, T. J., Moon, J. R., Esposito, E. N., & Cromartie, F. J. (2011). A coach's responsibility: Learning how to prepare athletes for peak performance. *Sport Journal, 14*(1), 1–3.

Jones, L. H. & Powrie, P. J. (1971). Instruction by correspondence courses. *Industrial and Commercial Training, 3*(10), 463–465. https://doi.org/10.1108/eb003165

Jorm, A. F. (2015). Why we need the concept of "mental health literacy." *Health Communication, 30*(12), 1166–1168. https://doi.org/10.1080/10410236.2015.1037423

Kaltman, S., Hurtado de Mendoza, A., Gonzales, F. A., Serrano, A., & Guarnaccia, P. J. (2011). Contextualizing the trauma experience of women immigrants from Central America, South America, and Mexico. *Journal of Traumatic Stress, 24*(6), 635–642. https://doi.org/10.1002/jts.20698

Kansky, B. (1987). Technology policy survey: A study of state policies supporting the use of calculators and computers in the study of precollege mathematics. ERIC. https://files.eric.ed.gov/fulltext/ED289728.pdf

Kaufmann, R., Sellnow, D. D., & Frisby, B. N. (2016). The development and validation of the online learning climate scale (OLCS). *Communication Education, 65*(3), 307–321. https://doi.org/10.1080/03634523.2015.1101778

Kaufmann, R. & Vallade, J. I. (2020). Exploring connections in the online learning environment: Student perceptions of rapport, climate, and loneliness. Interactive Learning Environments. https://doi.org/10.1080/10494820.2020.1749670

Keegan, D. J. (1980). On the nature of distance education. *ZIFF Papiere, 33*, 1–48.

Keller, J. M. (1983). Motivational design of instruction. In C. M. Reigeluth (Ed.), Instructional design theories and models: An overview of their current status. Erlbaum.

Kelly, R. (2016). 9 ed tech trends to watch in 2016. *Campus Technology*. https://campustechnology.com/Articles/2016/01/13/9-Ed-Tech-Trends-to-Watch-in-2016.aspx?Page=1

Kelly, S., & Westerman, D. K. (2016). New technologies and distributed learning systems. In P. L. Witt (Ed.), *Handbooks of communication science: Communication and learning* (Vol. 16, pp. 455–480). DeGruyter Mouton.

Kemp, S. (2021). Digital 2021: Global overview report. https://datareportal.com/reports/digital-2021-global-overview-report

Kentnor, H. E. (2015). Distance education and the evolution of online learning in the United States; curriculum and teaching dialogue. *Information Age Publishing, Charlotte, 17*, 21–34.

Kerr, A. M., Shaub, T., Casapulla, S., Smith, C., & Manzi, J. (2020). Addressing social justice and inclusion in the classroom: Using the principles of narrative medicine to discuss identity negotiation and passing. *Communication Teacher, 34*(2), 97–102. https://doi.org/10.1080/17404622.2019.1625939

Kerr, O. (1978). How to invite technology into the classroom without putting poetry in the corner. *The English Journal, 67*(4), 74–76. https://www.jstor.org/stable/815633

Kierkegaard, P. (2011). Electronic health record: Wiring Europe's healthcare. *Computer Law & Security Review, 27*(5), 503–515. https://doi.org/10.1016/j.clsr.2011.07.013

Killian, L., & Coletti, M. (2017). The role of universal health literacy precautions in minimizing "medspeak" and promoting shared decision making. *AMA Journal of Ethics, 19*(3), 296–303. https://doi.org/10.1001/journalofethics.2017.19.3.pfor1-1703

Kim, J., Merrill Jr, K., Xu, K., & Sellnow, D. D. (2021). I like my relational machine teacher: An AI instructor's communication styles and social presence in online education. *International Journal of Human–Computer Interaction, 37*(18), 1760–1770. https://doi.org/10.1080/10447318.2021.1908671

King, A. (1993). From sage on the stage to guide on the side. College Teaching, 41(1), 30–35. https://doi.org/10.1080/87567555.1993.9926781

Kirby, E. L. (2016). Encountering my privilege (and others' oppression). *Communication Teacher, 30*(3), 172–178. https://doi.org/10.1080/17404622.2016.1192659

Knisel, E., Rupprich, H., Wunram, A., Bremer, M., & Desaive, C. (2020). Promotion of elementary school students' health literacy. *International Journal of Environmental Research and Public Health, 17*(24), 9560. https://doi.org/10.3390/ijerph17249560

Korzenny, F. (1978). A theory of electronic propinquity: Mediated communication in organizations. *Communication Research, 5*(1), 3–24. https://doi.org/10.1177%2F009365027800500101

Kraiger, K. (2014). Looking back and looking forward: Trends in training and development research. *Human Resource Development Quarterly, 25*(4), 401–408. https://doi.org/10.1002/hrdq.21203

Krasker, A. (1943). A critical analysis of the use of educational motion pictures by two methods. *Science Education, 27*(1), 19–22. https://doi.org/10.1002/sce.3730270106

Krathwohl, D. R. (2002). A revision of Bloom's taxonomy: An overview. *Theory into Practice, 41*, 212–218.

Krause, D. A. (2000). "Among the greatest benefactors of mankind": What the success of the chalkboard tells us about the future of computers in the classroom. The Journal of Midwest Modern Language Association: Computers and the Future of the Humanities, 33(2), 6–16. Retrieved from http://www.jstor.org/stable/1315198

Kripalani, S., Jacobson, K. L., Brown, S., Manning, K., Rask, K. J., & Jacobson, T. A. (2006). Development and implementation of a health literacy training program for medical residents. Medical Education Online, 11(1), 4612. https://doi.org/10.3402/meo.v11i.4612

Kromka, S. M., & Goodboy, A. K. (2019). Classroom storytelling: Using instructor narratives to increase student recall, affect, and attention. Communication Education, 68(1), 20–43. https://doi.org/10.1080/03634523.2018.1529330

Kron, F. W., Fetters, M. D., Scerbo, M. W., White, C. B. Lypson, M. L., Padilla, M. A., Gilva-McConvey, G. A., Belfore, L. A., II, Westt, T., Wallace, A. M., Guetterman, T. C., Schleicher, L. S., Kennedy, R. A., Mangrulkar, R. S., Cleary, J. F., Marcella, S. C., & Becker, D. M. (2017). Using a computer simulation for teaching communication skills: A blinded multisite mixed methods randomized controlled trial. Patient Education and Counseling, 100(4), 748–759. https://doi.org/10.1016/j.pec.2016.10.024

Kuznekoff, J. H., & Titsworth, S. (2013). The impact of mobile phone usage on student learning. Communication Education, 62, 233–252. https://doi.org/10.1080/03634523.2013.767917

Kvareceus, W. C. (1961). Future classroom: An educational automat? Educational Leadership, 18, 288–292.

Kwitonda, J. C., & Singhal, A. (2018). Teaching and learning about positive deviance: Boosting metacognition to grasp global communication theory and practice. Journal of Intercultural Communication Research, 47(5), 382–391.

Kyaw, B. M., Saxena, N., Posadzki, P., Vseteckova, J., Nikolaou, C. K., George, P. P., Divakar, U., Masiello, I., Kononowicz, A. A., Zary, N., & Car, L. T. (2019). Virtual reality for health professions education: Systematic review and meta-analysis by the digital health education collaboration. Journal of Medical Internet Research, 21(1), e12959. https://doi.org/10.2196/12959

Lacka, E., & Wong, T. C. (2021) Examining the impact of digital technologies on students' higher education outcomes: The case of the virtual learning environment and social media. Studies in Higher Education, 46(8), 1621–1634. https://doi.org/10.1080/03075079.2019.1698533

Landau, J., & Johnson Thorton, D. (2015). Teaching rhetoric of health and medicine to undergraduates: Citizens, interdisciplinarity, and affect. *Communication Quarterly, 63*(5), 527–532. http://doi.org/10.1080/01463373.2015.1103602

Lanzieri, N., McAplin, E., Shilane, D., & Samelson, H. (2021). Virtual reality: An immersive tool for social work students to interact with community environments. *Clinical Social Work Journal, 49,* 207–219. https://doi.org/10.1007/s10615-021-00803-1

LeBlanc Farris, K., Houser, M. L., Hosek, A. M. (2018). Historical roots and trajectories of instructional communication. In M. L. Houser & A. M. Hosek (Eds.), *Handbook of instructional communication: Rhetorical and relational perspectives* (pp. 1–20). Taylor & Francis.

Lee, J., Kim, H., Kim, K. H., Jung, D., Jowsey, T., & Webster, C. (2020). Effective virtual patient simulators for medical communication training: A systematic review. *Medical Education, 54,* 786–795. https://doi.org/10.1111/medu.14152

Lesser, G. S. (1974). *Children and television: Lessons from Sesame Street.* Random House.

Lie, D., Carter-Pokras, O., Braun, B., & Coleman, C. (2012). What do health literacy and cultural competence have in common? Calling for a collaborative health professional pedagogy. Journal of Health Communication, 17(sup3), 13–22. https://doi.org/10.1080/10810730.2012.712625

Lillyman, S., & Farquharson, N. (2013). Self-care management education models in primary care. British Journal of Community Nursing, 18(11), 556–560. https://doi.org/10.12968/bjcn.2013.18.11.556

Limperos, A. M., Buckner, M. M., Kaufmann, R., & Frisby, B. N. (2015). Online teaching and technological affordances: An experimental investigation into the impact of modality and clarity on perceived and actual learning. *Computers & Education, 83,* 1–9. https://doi.org/10.1016/j.compedu.2014.12.015

Littlefield, R. (2015). Introduction to the dialectical tensions of risk and crisis communication. In R. Littlefield & T. Sellnow (Eds.), *Risk and crisis communication: Navigating the tensions between organizations and the public* (pp. 1–12). Lexington Books.

Littlefield, R., Beauchamp, K., Lane, D., Sellnow, D., Sellnow, T., Venette, S., & Wilson, B. (2014). Instructional crisis communication: Connecting ethnicity and sex in the assessment of receiver-oriented message effectiveness. *Journal of Management Strategy*, 5(3), 16–23.

Littlefield, R., & Sellnow, T. (2015). *Risk and crisis communication: Navigating the tensions between organizations and the public.* Lexington Books.

Liu, W. (2021). Does teacher immediacy affect students? A systematic review of the association between teacher verbal and non-verbal immediacy and student motivation. *Frontiers in Psychology: Educational Psychology.* https://doi.org/10.3389/fpsyg.2021.713978

Lloyd, A. S. (1972). Freire, conscientization, and adult education. Adult education, 23(1), 3–20. https://doi.org/10.1177/074171367202300101

Lukes, S. (1974) Power: A radical view, London: Macmillan (reprinted 2004, Basingstoke: Palgrave Macmillan)

Mackert, M., Champlin, S., Su, Z., & Guadagno, M. (2015). The many health literacies: Advancing research or fragmentation? *Health Communication*, 30(12), 1161–1165. https://doi.org/10.1080/10410236.2015.1037422

Mackert, M., Koh, H., Mabry, A., Champlin, S., & Beal, A. (2017). Domestic and international college students: Health insurance information seeking and use. *Journal of International Students*, 7(3), 542–561. https://doi.org/10.32674/jis.v7i3.287

Mackert, M., & Poag, M. (2011). Adult basic education and health literacy: Program efforts and perceived student needs. *Community Literacy Journal*, 5(2), 67–73. https://doi.org/10.25148/ clj.5.2.009413

Manning, J., Stern, D. M., & Johnson, R. (2018). Sexual and gender identity in the classroom. In M. L. Houser & A. M. Hosek (Eds.), *Handbook of instructional communication: Rhetorical and relational perspectives* (2nd ed. pp. 170–182). Routledge.

Marand, A. D., & Noe, R. A. (2018). Facilitating the development of expertise. In K. Brown (Ed.), *The Cambridge handbook of workplace training and employee development* (pp. 38–74). Cambridge University Press.

Martin, S., Carrington, N., & Muncie, N. (2017). Promoting user advocacy to shift technical communication identity and value. *Technical Communication*, 64(4), 328–344. https://www.ingentaconnect.com/content/stc/tc/2017/00000064/00000004/art00006

Mathis, R. S. (2020). Communicating influence: Positioning the trainer as an organizational leader. *Journal of Workplace Learning, 32*(8), 549–568. https://doi.org/10.1108/JWL-05-2020-0096.

Matusitz, J., & Breen, G-M. (2007). Telemedicine: Its effects on health communication. *Health Communication, 21*(1), 73–83. https://doi.org/10.1080/10410230701283439

Mayer, M. (2021). Navigating troubled waters: Applying the IDEA model to the Flint water crisis. *Proceedings of the International Crisis and Risk Communication Conference, 4,* 49–52. Nicholson https://doi.org/10.30658/icrcc.2021.12

Mazer, J. P. (2018). Instructor message variables. In M. L. Houser & A. M. Hosek (Eds.), *Handbook of instructional communication: Rhetorical and relational perspectives* (pp. 22–37). Taylor & Francis.

Mazer, J. P., McKenna-Buchanan, T. P., Quinlan, M. M., & Titsworth, S. (2014). The dark side of emotion in the classroom: Emotional processes as mediators of teacher communication behaviors and student negative emotions. *Communication Education, 63*(3), 149–168. https://doi.org/10.1080/03634523.2014.904047

McArthur, J. A. (2021). From classroom to Zoom room: Exploring instructor modifications of visual nonverbal behaviors in synchronous online classrooms. *Communication Teacher, 36*(3), 204–215. https://doi.org/10.1080/17404622.2021.1981959

McCarthy, D. M., Davis, T. C., King, J. P., Mullen, R. J., Bailey, S. C., Serper, M., Jacobson, K. L., Parker, R. M., & Wolf, M. S. (2013). Take-Wait-Stop: A patient-centered strategy for writing PRN medication instructions. Journal of Health Communication, 18(sup1), 40–48. https://doi.org/10.1080/10810730.2013.825675

McComas, K. (2006). Defining moments in risk communication research: 1996–2005. *Journal of Health Communication, 11,* 75–91.

McConnochie, K. M. (2019). Webside manner: A key to high-quality primary care telemedicine for all. *Telemedicine and E-Health, 25*(11), 1007–1011. http://doi.org/10.1089/tmj.2018.0274

McCroskey, J., & McCroskey, L. (2006). Instructional communication: The historical perspective. In T. Mottet, V. Richmond, & J. McCroskey (Eds.), *Handbook of instructional communication* (pp. 33–47). Pearson.

McCroskey, J. C., & Richmond, V. P. (1992). An instructional communication program for in-service teachers. *Communication Education, 41*(2), 215.

McCroskey, J. C., & Teven, J. J. (1999). Goodwill: A reexamination of the construct and its measurement. Communications Monographs, 66(1), 90–103. https://doi.org/10.1080/03637759909376464

McKeever, B. W. (2014). The status of health communication: Education and employment outlook for a growing field. *Journal of Health Communication, 19*(12), 1408–1423. https://doi.org/10.1080/10810730.2014.904024

Mikkelson, S., & Schweitzer, K. (2019). Hiring the formerly incarcerated: The mediating role of morality. Criminal Justice and Behavior, 46(12), 1757–1774. https://doi.org/10.1177/0093854819858373

Miller, K. E., & Wieland, M. (2019). Teaching metatheory through research application and design. *Communication Teacher, 33*(1), 21–25. https://doi.org/10.1080/17404622.2018.1530797

Millette, D. M., & Gorham, J. (2002). Teacher behavior and student motivation. In J. L. Chesebro & J. C. McCroskey (Eds.), *Communication for teachers* (pp. 141–154). Allyn & Bacon.

Milligin, S. (2020, June 2). Pandemic, recession, unrest: 2020 and the confluence of crises. *U.S. News & World Report.* https://www.usnews.com/news/national-news/articles/2020-06-02/pandemic-recession-unrest-2020-and-the-confluence-of-crises

Mirnig, N., Stollnberger, G., Miksch, M., Stadler, S., Giuliani, M., & Tscheligi, M. (2017). To err is robot: How humans assess and act toward an erroneous social robot. *Frontiers in Robotics and AI, 4,* 227. https://doi.org/10.3389/frobt.2017.00021

Morreale, S., Backlund, P., Hay, E., & Moore, M. (2011). Assessment of oral communication: A major review of the historical development and trends in the movement from 1975–2009. *Communication Education, 60*(2), 255–278.

Morreale, S., Backlund, P., & Sparks, L. (2014). Communication education and instructional communication: Genesis and evolution as fields of inquiry. *Communication Education, 63,* 344–354. https://doi-org/10.1080/03634523.2014.944926

Morreale, S. P., Osborn, M. M., & Pearson, J. C. (2000). Why communication is important: A rationale for the centrality of the study of communication. *Journal of the Association for Communication Administration, 29,* 1–25.

Morreale, S. P., & Pearson, J. C. (2008). Why communication education is important: The centrality of the discipline in the 21st century. *Communication Education, 57*(2), 224–240. https://doi.org/10.1080/03634520701861713

Morrow, D. G., Weiner, M., Young, J., Steinley, D., Deer, M., & Murray, M. D. (2005). Improving medication knowledge among older adults with heart failure: A patient-centered approach to instruction design. The *Gerontologist, 45*(4), 545–552. https://doi.org/10.1093/geront/45.4.545

Morton, T., & Duck, J. (2001). Communication and health beliefs. *Communication Research, 28*(5), 602–626.

Mostyn, A., Jenkinson, C. M., McCormick, D., Meade, O., & Lymn, J. S. (2013). An exploration of student experiences of using biology podcasts in nursing training. *BMC Medical Education, 13*, 12. https://doi.org/10.1186/1472-6920-13-12

Mottet, T. P., & Beebe, S. A. (2006). Foundations of instructional communication. In T. P. Mottet, V. P. Richmond, & J. C. McCroskey (Eds.), *Handbook of instructional communication* (pp. 3–32). Pearson.

Mottet, T. P., Frymier, A. B., & Beebe, S. A. (2006). Theorizing about instructional communication. In T. P. Mottet, V. P. Richmond, & J. C. McCroskey (Eds.), *Handbook of instructional communication* (pp. 255–282). Pearson.

Myers, S. A. (2010). Instructional communication: The emergence of a field. In D. Fassett & J. Warren (Eds.), *The SAGE handbook of communication and instruction* (pp. 149–160). SAGE.

Myers, S. A., Tindage, M. F., & Atkinson, J. (2016). The evolution of instructional communication research. In Paul L. Witt (Ed.), *Communication and learning* (pp. 13–42). De Gruyter Mouton.

Nadler, R. (2020). Understanding "Zoom fatigue": Theorizing spatial dynamics as third skins in computer-mediated communication. *Computers and Composition, 58*, 1–17. https://doi.org/10.1016/j.compcom.2020.102613

Nash, J. D. (1977). Frontiers in the communication curriculum: Health communication. *Association for Communication Administration Bulletin, 21*(1), 69–73.

National Research Council. (1989). *Improving risk communication.* National Academies Press.

Neuberger, L. (2017). Teaching health campaigns by doing health campaigns. *Communication Teacher, 31*(3), 143–148. https://doi.org/10.1080/17404622.2017.1314520

Neuhauser, L., & Kreps, G. L. (2008). Online cancer communication: Meeting the literacy, cultural and linguistic needs of diverse audiences. Patient Education and Counseling, 71(3), 365–377. https://doi.org/10.1016/j.pec.2008.02.015

Ng, W. (2012). Can we teach digital natives digital literacy? *Computers & Education, 59*(3), 1065–1078. https://doi.org/10.1016/j.compedu.2012.04.016

Niculescu, A., van Dijk, B., Nijholt, A., Li, H., & See, S. L. (2013). Making social robots more attractive: The effects of voice pitch, humor and empathy. International Journal of *Social Robotics, 5*, 171–191. https://doi.org/10.1007/s12369-012-0171-x

Nielsen-Bohlman, L., Panzer, A. M., & Kindig, D. A. (Eds.). (2004). *Health literacy: A prescription to end confusion.* National Academies Press. https://doi.org/10.17226/10883

Nielsen, J. (2006, November 19). Digital divide: The 3 stages. *Nielsen Norman Group.* https://www.nngroup.com/articles/digital-divide-the-three-stages/

Noland, C. M. (2014). Baccalaureate nursing students' accounts of medical mistakes occurring in the clinical setting: Implications for curricula. *Journal of Nursing Education, 53*(3), S34–37. https://doi.org/10.3928/01484834-20140211-04

Noland, C. M., & Carmack, H. J. (2015). "You never forget your first mistake": Nursing socialization, memorable messages, and communication about medical errors. *Health Communication, 30*(12), 1234–1244. https://doi.org/10.1080/10410236.2014.930397

Noordman, J., Verhaak, P., van Beljouw, I., & van Dulmen, S. (2010). Consulting room computers and their effect on general practitioner-patient communication. *Family Practice, 27*(6), 644–651. https://doi.org/10.1093/fampra/cmq058

Nowell, S. D. (2014). Using disruptive technologies to make digital connections: Stories of media use and digital literacy in secondary classrooms. *Educational Media International, 51*(2), 109–123. https://doi.org/10.1080/09523987.2014.924661

Nussbaum, J., & Friedrich, G. (2005). Instructional/developmental communication: Current theory, research, and future trends. *Journal of Communication, 55*(3), 578–593. https://doi.org/10.1111/j.1460-2466.2005.tb02686.x

O'Hair (eds.) *Handbook of Risk and Crisis Communication* (pp. 99–118). New York: Routledge.

Oklahoma State Department of Education. (2021, February 16). *Educators embrace trauma-informed instruction in fourth statewide summit.* https://content.govdelivery.com/accounts/OKSDE/bulletins/2c1df94

Ombres, R., Montemorano, L., & Becker, D. (2017). Death notification: Someone needs to call the family. *Journal of Palliative Medicine, 20*(6), 672–675. https://dx.doi.org/10.1089/jpm.2016.0481

Onuka, A. O., & Ajayi, K. O. (2012). Effect of manpower development on workers' job performance. In. T. Stoilov (Ed.), *Time management* (pp. 77–88). InTech.

Paasche-Orlow, M. K., & Wolf, M. S. (2007). The causal pathways linking health literacy to health outcomes. *American Journal of Health Behavior, 31*(1), S19–S26. https://doi.org/10.5555/ajhb.2007.31.supp.S19

Pagano, M. P. (2016). Learning about dying and living: An applied approach to end-of-life communication. *Health Communication, 31*(8), 1019–1028. https://doi.org/10.1080/10410236.2015.1034337

Paige, R. M., & Martin, J. N. (1996). Ethics in intercultural training. In D. Landis, & R. S. Bhagat (Eds.), *Handbook of intercultural training* (2nd ed., pp. 35–60). SAGE.

Pain, P. (2021). Teaching gender and race online. In S. Kelly (Ed.), *Online instructional communication* (pp. 44–58). Cambridge Scholars Publishing.

Palumbo, M. V., Sandoval, M., Hart, V., & Drill, C. (2016). Teaching electronic health record communication skills. *CIN: Computers, Informatics, Nursing, 34*(6), 254–258. https://doi.org/10.1097/CIN.0000000000000238

Panke. S. (2017, July 7). Crossover learning. *Association for the Advancement of Computing in Education.* https://www.aace.org/review/crossover-learning/

Patil, U., Kostareva, U., Hadley, M., Manganello, J. A., Okan, O., Dadaczynski, K., Massey, P. M., Agner, J., & Sentell, T. (2021). Health literacy, digital health literacy, and COVID-19 pandemic attitudes and behaviors in U.S. college students: Implications for interventions. *International Journal of Environmental Research and Public Health, 18*(63301). https://doi.org/10.5555/ajhb.2007.31.supp.S19

Perlberg, A., & Resh, M. (1967). Evaluation of the effectiveness of the overhead projector in teaching descriptive geometry and hydrology. The Journal of Education Research, 61(1), 14–18. https://doi.org/10.1080/00220671.1 967.10883567

Petronio, S. (2002). Boundaries of privacy: Dialectics of disclosure. Suny Press.

Plein, C., & Cassels, A. (2021). The military families learning network: A model for extension-based virtual learning communities. *Journal of Extension, 57(6)*, 22.

Plimpton, G. A. (1916). The hornbook and its use in America. *Proceedings of the American Antiquarian Society, 26*, 264–272.

Pomerantz, H. (1997, December). The role of calculators in math education. Urban Systematic Initiative/Comprehensive Partnership for Mathematics and Science Achievement. Dallas.

Popova, L. (2012). The extended parallel process model: Illuminating the gaps in research. *Health Education & Behavior, 39(4)*, 455–473.

Post, D. M., Cegala, D. J., & Miser, W. F. (2002). The other half of the whole: Teaching patients to communicate with physicians. Family Medicine, 34(5), 344–352. https://www.ncbi.nlm.nih.gov/pubmed/12038716

Powell, R. G., & Harville, B. (1990). The effects of teacher immediacy and clarity on instructional outcomes: An intercultural assessment. Communication Education, 39, 369–379. https://doi.org/10.1080/ 03634529009378816

Prakash S. S., Muthuraman, N., & Anand, R. (2017). Short-duration podcasts as a supplementary learning tool: Perceptions of medical students and impact on assessment performance. *BMC Medical Education, 17*, 167. https://doi.org/10.1186/s12909-017-1001-5

Preiss, R. W., & Wheeless, L. R. (2014). Perspectives on instructional communication's historical path to the future. *Communication Education, 63(4)*, 308–328. http://doi.org/10.1080/03634523.2014.910605

Prensky, M. (2001). Digital natives, digital immigrants. *On The Horizon, 9(5)*. https://doi.org/10.1108/10748120110424816

Price, S., Carmack, H. J., & Kuang, K. (2021). Contradictions and predicaments in instructors' boundary negotiation of students' health disclosures. *Health Communication, 36(7)*, 795–803. *https://doi.org/10.1080/1041023 6.2020.1712525*

Pula, F. J. (1968). *Application and operation of audiovisual equipment in education*. Wiley.

Quote Investigator. (2012, April 21). Students today can't prepare bark to calculate their problems. https://quoteinvestigator.com/2012/04/21/students-bark/

Rababah, J. A., Al-Hammouri, M. M., Drew, B. L., & Aldalaykeh, M. (2019). Health literacy: Exploring disparities among college students. *BMC Public Health, 19*(1), 1401. https://doi.org/10.1186/s12889-019-7781-2

Ramamoorthy. (1986). Computer science and engineering education. *IEEE Transactions on Computers, 25*(12), 1200–1206. https://doi.org/10.1109/TC.1976.1674588

Randall, J. (2018, May 21). Why communication manors are winning in business. Study Breaks. https://studybreaks.com/college/communication-majors/

Ratzan, S. C., & Parker, R. M. (2000). Introduction. In C. R. Selden, M. Zorn, S. C. Ratzan, & R. M. Parker (Eds.), National Library of Medicine Current Bibliographies in Medicine: Health Literacy. National Institutes of Health, US Dept of HHS. NLM Pub. No. CBM 2000-1

Rey, R. T., & Johnson, Z. D. (2021). "Detrimental to the team dynamic": Exploring college student-athlete dissent. *Communication & Sport*. https://doi.org/10.1177/21674795211001938

Reynolds, B., & Seeger, M. (2005). Crisis and emergency risk communication as an integrative model. *Journal of Health Communication, 10*, 43–55.

Reynolds, E. J. (1975). The development of a computer controlled super 8 motion picture projector. https://files.eric.ed.gov/fulltext/ED115213.pdf

Rice-Bailey, T. (2016). The role and value of technical communicators: Technical communicators and subject matter experts weigh in. Technical Communication Quarterly, 25(4), 230–243. http://doi.org/10.1080/10572252.2016.1221140

Richardson, J. C., Maeda, Y., Lv, J., & Caskurlu, S. (2017). Social presence in relation to students' satisfaction and learning in the online environment: A meta-analysis. *Computers in Human Behavior, 71*, 402–417. https://doi.org/10.1016/j.chb.2017.02.001

Ricketts, M., Shanteau, J., McSpadden, B., & Fernandez-Medina, K. M. (2010). Using stories to battle unintentional injuries: Narratives in safety and health communication. Social Science & Medicine, 70(9), 1441–1449. https://doi.org/10.1016/j.socscimed.2009.12.036

Risser, H. S. (2011). What are we afraid of? Arguments against teaching mathematics with technology in the professional publications of organisations for US mathematicians. International Journal for Technology in Mathematics Education, 18(2), 91–101. https://www.learntechlib.org/p/109511/

Robinson, R. (2019). Trainer persona: Instructional communication strategies promoting employee online learning. In S. Kelly (Ed.), Computer-mediated communication for business: Theory to practice (pp. 172–184). Cambridge Scholars Publishing.

Robson, D., Sodowsky, K., & Cates, C. M. (2013). Advocating offering health communication certificates: Answering America's needs. Journal of the Association for Communication Administration, 32(1/2), 69–78.

Rodriguez, J. I., & Plax, T. G. (1996). Clarifying the relationship between teacher nonverbal immediacy and student cognitive learning: Affective learning as the central causal mediator. Communication Education, 45, 293.

Root, E. (2018). Staging scenes of co-cultural communication: Acting out aspects of marginalized and dominant identities. Communication Teacher, 32(1), 13–18. https://doi.org/10.1080/17404622.2017.1372617

Rosenshine, B., & Furst, N. (1971). Research on teacher performance criteria. In B.O. Smith (Ed.), Research in teacher education (pp. 37–72). Prentice Hall.

Rosenzweig, M. Q. (2012). Breaking bad news: A guide for effective and empathetic communication. The Nurse Practitioner, 37(2), 1–4. https://doi.org/10.1097/01.NPR.0000408626.24599.9e

Rudick, C. K., & Golsan, K. B. (2016). Difference, accountability, and social justice: Three challenges for instructional communication scholarship. Communication Education, 65(1), 110–112. https://doi.org/10.1080/0363 4523.2015.1096947

Russo, T., & Benson, S. (2003). Learning with invisible others: Online presence and its relationship to cognitive and affective learning. Conference Papers—International Communication Association, 1–27. http://hdl.handle.net/1808/13159

Saettler, P. (1968). A history of instructional technology. Random House.

Salazar, E. (2021). The IDEA model as an effective instructional crisis and risk communication framework to analyze the CDC's messages aimed at Hispanics in the COVID-19 era. *Proceedings of the International Crisis and Risk Communication Conference, 4,* 45–48. https://doi.org/10.30658/icrcc.2021.11

Salazar, E., & Sellnow, D. (2021). When the pandemic impacts the most vulnerable: Analyzing crisis and risk messages aimed at Latinx individuals about COVID-19. *Proceedings of the International Crisis and Risk Communication Conference, 4,* 41–44. https://doi.org/10.30658/icrcc.2021.11

Salem, M., Lakatos, G., Amirabdollahian, F., & Dautenhahn, K. (2015, March). Would you trust a (faulty) robot?: Effects of error, task type and personality on human-robot cooperation and trust. In J. A. Adams & W. Smart (Chairs), *Proceedings of the Tenth Annual ACM/IEEE International Conference on Human-Robot Interaction* (pp. 141–148). ACM. https://doi.org/10.1145/2696454.2696497

Sanchez, G. R., & Foxworth, R. (2021, July 29). *Native Americans and COVID-19 vaccine hesitancy: Pathways toward increasing vaccination rates for Native communities.* Health Affairs Blog. https://www.healthaffairs.org/do/10.1377/hblog20210723.390196/full/

Sanders, J. A., & Wiseman, R. L. (1990). The effects of verbal and nonverbal teacher immediacy on perceived cognitive, affective, and behavioral learning in the multicultural classroom. Communication Education, 39(4), 341–353. https://doi.org/10.1080/03634529009378814

Schmitt, M., Blue, A., Aschenbrener, C. A., & Viggiano, T. R. (2011). Core competencies for interprofessional collaborative practice: Reforming health care by transforming health professionals' education. *Academic Medicine,* 86(11), 1351. https://doi.org/10.1097/acm.0b013e3182308e39

Schramm, W. (1997). The beginnings of communication study in America: A personal memoir (S. H. Chaffee & E. M. Rogers, Eds.). SAGE.

Schrodt, P., & Witt, P. L. (2006). Students' attributions of instructor credibility as a function of students' expectations of instructional technology use and nonverbal immediacy. *Communication Education, 55*(1), 1–20. https://doi.org/10.1080/03634520500343335

Schulz, P. J., & Jiang, S. (2021). Theoretical frameworks of provider-patient interaction. In T. L. Thompson & P. J. Schulz (Eds.), *Health communication theory* (pp. 108–130). Wiley.

Seeger, M. (2018). Response to special issue on communication and instruction beyond the traditional classroom. *Communication Education, 67*(4), 491–494.

Seeger, M. W., Sellnow, T. L., & Ulmer, R. R. (1998). Communication, organization, and crisis. Annals of the International Communication Association, 21(1), 231–276. https://doi.org/10.1080/23808985.1998.11678952

Seeger, M., Sellnow, T., & Ulmer, R. (2001). Public relations and crisis communication: Organizing and chaos. In R. L. Heath (ed.), *Handbook of public relations* (pp. 155–166). SAGE.

Seeger, M., Sellnow, T., & Ulmer, R. (2003). *Communication and organizational crisis*. Praeger.

Seeger, W., & Sellnow, T. (2016). *Narratives of crisis: Telling stories of ruin and renewal*. Stanford University Press.

Selfe, C. L. (1988). The humanization of computers: Forget technology, remember literacy. The English Journal, 77(6), 69–71. https://doi.org/10.2307/818623

Selfie, C. L. (1988). Computers in the classroom: The humanization of computers: Forget technology, remember literacy. *The English Journal, 77*(6), 69–71. https://www.jstor.org/stable/818623

Sellnow, D., & Kaufmann, R. (2018). Instructional communication and the online learning environment: Then, now, next. In M. L. Houser & A. M. Hosek (Eds.), *Handbook of instructional communication* (pp. 195–206). Routledge.

Sellnow, D., & Sellnow, T. (2014). Risk communication: Instructional principles. In T. Thompson (Ed.), *Encyclopedia of health communication* (Vol. 1, p. 1181). SAGE.

Sellnow, D., & Sellnow, T. (2018). Introduction to this special issue on communication and instruction beyond the classroom. *Communication Education, 67*(4), 409–413.

Sellnow, D., & Sellnow, T. (2019). The IDEA model for effective instructional risk and crisis communication by emergency managers and other key spokespersons. *Journal of Emergency Management, 17*(1), 67–78. https://doi.org/10.5055/jem.2019.0399

Sellnow, D., & Sellnow, T. (2020, August 3). Effective communication in times of risk and crisis. Research Outreach. https://doi.org/10.32907/RO-115-3437

Sellnow, D., Lane, D., Littlefield, R., Sellnow, T., Wilson, B., Beauchamp, K., & Venette, S. (2015). A receiver-based approach to effective crisis communication. *Journal of Contingencies and Crisis Management, 23*(3), 149–158.

Sellnow, D., Lane, D., Sellnow, T., & Littlefield, R. (2017). The IDEA model as a best practice for effective instructional risk and crisis communication. *Communication Studies, 68*(5), 552–567.

Sellnow, D., Limperos, A., Frisby, B. N., Sellnow, T. L., Spence, P. R., & Downs, E. (2015). Expanding the scope of instructional communication research: Looking beyond classroom contexts. *Communication Studies, 66*(4), 417–432. https://doi.org/10.1080/10510974.2015.1057750

Sellnow, D., Sellnow, T., & Martin, J. (2019). Strategic message convergence in communicating biosecurity: The case of the 2013 Porcine Epidemic Diarrhea virus. *Communication Reports, 32*(3), 125–136.

Sellnow, T. (2015). Crisis communication. In H. Cho, T. Reimer, & K. McComas (Eds.), *The SAGE handbook of risk communication* (pp. 10–23). SAGE.

Sellnow, T., & Seeger, M. (2013). *Theorizing crisis communication.* Wiley.

Sellnow, T., Parker, J., Sellnow, D., Littlefield, R., Helsel, E., Getchell, M., Smith, J., & Merrill, S. (2017). Improving biosecurity through instructional crisis communication: Lessons Learned from the PEDv outbreak. *Journal of Applied Communications, 10*(4). https://doi.org/10.4148/1051-0834.1298

Sellnow, T., & Sellnow, D. (2010, April). The instructional dynamic of risk and crisis communication: Distinguishing instructional messages from dialogue. *The Review of Communication, 10*(2), 112–126.

Sellnow, T., Sellnow, D., Lane, D. R., & Littlefield, R. S. (2012). The value of instructional communication in crisis situations: Restoring order to chaos. *Risk Analysis: An International Journal, 32*(4), 633–643. https://doi.org/10.1111/j.1539-6924.2011.01634.x

Sellnow, T., Sellnow, D., Lane, D., Littlefield, R. (2012). The value of instructional communication in crisis situations: Restoring order to chaos. *Risk Analysis, 32*(4), 633–643.

Sellnow-Richmond, D., George, A., and Sellnow, D. (2018). An IDEA model analysis of instructional risk communication in the time of Ebola. *Journal of International Crisis and Risk Communication Research, 1*(1), 135–166. https://doi.org/10.30658/jicrcr.1.1.7

Sharma, R., Nachum, S., Davidson, K. W., & Nochomovitz, M. (2019). It's not just FaceTime: Core competencies for the medical virtualist. *International Journal of Emergency Medicine, 12*(1), 1–5. https://doi.org/10.1186/s12245-019-0226-y

Shay, J. E., & Pohan, C. (2021). Resilient instructional strategies: Helping students cope and thrive in crisis. *Journal of Microbiology & Biology Education, 22*(1), ev22i1–2405. https://doi.org/10.1128/jmbe.v22i1.2405

Short, J., Williams, E., & Christie, B. (1976). *The social psychology of telecommunications.* Wiley.

Simpson, E. J. (1966). *The classifications of educational objectives, psychomotor domain.* University of Illinois.

Singhal, A. (2002). A theoretical agenda for entertainment-education. *Communication Theory, 12,* 117.

Singhal, A., Cody, M. J., Rogers, E. M., & Sabido, M. (2003). *Entertainment education and social change: History, research, and practice.* Routledge.

Smith, D. K. (1954). Origins and development of departments of speech. In K. R. Wallace (Ed.), *A history of speech education in America: Background studies* (pp. 447–470). Appleton-Century-Crofts, Inc.

Smith, E. E. (1987). Interactive video: An examination of use and effectiveness. *Journal of Instructional Development, 10*(2), 2–10.

Smith, R. A. (1976, April). Educational games in today's learning. ERIC. https://files.eric.ed.gov/fulltext/ED129304.pdf

Smith, W. R., Atala, A. J., Terlecki, R. P., Kelly, E. E., & Matthews, C. A. (2020). Implementation guide for rapid integration of an outpatient telemedicine program during the COVID-19 pandemic. *Journal of the American College of Surgeons, 231*(2), 216–222. https://doi.org/10.1016/j.jamcollsurg.2020.04.030

Soricone, L. Rudd, R., Santos, M., Capistrant, B. (2007) *Health literacy in adult basic education: Designing lessons, units, and evaluation plans for an integrated curriculum.* https://cdn1.sph.harvard.edu/wp-content/uploads/sites/135/2012/09/healthliteracyinadulteducation.pdf

Soto Mas, F., Ji, M., Fuentes, B. O., & Tinajero, J. (2015). The health literacy and ESL study: A community-based intervention for Spanish-speaking adults. *Journal of Health Communication, 20*(4), 369–376. https://doi.org/10.1080/10810730.2014.965368

Spence, P. R., Westerman, D., Edwards, C., & Edwards, A. (2014). Welcoming our robot overlords: Initial expectations about interaction with a robot. Communication Research Reports, 31(3), 272–280. https://doi.org/10.1080/08824096.20

Sprague, J. (1992). Expanding the research agenda for instructional communication: Raising some unasked questions. *Communication Education*, 41, 1, 1–25. https://doi.org/10.1080/03634529209378867

Sprague, J. (2002). Communication education: The spiral continues. *Communication Education*, 51(4), 337–354. https://doi.org/10.1080/03634520216532

Steinfeld, C. W. (1986). Computer-mediated communication in an organizational setting: Explaining task-related and socioemotional uses. In M. L. McLaughlin (Ed.), *Communication Yearbook*, 9 (pp. 777–804). SAGE.

Stevens, D. J. (1982). How educators perceived computers in the classroom. *Association for Educational Data Systems (AEDS) Journal*, 16, *https://doi.org/10.1080/00011037.1980.11008276*

Stoll, C. (1995, February 26). Why the web won't be nirvana. Newsweek. https://www.newsweek.com/clifford-stoll-why-web-wont-be-nirvana-185306

Storz, M. G., & Hoffman, A. R. (2013). Examining response to a one-to-one computer initiative: Student and teacher voices. *Research in Middle Level Education*, 36(6). https://files.eric.ed.gov/fulltext/EJ995733.pdf

Strawser, M. G., & Sellnow, D. D. (2019). Problem-solvers in the academy and beyond. *Communication Education*, 68(4), 475–480. https://doi.org/10.1080/03634523.2019.1646919

Strawser, M. G., Hannah, M., & Densmore, C. (2022) Communication education in K–12 contexts: Strategic initiatives to engage student and instructor stakeholders, *Communication Education*, 71(3), 246–250. https://doi.org/10.1080/03634523.2022.2069835

Street, R. L., O'Malley, K. J., Cooper, L. A., & Haidet, P. (2008). Understanding concordance in patient-physician relationships: Personal and ethnic dimensions of shared identity. The Annals of Family Medicine, 6(3), 198–205. https://doi.org/10.1370/afm.821

Sullivan, P. A. (1993). Communication skills training for interactive sports. The Sport Psychologist, 7(1), 79–91.

Suojanen, K., Woodall, K., Hammonds, J. R., Monie, D., Scribani, M., Krupa, N., Jenkins, P., Weil, H., & Frye, J. J. (2018). Teaching future doctors to communicate: A communication intervention for medical students in their clinical year. *Journal of Communication in Healthcare, 11*(4), 263–277. https://doi.org/10.1080/17538068.2018.1507082

Sutton, J., League, C., Sellnow, T., & Sellnow, D. (2015). Terse messaging and public health in the midst of natural disasters: The case of the Boulder floods. *Health Communication, 30*(2), 135–143.

Suydam, M. N. (1981). The use of calculators in pre-college education: Third and fourth annual state-of-the-art reviews. ERIC. https://files.eric.ed.gov/fulltext/ED220273.pdf

Swan, M. K., & Brehmer, J. (1994). Educational instruction via interactive video network. *Journal of Agricultural Education, 35*(1), 13–20. https://doi.org/10.5032.jae.1994.01013

Taneja, A., Fiore, V., & Fischer, B. (2015). Cyber-slacking in the classroom: Potential for digital distraction in the new age. Computers & Education, 82, 141–151. https://doi.org/10.1016/j.compedu.2014.11.009

Tatum, N. T., Martin, J. C., & Kemper, B. (2018). Chronemics in instructor–student e-mail communication: An experimental examination of student evaluations of instructor response speeds. *Communication Research Reports, 35*(1), 33–41. https://doi.org/10.1080/08824096.2017.1361396

Thompson, T. L. (2018). Health communication as an instructional communication context beyond the classroom. *Communication Education, 67*(4), 488–490. https://doi.org/10.1080/03634523.2018.1504095

Titsworth, S., Hosek, A. M., Pearson, J. C., & Nelson, P. E. (2020). *Human communication* (7th ed.). McGraw-Hill.

Titsworth, S., McKenna, T., Mazer, J., & Quinlan, M. (2013). The bright side of emotion in the classroom: Do teachers' behaviors rredict students' enjoyment, hope, and pride? *Communication Education, 62*, 191–209. https://doi-org.proxy.library.ohio.edu/10.1080/03634523.2013.763997

Titsworth, S., Quinlan, M. M., & Mazer, J. P. (2010). Emotion in teaching and learning: Development and validation of the classroom emotions scale. *Communication Education, 59*, 431–452. https://doi.org/10.1080/03634529909379152

Toronto, C. E., & Weatherford, B. (2015). Health literacy education in health professions schools: An integrative review. *Journal of Nursing Education*, 54(12), 669–676. https://doi.org/10.3928/01484834-20151110-02

Treisman, R. (2021). *Outpacing the U.S., hard-hit Navajo Nation has vaccinated more than half of adults, NPR Coronavirus updates.* https://www.npr.org/sections/coronavirus-live-updates/2021/04/26/990884991/outpacing-the-u-s-hard-hit-navajo-nation-has-vaccinated-more-than-half-of-adults

Tullis, J. A., & Ryalls, E. D. (2019). SNAP challenge in the communication classroom. *Communication Teacher, 33*(4), 304–308. https://doi.org/10.1080/17404622.2019.1575439

Turner, J. W., Robinson, J. D., Tian, Y., Neustadtl, A., Angelus, P., Russell, M., Mun, S. K., & Levine, B. (2013). Can messages make a difference? Association between e-mail messages and health outcomes in diabetes patients. *Human Communication Research, 39*, 252–268. https://doi.org/10.1111/j.1468-2958.2012.01437.x

Ulmer, R., Sellnow, T., & Seeger, M. (2019). *Effective crisis communication: Moving from crisis to opportunity* (4th ed.). SAGE.

Vahabi, Sh. (2006). The relationship between EFL Learners FD/FI cognitive style, proficiency, and communication strategies in writing. *ILI Language Teaching Journal, 2*, 145–150.

Valenzano, J., III, & Wallace, S. (2017). Expanding and exporting instructional communication scholarship: A necessary new direction. *Communication Education, 66*(4), 483–484. https://doi.org/10.1080/03634523.2017.1346264

Valverde, H. H. (1968). *Flight simulators: A review of the research and development.* Aerospace Medical Research Laboratory. https://apps.dtic.mil/sti/pdfs/AD0855582.pdf

Vareberg, K. R. (2021). *"Cause you don't really need a teacher to learn stuff": Theorizing a "lanes of learning" model of informal, self-directed learning* (No. 28647125) [Dissertation, North Dakota State University]. ProQuest Dissertations & Theses Global (2572606721).

Vareberg, K. R., & Platt, C. A. (2019). Little tech on the prairie: Understanding teachers' adoption of and resistance to technology in the rural classroom. *Journal of the Communication, Speech, and Theatre Association of North Dakota, 32*, 27–42.

Vareberg, K. R., & Westerman, D. K. (2020). To :-) or to, that is the question: A study of students' initial impressions of instructors' paralinguistic cues. *Education and Information Technologies, 25*(5), 4501–4516. https://doi.org/10.1007/s10639-020-10181-9

Vareberg, K. R., Luo, Z., Westerman, D., Bartels, M., & Lindmark, P. (2020). For a good class, e-mail: Technologically mediated outside-of-class communication and instructional outcomes. *The Internet and Higher Education, 47*. https://doi.org/10.1016/j.iheduc.2020.100761

Verdoux, P. (2009). Transhumanism, progress and the future. *Journal of Evolution and Technology, 20*(2), 49–69. https://jetpress.org/v20/verdoux.htm

Vernon, J. A., Trujillo, A., Rosenbaum, S., & DeBuono, B. (2007). Low health literacy: Implications for national health policy. Department of Health Policy, School of Public Health and Health Services, The George Washington University. https://hsrc.himmelfarb.gwu.edu/cgi/viewcontent.cgi?article=1173&context=sphhs_policy_facpubs

Villagran, M., Goldsmith, J., Wittenberg-Lyles, E., & Baldwin, P. (2010). Creating COMFORT: A communication-based model for delivering bad news. Communication Education, 59(3), 220–234. https://doi.org/10.1080/03634521003624031

Vince, R. (2014). What do HRD scholars and practitioners need to know about power, emotion, and HRD? *Human Resource Development Quarterly, 25*(4), 409–420. https://doi.org/10.1002/hrdq.21191

Vrchota, D. (2011). Communication in the disciplines: Interpersonal communication in dietetics. *Communication Education, 60*(2), 210–230. https://doi.org/10.1080/03634523.2010.523475

Waldeck, J. H. (2008). The development of an industry-specific online learning center: Consulting lessons learned. *Communication Education, 57*(4), 452–463. https://doi.org/10.1080/03634520801894747

Waldeck, J. H., Kearney, P., & Plax, T. G. (2001). Instructional and developmental communication theory and research in the 1990s: Extending the research agenda for the 21st century. In William B. Gudykunst (Ed.), *Communication yearbook* (pp. 207–229). SAGE.

Wallace, K. R. (Ed.). (1954). *History of speech education in America: Background studies*. Appleton-Century-Crofts, Inc.

Wallerstein, N. B., & Duran, B. (2006). Using community-based participatory research to address health disparities. *Health Promotion Practice, 7*(3), 312–323. https://doi.org/10.1177/1524839906289376

Walters, R., Leslie, S. J., Polson, R., Cusack, T., & Gorely, T. (2020). Establishing the efficacy of interventions to improve health literacy and health behaviours: A systematic review. *BMC Public Health, 20*(1), 1–17. https://doi.org/10.1186/s12889-020-08991-0

Walther, J. B. (1992). Interpersonal effects in computer-mediated interaction: A relational perspective. *Communication Research, 19*(10, 52–90. http://doi.org/10.1177/009365092019001003

Walther, J. B. (1996). Computer-mediated communication: Impersonal, interpersonal, and hyperpersonal interaction. *Communication Research, 23*(1), 3–43. https://doi.org/10.1177%2F009365096023001001

Walther, J. B. (2007). Selective self-presentation in computer-mediated communication: Hyperpersonal dimensions of technology, language, and cognition. Computers in Human Behavior, 23(5), 2538–2557. https://doi.org/10.1016/j.chb.2006.05.002

Walther, J. B., & Bazarova, N. N. (2008). Validation and application of electronic propinquity to computer-mediated communication in groups. Communication Research, 35(5), 622–645. https://doi.org/10.1177/0093650208321783

Walther, J. B., & Parks, M. R. (2002). Cues filtered out, cues filtered in: Computer-mediated communication and relationships. In M. L. Knapp & J. A. Daly (Eds.), Handbook of interpersonal communication (3rd ed., pp. 529–563). SAGE.

Wanzer, M. B., Booth-Butterfield, M., & Gruber, K. (2004). Perceptions of health care providers' communication: relationships between patient-centered communication and satisfaction. Health communication, 16(3), 363–384. https://doi.org/10.1207/S15327027HC1603_6

Warren, J. L., Clancy, K., Brady, C. F., Rump, K., & New-Oglesby, T. (2021). Toward improving physician/patient communication regarding invisible chronic illness (ICI): The potential of mHealth technology in instructional communication. *Journal of Communication Pedagogy, 4*, 3–20. https://doi.org/10.31446/JCP.2021.1.02

Wayne, T. (2014, June 13). *At the tone, leave a what?* The New York Times. https://www.nytimes.com/2014/06/15/fashion/millennials-shy-away-from-voice-mail.html

Webb, N. G., & Barrett, L. O. (2014). Student views of instructor-student rapport in the college classroom. *Journal of the Scholarship of Teaching and Learning, 14*(2), 15–28. https://doi.org/10.14434/josotl.v14i2.4259

Westerman, D., Daniel, E. S., & Bowman, N. D. (2016). Learned risks and experienced rewards: Exploring the potential sources of students' attitudes toward social media and face-to-face communication. *The Internet and Higher Education, 31,* 52–57. https://doi.org/10.1016/j.iheduc.2016.06.004

Westerman, D., & Skalski, P. D. (2010). Computers and telepresence: A ghost in the machine? In C. C. Braken and P. D. Skalski (Eds.), *Immersed in media: Telepresence in everyday life* (pp. 63–86). Routledge.

Whitaker, A. (2021, July 15). "Sesame Street" corporate deals have upset fans. But they keep the show alive. *Washington Post.* https://www.washingtonpost.com/outlook/2021/07/15/sesame-street-corporate-deals-have-upset-fans-they-keep-show-alive/

Whiteley, A., Price, C., & Palmer, R. (2013). Corporate culture change: adaptive culture structuration and negotiated practice. *Journal of Workplace Learning, 25*(7), 476–498. https://doi.org/10.1108/JWL-09-2012-0069

Wickline, M., & Sellnow, T. (2013). Expanding the concept of significant choice through consideration of health literacy during crises. *Health Promotion Practice, 14,* 809–815. https://doi.org/10.1177/1524839913498752

Wilson, G., & Wolford, R. (2017). The technical communicator as (post-postmodern) discourse worker. *Journal of Business and Technical Communication, 31*(1), 3–29. https://doi.org/10.1177%2F1050651916667531

Witt, P. L. (2017). Making tough choices to continue instructional communication research. *Communication Education, 66*(4), 494–496. https://doi.org/10.1080/03634523.2017.1350872

Witte, K. (1992). Putting fear back into fear appeals: The extended parallel process model. *Communication Monographs, 59*(4), 329–349.

Wittenberg, E., & Goldsmith, J. (2021). Palliative care and end-of-life communication. In T. L. Thompson & N. Grant Harrington (Eds.), *The Routledge handbook of health communication* (3rd ed., pp. 1194–1235). Routledge.

Wulf, S. (1987). Opportunity knocks (NCAA to work for black coaches). *Sports Illustrated, 5.*

Xu, Y., Margolin, D., & Niederdeppe, J. (2021). Testing strategies to increase source credibility through strategic message design in the context of vaccination and vaccine hesitancy. *Health Communication, 36*(11), 1354–1367.

Yarwood, J. (2015, October 22). The making of *The Oregon Train:* An interview with Don Rawitsch. *Paste Magazine.* https://www.pastemagazine.com/games/oregon/the-making-of-the-oregon-trail-an-interview-with-d/

Yen, P. H., & Leasure, A. R. (2019). Use and effectiveness of the teach-back method in patient education and health outcomes. *Federal Practitioner, 36*(6), 284–289.

Zengaro, E., Carmack, H. J., Buzzelli, N., Towery, N. A. (2020). Disclosure catalysts in student disclosures of personal health information to college instructors. *Health Communication, 37*(1), 55–63. https://doi.org/10.1080/10410236.2020.1816310

Zhang, C. W., Hurst, B., & McLean, A. (2016). How fast is fast enough? Education students' perceptions of email response time in online courses. *Journal of Educational Technology Development and Exchange, 9*(1). https://doi.org/10.18785/JETDE.0901.01

Zheng, B., Arada, K., Niiya, M., & Warschauer, M. (2014). One-to-one laptops in K–12 classrooms: Voices of students. *Pedagogies: An International Journal, 9*(4), 279–299. https://doi.org/10.1080/1554480X.2014.955499

Zirkel, G. (1978). Probable quotes from history. *Mathematics Associations of Two-Year Colleges, 12*(3), 189.

Zourbanos, N., Hatzigeorgiadis, A., Tsiakaras, N., Chroni, S., & Theodorakis, Y. (2010). A multimethod examination of the relationship between coaching behavior and athletes' inherent self-talk. *Journal of Sport and Exercise Psychology, 32*(6), 764–785. https://doi.org/10.1123/jsep.32.6.764

Index